Democracy, Inc.

THE HISTORY OF COMMUNICATION

Robert W. McChesney and
John C. Nerone, editors

*A list of books in the series appears
at the end of this book.*

Democracy, Inc.

The Press and Law in the Corporate
Rationalization of the Public Sphere

DAVID S. ALLEN

UNIVERSITY OF ILLINOIS PRESS
Urbana and Chicago

Library of Congress Cataloging-in-Publication Data

Allen, David S., 1955–
Democracy, inc. : the press and law in the corporate rationalization
of the public sphere / David S. Allen.
p.   cm. — (The history of communication)
Includes bibliographical references and index.
ISBN 0-252-02975-5 (cloth : alk. paper)
1. Press law—United States. 2. Corporate state—United States.
3. Democracy—United States. I. Title: Democracy, incorporated.
II. Title. III. Series.
KF2750.A9395   2005
343.7309'98—dc22   2004023676

For my parents, Stan and Bea, for their guidance,
and my daughters, Meg and Carrie,
for their hope for the future.

Contents

Acknowledgments

It is difficult to claim ownership of the ideas expressed on the following pages. All research is a curious mix of old and new, original and unoriginal ideas, and mine is no different. My ideas about what democracy is and ought to be and what role the press and the law play in the realization of democracy are indebted to the writers and scholars who have preceded me. Their work has spurred questions and directed me to seek answers that I believe are vital for us as citizens to answer. The pages that follow are presented not as a definitive statement but rather as my attempt to engage in a conversation with readers about the foundation of democratic society. This book represents my attempt to try to find answers to the questions of why American public life is structured the way it is and whether that structure aids or hinders an active citizenry.

In many ways, the roots of this book can be traced to the questions asked by my students over the years. From my graduate student years at the University of Minnesota, through my time among the faculty at Illinois State University, to my current academic home at the University of Wisconsin–Milwaukee, students have always asked the questions that spur my research. Over the years, students in my graduate seminars have played an important role in framing my analysis. At Illinois State University, conversations with Guillermo K. Collado-Madcur, Mark Fromson, Jude Geiger, Georgia Gotsis, Jeff Grabb, and Chris Grove greatly aided my thinking. At the University of Wisconsin–Milwaukee, I am particularly indebted to students in my Politics and the Media graduate seminar in spring 2003, who generously allowed me to talk about some of my ideas and provided valuable critiques—some of which I am still struggling to address. Participants in that seminar were Frizell Bailey, Carlos Fierro, Jessi Hafer, Jessica McBride, Heather Powers, and Chris Terry. I have also benefited from discussions with March Jacques and Lisa Nalbandian.

The writing of this book began during a sabbatical in spring 2000 at Illinois State University. I would like to thank Dean Paul Schollaert for his encouragement of this project, as well as my colleagues in the Department of Communication who generously supported that valuable research opportunity. Numerous people at Illinois State University supported my work by listening patiently to my ideas and providing the friendship to see me through those days when I never thought this book would get finished. I'd like to particularly thank Patricia Carlson, Ana Floriani, Margaret Haefner, John Gill, Virginia Gill, Cynthia Hoffner, Dan Holland, Rebecca Houtsma, Willie Hunter, Ken Levine, Patrick O'Sullivan, George Seelinger, and Roberta Seelinger Trites.

My move to the University of Wisconsin–Milwaukee in 2001 provided the needed impetus to finish the work. I'll be forever grateful for the help of my colleagues in the Department of Journalism and Mass Communication, but also to the many scholars outside of the department who have influenced my thinking. Jeff Smith and Dave Pritchard provided valuable guidance, unflagging support, and friendship. A year-long research fellowship at the Center for 21st Century Studies at UW-Milwaukee provided me with the environment and the stimulation to finish the book. I'd like to thank the center's staff: Dan Sherman, director; Carol Tennessen, executive director; William Turner, assistant director (for our many wonderful discussions); and Maria Liesegang, office manager. My year at the center was one of my most rewarding experiences since joining the academy. Dean Richard Meadows and Associate Dean Ellie Miller of the University of Wisconsin–Milwaukee's College of Letters and Science have provided encouragement and research support, for which I am most grateful.

Over the years, many friends and colleagues have read and commented on parts of this book in some form. While not always agreeing with my argument, each generously provided feedback, gentle criticism, and friendship. They include Ann Haugland, Beth Blanks Hindman, Doug Hindman, Bob Jensen, Don Gillmor, Ted Glasser, Don McComb, Steve Rhodes, and Tom Streeter. I'd especially like to thank John Nerone for his thorough, careful critique of this work and for his encouragement. Kerry Callahan at the University of Illinois Press was excellent at guiding this book through the editorial process and provided constant, calming reassurance that things would come together.

Many friends in Milwaukee have also provided support and friendship during the writing of this book. I'm especially grateful to Jon Margolies, Margie Margolies, Margaret Pedrick, Sandy Stehling (who suggested the title), and Ruth Williams.

I would also like to thank Sage Publications Ltd. for granting me permission to use portions of my essay, "The First Amendment and the Doctrine of Corporate Personhood: Collapsing the Press-Corporation Distinction" (*Journalism: Theory, Practice and Criticism* 2 [2001]: 255–78), in chapter 5; the National Communication Association for allowing me to use portions of my essay, "The Institutional Press and Professionalization: Defining the Press Clause in Journalist's Privilege Cases" (*Free Speech Yearbook* 34 [1996]: 49–62), in chapter 4; and Lawrence Erlbaum Associates, Inc., for allowing me to use portions of my essay, "Merging Law and Ethics: Discourse Legal Theory and Freedom of Expression in *Hurley*" (*Communication Law and Policy* 4 [1999]: 403–30), in chapter 6.

And finally, I'd like to thank my family for their love and encouragement. Most of the good ideas in this book can be attributed to Laura Pedrick, who remains the love of my life, my best friend, my best critic, and my best editor. She always found time in our hectic lives to listen to my ideas and provide the encouragement I needed to finish this project. My parents, Beatrice Allen and the late Stanley Allen, instilled in me the values that ground my work. And finally, I want to thank my two wonderful daughters, Meg and Carrie, who allowed me to upend their lives with our move to Milwaukee. In ways that they might not understand at this point, this book was written for them—to try and change a little bit of the world so that they might have a better future.

Introduction

This book examines the complex relationship between corporations and the public sphere. While most critiques of corporate ownership focus on the product, this book attempts to uncover how the corporate form has changed the way we think and talk about democracy. It argues that corporations have altered the culture of democracy by changing the language and logic that we use to evaluate public life. In a sense, this work examines the ideology of modern-day democracy. It questions why democracy is structured the way it is and why civil society's dominant institutions evaluate public life through the lens that they do. This book seeks to identify how the logic of corporations has been made into the logic of the public sphere—how corporate ideology has become public ideology, and how law and the press have played a crucial role in that transfer.

This ideological transfer is perhaps best reflected in the way we talk about free speech in the United States. Since at least the 1920s, an area where people come together to exchange ideas in our democratic society has typically been referred to as "the marketplace of ideas," a phrase linked to U.S. Supreme Court Justice Oliver Wendell Holmes.[1] Democracy, as envisioned in Holmes's metaphor, is a market in which competing forces battle for acceptance and the winner takes all. So what's wrong with that vision? Watching the entertainment programming that passes for political discussion in today's society, from Bill O'Reilly and Rush Limbaugh to their multitude of imitators, it can be argued that the marketplace is an apt description of our political culture. Today's democracy does seem to be about attracting an audience, making money, and winning. When one tries to envision democracy as something else, however, the marketplace metaphor seems misguided, or at least empty. What if democracy is not about attracting an audience, making money, and winning? What if it is more accurately defined as the need to find common ground, as the exchange of ideas between citizens in an attempt to reach understanding? Those ideas are often associated with a different theory of democracy, discourse democracy.[2] Very broadly, discourse democracy theorists believe that one of the problems facing modern life is the increasing alienation of citizens from the forces that govern their lives. Discourse democracy seeks to identify ways to make possible an open dialogue among citizens through the creation of public space absent governmental and corporate interference. It seeks less to alter the fundamental structure of democratic societies than to influence the values that guide democracy and how those values are determined. Public life in discourse democracy is less like a market and more like what Jürgen Habermas calls a public sphere, where private people come together to fashion true public opinion.[3]

Why has the marketplace metaphor come to dominate our description of public life? It will be argued that at least part of the reason is that the values of corporations, which emphasize efficiency, maximizing profits, scientific reasoning, and winning as opposed to understanding, have become the values of the public sphere. While other works have looked at how corporations have influenced public life,[4] this book is unique in that it investigates the transfer, or what might be called the ideological drift, of ideas from corporations to the public sphere. I have labeled that process of ideological drift "corporate rationalization." I will argue that two institutions—the press and the law—have played a fundamental role in this process. Both institutions are vital to the functioning of the public sphere, providing cultural support and institutional legitimacy as well as shaping the structure of public life.

Corporations and Rationalization

The term "corporate rationalization" calls out for clarification; the terms "corporate" and "corporation" are ambiguous at best. In today's society, "corporation" is often used as a form of criticism. Truth be told, however, corporations are not all alike. There are large, multinational corporations, and there are small corporations that are sometimes organized around family businesses. There are for-profit corporations, and there are nonprofit corporations. In fact, the number of small corporations in the United States far exceeds the number of large corporations. According to U.S. Internal Revenue Service statistics, about five million corporations filed tax returns in 2000. That is up from about 2.7 million corporate tax returns in 1980. About 2.9 million of the corporations that filed tax returns in 2000 reported assets under a hundred thousand dollars, and about 1.6 million reported assets between a hundred thousand and a million dollars. About eleven thousand corporations reported assets greater than $250 million.[5] Such statistics demonstrate not only the tremendous growth of corporations in the United States over the last several decades but also their increasing relevance to various demographic sectors. At some level, the diversity of the corporate form can be seen as evidence of its connection with various parts of American life. The corporation permeates practically all levels of society.

Admittedly, it is difficult to discuss corporations as a single entity. However, this work is less concerned with the structural features of a corporation (what makes something a corporation) than with the ideas that have come to be associated with a corporation. The main advantages of the corporation lie in their ability to protect shareholders from financial problems, known as limited liability, and the associated tax benefits. As such, it is first an economic structure. However, it is more than that due to the ideas and developments that are associated with it. The corporate form is linked to notions about the role of bureaucracies in democratic life, the importance of efficient means of production, a certain definition of individualism, the fragmentation of the public, and the importance of social control. As R. Jeffrey Lustig notes, however, a fundamental principle associated with the corporate form is the inversion of democratic principles: "Since ancient times statesmen have attempted to create a polity that could harness private interests to the public welfare. The corporation succeeds, by contrast, in harnessing vast publics to a private interest. It subordinates plurality to singularity, the many to the few."[6]

This study is not really concerned with the question, What is a corporation? It is more interested in the questions, What does it mean to be a corporation? And what is the impact of the spread of the corporate form on democracy? It agrees with Lustig in suggesting that corporations are less about money and charters than about "ways of structuring relations between *people*."[7]

The term "corporate rationalization" attempts to capture the process that is the focus of this book. The term has close links with several other concepts, such as market rationalization and corporate liberalism, but it differs from those terms in important ways. "Market rationalization" describes the influence of market logic on private and public sectors of life. The term seeks to capture how the need for profitability overrides all other concerns. It does not, however, focus our attention on the corporate form of ownership or related ideas that are often associated with that form. I argue that it is not simply the market that has changed democracy but rather the corporate form and the ideas associated with it. This contention is supported by the fact that most critics of the current state of democracy do not focus on capitalism in general but on how corporations have changed capitalism. Corporate domination of public life, as Martin J. Sklar has written, is best understood "not simply as an 'external force' or an 'objective' economic or organizational phenomenon, but as a social movement."[8] In that way, corporate rationalization involves far more than structuring democracy so that it mirrors the economic sector of society: it changes the assumptions and the guiding ideals that are central to how democracy functions.

Corporate liberalism also has clear connections to the ideas expressed in this book. The term nicely identifies a way of organizing democracy—a structure that values corporations as individuals and uses expanded governmental oversight as a way to legitimate corporate actions. As Thomas Streeter explains, corporate liberal thought is not a dominant ideology in the sense that it is a "monolithic framework imposed on a hapless populace by the ruling elite."[9] Rather, he sees it as a set of values that is constantly changing to meet challenges: "As an underlying framework for understanding and legitimating the U.S. political economy, corporate liberalism has persisted, with variations, . . . providing a set of shared values and assumptions to the mainstreams of the business community and the Republican and Democratic parties."[10]

While the term "corporate liberalism" captures the form of democracy that is examined here, it doesn't help us understand the process by which that form is made dominant. My use of the term "corporate rationalization" leans more towards Lustig's idea of identifying a "cultural logic" that informs and shapes political institutions within democratic society and how that logic has been made dominant in America public life.[11] In important ways, corporate rationalization links the idea of corporate liberalism with the process of rationalization discussed by Max Weber and, more recently, Habermas.

Some might also question the connection between elements of what I refer to as corporate ideology and corporate ownership. For example, it would be valid to suggest that efficiency standards did not begin with corporate ownership—that the desire for efficiency has long been a cultural value in the United States. This book does not suggest that corporations initiated the ideas associated with corporate rationalization, but they have used them—often in unique ways—to their benefit. Corporations did not necessarily begin the process, but they have managed to do it "better" than anyone or anything else. Whereas classical liberalism saw government as the greatest threat to freedom, today corporations embody the problems that face modern democracy more than any other institution. I do not make corporations the focus of this study because they are an inherently evil form of association. Rather, they are a rhetorical tool to help identify the fundamental challenges to discourse democracy. Ending corporate ownership of property in the United States would not solve all the problems that face democracy, though it might be a step in the right direction. The more difficult problem facing democracy is how to rethink the structure of public life in ways that differ from corporate liberal values.

Corporate Rationalization, the Press, and the Law

Some may also wonder why this book focuses on the press and the law. Admittedly, these are not the only institutions that play a role in structuring democracy. Too often in scholarly studies, the problems that face democracy are portrayed as being either press problems or law problems. The argument often seems to be that if only we could create a better press or legal system, the problems facing democracy will vanish. I agree that the press and law are vital institutions in the creation of public life, but the central problem facing democracy is neither solely journalistic nor legal. The problem facing democracy today is the loss of public life, and the press and law are important because of the role they play in that loss. While corporations have influenced all sectors of life, their ability to capture the press and the law has the most serious impact on public life because the press exists to give life to and aid in the development of political discourse among citizens, while the law sets the legal and ethical standards of how public life will be conducted.

I understand that for many people, those definitions might be problematic. Countless examples reveal the press playing a far different role in American society. One could argue that its primary purpose is to entertain us, to make money for its shareholders, or to simply inform us about the day's events. All of these need to be considered to understand how the press functions in today's society. This book focuses only on the press, the information-gathering media. And while even its most avid defenders admit that today's press is about making money and entertaining its audience, they don't see either as being its primary mission. I argue that public life is broken, and a status-quo press system is unlikely to fix that problem. This is not only a study of where we have been but also an argument about where we ought to go. If we are to capture any sense of a democracy based on discursive principles, we need to figure out ways to revitalize the public sphere. This book begins from the assumption that the press is a vital institution in the creation of the public sphere. Without its institutional support, reform will be difficult. Besides, if we are to believe that the press ought to play a unique role in our society—an argument that most observers in American society seem willing to accept—it is not because of entertainment or profits. It is based on the press's role in democracy.

My definition of the judiciary's role is likely to be equally troubling to some readers. For many, the role of the courts is to interpret laws and impose justice in a fair (or equal) manner. But as the law professor James Boyd White has noted, legal decisions do far more than simply decide disputes between parties. Judicial decisions define the ethical standards of society and the relationship between citizens and the institutions within society. Law is, in White's words, the "constitution of a world,"[12] one of the primary areas in society where roles and relationships are established. Law takes what may seem to be trivial events and turns them into narratives "that touch our largest concerns as a people engaged in self-government under law."[13] Judicial opinions are texts that have an ethical and political dimension. They establish relationships between at least two people (the writer and the reader), defining what role each will play in that relationship and what power individuals will enjoy.[14]

Judicial decisions, while closely tied to the power that is vested in the judiciary, are not simply an isolated exercise of power. Judicial opinions are a continuing conversation, with the judges looking to the past for their authority and to the future as a guide to their decisions.[15] The courts can be seen as writing a drama of public significance.[16]

This is not to suggest that the press and the law function independently and authoritatively. In important ways, the press and the law are socially constructed. But perhaps even more importantly, the two institutions at times come together to implement the ideals of corporate rationalization. Some of those instances will be highlighted in the chapters that follow.

This book attempts to identify developments within the press and the law that have aided in the creation of an inactive public sphere. It will not be suggested that this is the result of a massive corporate conspiracy, nor will it be suggested that all decisions at all times favor corporate liberal beliefs—there are no doubt cases in which the press and courts have acted contrary to corporate-liberal values. This work argues that we are engaged in an ongoing process of corporate rationalization. This exists at a deep ideological level and began long ago.

Choices about how to structure public life are guided by an unarticulated and undebated ideology that has its roots in the development of corporate-liberal culture. The structure of public life seems so entirely natural to most Americans that few question the fundamental assumptions of modern corporate ideology, including the idea that media content should be driven solely by questions of popularity, that larger corporations will provide better and more efficient service than smaller corporations, that technology can solve society's problems, and that an ideological individualism that values confrontation, winning, and capitalism is preferable to an ideological community that values discourse and understanding.

I say "ideological" individualism because today's corporate climate does not truly value individualism. As historians and social critics have noted, inherent in corporate liberalism is the idea that the corporation, not the individual, is at the center of protection. In fact, it can be argued that corporations have used individualism to destroy the very essence of individualism in American society.

This book is a work of critical theory. This is not an attempt to link the pages that follow to a specific school of thought but rather to alert the reader to the methodology that drives this work. To quote Max Horkheimer's classic definition of critical theory, the goal is people's "'emancipation from the relationships that enslave'" them.[17] The methodology that drives this work is interdisciplinary in nature. It is part history, part political philosophy, part sociology, and part legal analysis. The goal is to analyze the stories that journalists and judges tell about public life to try and discern their vision of how democracy ought to work and ultimately what role citizens and institutions should play in democracy.

The analysis is guided by what I call a discourse model of democracy, which has direct ties to the writings of Habermas. While the ideas central to that form of democracy will be laid out in more detail later in the book, it assumes that finding the discursive space for citizens to come together, absent the coercive force of government and corporations, is the fundamental problem facing society today and that finding and protecting that space is central to the survival of democracy. Not all will agree with that assessment, and some have offered powerful arguments for why discourse democracy will either fail or not be good for society.[18] In the end, we need to realize that how we define democracy says a lot about how we envision public life. Democracy comes in many forms, from its elitist models to its more participatory forms. Each has something to offer. Elitist forms offer the security of expert knowledge and efficient decision-making processes, with little room for citizen participation; participatory models offer the opportunity for citizens to be directly involved in the governmental process but are difficult to implement in large societies. Discourse democracy attempts to overcome those and other limitations, maintaining an administrative apparatus that is responsive to the discursively formed needs of citizens. But it is more than simply a different way to organize society: It is about citizens making a commitment to relate to each other in different ways than they currently do. Discourse is viewed as necessary for citizens to come together and realize what problems they have in common without losing individual identity, to resist forces within society that seek to divide people, and to begin treating others with respect and dignity. The democracy we live in today is fundamentally at odds with those beliefs. One needs only to listen to political talk shows in the United States to realize that concepts such as understanding, respect, and civility are not central elements of our political culture. Perhaps they never have been. But if we are serious about revitalizing public life in the United States, we have to give people a reason and an opportunity to get involved.

One example nicely illustrates how the press reduces opportunities for citizen involvement through news choices. Several years ago, during a public meeting with the managing editor of a large midwestern newspaper, the editor was asked about the paper's coverage of the reapportionment process, the once-a-decade exercise where voting districts are redrawn. She was asked to envision two stories: a story about the final vote on the redistricting plan by a governmental body, and another about an upcoming mandatory public hearing on a proposed redistricting plan. Which would be a front-page story, and which would be placed inside the paper? With no hesitation, she said that the story about the final vote would be a front-page story, and the public hearing would be placed inside, if covered at all. Why? No one cares about reapportionment, she said. Perhaps her assessment of citizens' interests is correct, but she fails to recognize that the press plays a role in activating citizens and determining how those news choices impact citizenship. It is important to note that the most important story, in her eyes, is the one that not only requires no citizen involvement but provides no opportunity for citizen involvement. Story choice in this instance reflects deeply held values about the role of citizens in a democratic society—values that have important links to corporate rationalization and the management and control of public opinion.

As I hope will be demonstrated over the next pages, corporate rationalization processes are inherently not discursive. Corporate values are dominated by ideas that are destructive of public life and at odds with discourse democracy. This book investigates the decisions and stories that journalists and judges make and tell—sometimes together, sometimes separately—in an attempt to understand whether they help us achieve the goal of discourse democracy. In other words, the central question faced in this book is, in the words of White, "Is this an invitation to a conversation in which democracy begins (or flourishes)? Or to one in which it ends?"[19]

*   *   *

This book is divided into three sections. The first provides historical and theoretical background. Chapter 1 is historical in nature and attempts to bring together a number of concepts vital to understanding the idea of corporate rationalization. I will look at the rise of the corporate form and how other developments contributed to that rise, and I will argue that the merger of movements such as Taylorism, Fordism, and Progressivism were influential in legitimating corporate rationalization. The Progressives, with their belief in science and a strong bureaucracy, perhaps unwittingly created the foundation for the rise of corporate rationalization. Corporate rationalization is not necessarily a conservative movement but rather a technocratic form that is more concerned about social control than political beliefs.

In chapter 2 the rise of corporations will be connected with the rationalization process, building off of the work of Weber and Habermas. Weber's idea of formal rationalization will be examined, and it will be linked to Habermas's concept of communicative action and his colonization thesis, according to which the interests of the system have come to dominate the interests of the lifeworld. The final part of this chapter will describe the theory of discourse democracy that will guide the analysis. Discourse theory builds on the distinction between an active and an informed public. Today we have a public that is informed by dominant institutions. Discourse theory seeks an active public that works to create its own meaning. Working off of critical and cultural theory, the model of discourse democracy put forward here emphasizes the creation of conditions that will allow the public to create meaning by opening public spaces to discursive activities, breaking from the liberal understanding of the right of association and reconceptualizing the role that institutions play in that process.

Part 2 examines the relationship between corporate rationalization and the two institutions central to a functioning public sphere, the press and the law. It uses the professionalization process as a framework for analyzing the relationship between these institutions and the public sphere. Chapter 3 opens with an examination of the relationship between professionalization and corporate rationalization. The professionalization movement is less about finding ways to improve public life than about allowing an occupation to capture control of an area of work. Professionalization has served to separate the press and the law from the public sphere. With an emphasis on expertise and scientific reasoning, both institutions have served as an avenue for corporate-liberal values to be disseminated to the public. As the press and law come to value expertise and institutional knowledge as expressed through professionalization, those values are also prominently displayed for public consumption. The second part of chapter 3 will examine how professionalization as corporate rationalization has changed the press and the law. Press professionalization, with its emphasis on objectivity, routines, and efficiency, has led to a watchdog role for the press—the press serves as a stand-in for an inactive public sphere. Professionalization, as reflected in the dominant intellectual ideas, also influences how the law relates to the public sphere. Beginning with legal formalism, law has engaged in a campaign to become more scientific and to separate itself from the public sphere. It will be argued that today's law-and-economics movement is the culmination of a long attempt to promote the law as a scientific practice, but it is also a way to use those standards to structure public space. Law-and-economics is not a political movement but rather a form of technocracy that emphasizes efficiency and predictability to disguise its moral choices. It replaces questions of justice with questions of procedural fairness. Professionalization, then, allows corporate values to enter the public sphere through its dominant institutions.

Chapter 4 demonstrates how those values are used to structure not only public life but also the institutions and their relationship to the public sphere. One of the strongest indicators of professional status in our society is a privilege that grants members of an occupation a right to withhold information from the state. Journalists have long sought this standing, often called shield laws or their common-law equivalent, journalist's privilege. Through an analysis of more than a hundred years of case law, I will describe how the press and the courts have battled to define their roles in democracy. Over time, the stories journalists tell about their place in democracy have changed from claiming rights enjoyed by all citizens to rights enjoyed by a privileged professional group. This chapter traces a tricky move by journalists as they go from being *of* the public sphere to standing outside the public sphere, while still retaining their ties to the public sphere. The courts acknowledge a public sphere that is generally uninterested and inactive in public life—a public that lives democracy through its institutions. The primary fight displayed in the journalist's-privilege cases and hearings is not about finding what's best for the public sphere, but rather what institutional body—government or the press—is able to stake claim to being the true representative of an inactive and depoliticized public sphere.

The book turns in the third part to an examination of how the courts have shaped our understanding of public life. Chapter 5 looks at how the U.S. Supreme Court has allowed corporations to gain access to the public sphere by granting them First Amendment rights. While the Supreme Court's decision in *First National Bank of Boston v. Bellotti*[20] has been closely scrutinized, this chapter looks at how that decision has been used to collapse distinctions between the press and corporations. The idea of corporate personhood has led the Court to struggle with defining exactly how "corporations" are different from "the press" under the First Amendment. Over the years, the Court has distinguished the press from corporations by looking at the form of the publication as well as the press's information-providing function in society. However, in recent years the Court has moved toward leveling press rights and corporate rights, arguing that the press as an institution does not enjoy special protection under the First Amendment. The Court has recognized and accepted the economic reality of today's democracy: There is little difference between the press and corporations. By collapsing and institutionalizing those differences, the Court dilutes press protections and expands the rights of corporations while hurting the public sphere's ability to insulate itself from corporate influence. The Court sees democracy as a battle for dominance between institutions, ignoring the more fundamental question about what the public sphere needs to thrive in modern society.

Chapter 6 examines how the Supreme Court has sought to limit the use of public space in the United States. By looking for easy decisions that revolve around property and the efficient management of public space and by avoiding difficult political questions, the Court has allowed corporate values to dominate. The Court turns to property issues in an attempt to make value-free decisions, emphasizing a managerial function. This chapter will examine several recent issues—political debates on a state-owned television network, speech in national parks, participation in parades on city streets, and expression at rest areas along interstate highways—and argue that relying on property to resolve First Amendment questions damages the public sphere. The courts view the meaning of speech through an authoritarian framework that allows the property owner to determine what the event means for citizens. By relying on property rights rather than the public's right to determine the meaning of a public event on its own terms, courts emphasize social control and the efficient management of public space at the expense of discourse. The chapter argues that discourse democracy will never flourish until the courts break away from property arguments and begin making independent assessments of the value of the speech to discourse. It will be argued that only by opening up public arenas—those that are publicly owned and those that are also privately owned but generally open to the public—to discursive activity can an active public begin to flourish.

Chapter 7 will offer concluding remarks and suggest some ways that we might undo the damage done to the public sphere through corporate rationalization. It will call on the press to adopt a new professional mission that serves the needs of the public sphere. While we have long worried about securing the rights of individual access to information, we have ignored concerns about enabling citizens to convert that information to action. We need to rethink First Amendment rights to identify ways that value the associational freedoms of individuals and devalue the powers of corporate entities. This would include valuing action as well as expression, carving out public space free from the coercive influence of government and corporate interests, not allowing property issues to determine First Amendment rights, and reconsidering the idea that corporations are people under the Constitution. Empowering the public sphere is not simply a job for institutions but work that must engage all citizens. It requires citizens to adopt a new ethic of public discourse that promotes understanding rather than winning.

This book is not only a study of how institutions have limited the role and function of the public sphere in democracy; it also presents a tentative framework for rethinking the structure of that democracy. Lustig notes that Americans find themselves living in a world that is "collective without being cooperative."[21] This book attempts to help citizens not only understand how that has happened but also to begin thinking about how we might recapture the collective nature of democracy.

PART 1

The Corporation
and Democracy

1

The Rise of Corporate Rationalization

The examination of corporate influence on public life in the United States is not lacking in literature. From Alexis de Tocqueville through the Progressive movement to today's corporate critics, the corporate form—or what Tocqueville called the "manufacturing aristocracy"[1]—has attracted more than its share of attention. Much of that literature can be divided into two camps. On one side are those who see little good in the corporate form and what that form has wrought for today's society. While most Progressives stopped short of calling for an end to corporations, preferring administrative rules, today's critics tend to see little if any good in corporations. In the words of the media critic Robert W. McChesney, "The wealthier and more powerful the corporate media giants have become, the poorer the prospects for participatory democracy."[2]

On the other side are those who argue in favor of expertise, efficiency, and the popular. The rise of corporate America, with its emphasis on scientific management styles, has created a business sector that is better able to serve the needs of democracy by providing "what people want" and by giving voice to citizens, helping us understand our world. In the area of the media, these advocates point to the tremendous amount of information that is available to today's consumers through the Internet, cable television, and publishing outlets. Not only that, the argument goes, but those media outlets are staffed by the best trained, most professional workforce that has ever occupied those offices of culture.[3] Through an emphasis on profitability, efficiency, expertise, and professionalism, the needs of democracy are more than being met.

The debate between these groups is interesting not only because of what it says about modern-day American democracy but because of what issues go unchallenged. The two sides seem to agree that the values of corporations have come to be the values of the public sphere; there is a disagreement about whether that is good or bad, but few seriously dispute the centrality of corporations in modern democracy. No one seemingly challenges the idea that corporations now dominate public life.

Take, for example, the comment by the publisher of the *New York Times,* Arthur Sulzberger Jr.: "'New media are by definition transactional. We need to work more closely with advertisers and marketers to create content that meets their needs. We must develop new ground rules.'"[4] Corporate critics would argue that such claims collapse the distinction between journalism and advertising; corporate advocates would acclaim Sulzberger's forward-thinking mission for making the press more financially sound, thus allowing it to better serve the public by providing what people want.

The point of this chapter is not to rehash this debate. Instead, this book attempts to understand how corporate values have come to play that dominant role by investigating how those values have become ideological. Like most questions concerning public life, there are no easy answers. Still, if we believe that all human developments—including intellectual endeavors—have a history, then we ought to be able to uncover some parts of how this transformation took place. This chapter links the historical development of corporations with corporate liberalism and the Progressive movement in an attempt to provide a foundation for an understanding of that transformation.

Much has been written about the American development of a democracy based on corporate-liberal principles. Historians have tracked how a liberalism based on individualism eventually morphed into a liberalism that was primarily aimed at protecting and enhancing corporate rights. This study explores not the development of that political ideology but rather the hegemonic process that has allowed it to be transferred to the public sphere.

The Growth of Corporations

The threat that corporate power potentially might pose was identified long before the transformation actually began. As Tocqueville wrote in 1831, "I think that all in all, the manufacturing aristocracy that we see rising before our eyes is one of the hardest that has appeared on earth; but it is at the same time one of the most restrained and least dangerous. Still, the friends of democracy ought constantly to turn their regard with anxiety in this direction; for if ever permanent inequality of conditions and aristocracy are introduced anew into the world, one can predict that they will enter by this door."[5]

Despite Tocqueville's warning, the history of corporations in the United States is a long one. Prior to 1800, few corporations existed in the United States.[6] Those that did exist, according to the law historian Lawrence M. Friedman, were churches, charities, or cities. Friedman reports that in the eighteenth century, only 335 businesses were chartered as corporations.[7]

The nineteenth century saw a tremendous growth in the formation of corporations. That growth was tied to the rising economic interests in the United States. As Friedman writes, "[A]s the economy developed, entrepreneurs made more and more use of the corporation, especially for transport ventures. The corporate form was a more efficient way to structure and finance their ventures."[8]

Interestingly, in the early part of the nineteenth century people equated chartered corporations with monopolies, and because of that they were subject to a higher degree of regulation. Corporations were clearly viewed as entities created by the state that hold a special privilege. In Friedman's terms, corporations "were in a sense parasitic, and yet unduly powerful."[9] During these early years of the corporations, legislatures had to routinely grant special charters to what they considered to be deserving corporations. By the 1840s and 1850s, most legislatures had ended that practice and instead granted a general law to oversee the formation of all corporations. As Friedman notes, the special charters were seen as being increasingly inefficient. But perhaps more importantly, it turned the "corporate form into a freely available right, rather than a privilege of the few."[10]

Such changes made the formation of corporations far more accessible to the general public but also increased the potential for abuse. With no limits put on the length of the life or size of corporations, they soon would become powerful players in American law and politics.

The courts began granting rights and privileges to corporations in the early 1800s. In *Dartmouth College v. Woodward*[11] in 1819, the Court granted corporations their first protection under the U.S. Constitution, recognizing contract clause protection. In the case, the New Hampshire legislature attempted to alter a charter for the college—a charter that dated back to George III in 1769. In 1816, the state attempted to bring the college under public control by taking authority away from its trustees. The Court, led by Chief Jus-

tice Marshall, decided that the college's original charter was in effect a contract under the meaning of the Constitution.

It is important to note, however, that Marshall's intent, at least in the eyes
of some observers, was less to carve out protections for corporations than
to protect investors. As such, his purpose was to "assure capitalists the expectation of a reasonable return on their investment in return for providing
public improvements and services useful to the community at large."[12]

While *Dartmouth College v. Woodward* recognized corporations under
contract law, they had not yet been granted broader protection under the
Constitution. Most writers trace the development of the Supreme Court's
recognition of corporations as people to its 1886 decision in *Santa Clara v.
Southern Pacific Railroad.*[13] The question before the Court was whether the
Fourteenth Amendment barred California from taxing the corporate property of a railroad differently from how it taxed the property of individuals.
In siding with the railroad, the Court noted, "The court does not wish to hear
argument on the question whether the provision of the Fourteenth Amendment to the Constitution, which forbids a State to deny to any person within its jurisdiction the equal protection of the laws, applies to these corporations. We are all of opinion that it does."[14]

In the eyes of many, the Court's *Santa Clara* decision was the foundation
for future decisions expanding the rights of corporations. The law professor
Morton Horwitz has argued that *Santa Clara* does not break with precedent
that can be traced back to *Dartmouth College,* however. He sees the Court as
not necessarily accepting corporations as people (often referred to as the
theory of corporate personhood, examined in more detail in chapter 5) but
rather as trying to protect the property rights of individual shareholders,
much as it did in *Dartmouth College.* Horwitz argues that "corporate personhood" theory had not even been developed at the time of the *Santa Clara*
decision and that personhood theory has been gradually absorbed into the
meaning of the *Santa Clara* decision "to establish dramatically new constitutional protections for corporations."[15]

It is clear that as the corporate form developed in the latter part of the
nineteenth century, the legal grounds had been established for an expansion
of corporate rights in the United States. And while the intent of the *Dartmouth College* and *Santa Clara* decisions might have been to protect investors rather than corporate rights per se, those developments when coupled
with other intellectual movements produced an important foundation for
the expansion of corporate rights.

Competitive Capitalism to Corporate Liberalism

As with most thing things involving business after the Civil War, John D. Rockefeller seemed to understand it best. While we often associate the public cry for free and open competition in the marketplace with American business, the death of competitive capitalism was initiated by Rockefeller and other captains of industry.[16] Rockefeller recognized far earlier than most that corporations could not withstand the economic booms and busts associated with growing markets. Following the Civil War he began the move away from competition and toward cooperation and control. As Rockefeller put it, "'This movement was the origin of the whole system of economic administration. It has revolutionized the way of doing business all over the world. The time was ripe for it. It had to come, though all we saw at the moment was the need to save ourselves from wasteful conditions. . . . The day of combination is here to stay. Individualism has gone, never to return.'"[17]

Rockefeller's idea in many ways eerily coincided with the views of many reformers as America neared the twentieth century. Those reformers, loosely organized around the Progressive movement, also recognized that unbridled competition was not the answer to economic problems. As the historian Ron Chernow writes, "Standard Oil has taught the American public an important but paradoxical lesson: Free markets, if left completely to their own devices, can wind up terribly unfree."[18] The vital question was, of course, how to regulate the economy to rein in the undemocratic nature of corporations while still preserving and allowing economic growth. For that, the Progressives turned to regulation and scientific management skills. The hope was that social science would enable the government to manage corporate growth and control its impact on democracy.

As the corporate form began to dominate American capitalism, the Progressives sought to control that power from within. This is evident in many areas of public life, especially in the law and journalism. As will be examined in subsequent chapters, the push to make the law and journalism more scientific has had a powerful impact on those professions. However, in more general terms, Progressive reform worked from the belief that corporations could be controlled and therefore need not be eliminated. As the historian Robert H. Wiebe has written, "In particular, national progressivism had been predicated upon the existence of the modern corporation and its myriad relationships with the rest of American society."[19] The corporations encompassed many of the values that the Progressives also coveted: efficiency, technology, and administrative expertise. As Wiebe writes, "In a way only a few of them fathomed, their alteration strengthened a scheme they disliked by weaving its basic elements into an ever-tighter and more sophisticated national system. A public bureaucracy sheltered as it regulated."[20]

One of the most important ways in which this was done was through alliances with government. Whereas before business had expressed distrust of government, now it turned to government for protection, using cooperation as a way of staving off destructive competitive forces. Wiebe writes of corporations during the Progressive Era, "They wanted a powerful government, but one whose authority stood at their disposal; a strong, responsive government through which they could manage their own affairs in their own way."[21]

To accomplish this task, Progressives and corporations turned to scientific management techniques. Business had long become enamored with the scientific management ideas associated with Frederick Winslow Taylor. Taylor's idea was that the adoption of scientific techniques within the workplace would make business more profitable while improving the lot of workers. The goal was to establish "absolute uniformity" for workers and place more of the burden of making choices in the hands of managers. As Taylor wrote, "The managers assume new burdens, new duties, and responsibilities never dreamed of in the past. The managers assume, for instance, the burden of gathering together all of the traditional knowledge which in the past has been possessed by the workmen and then of classifying, tabulating, and reducing this knowledge to rules, laws, and formulae which are immensely helpful to the workmen in doing their daily work."[22]

The development of these formulae allows management to "replace the judgment of the individual workers" with the expertise of managers.[23] As Taylor noted, "every single act of every workman can be reduced to a science."[24] Of course, Taylor's ideas were accompanied with a particularly unflattering and elitist view of the working class. He believed that one of the greatest problems facing business was "soldiering," or loafing, by workers. He believed this was due not only to the "natural instinct and tendency of men to take it easy" but also to systematic effects—industrious workers will inherently work at the pace and level of the slowest, least productive member of the workforce. As Taylor wrote, "So universal is soldiering for this purpose that hardly a competent workman can be found in a large establishment, whether he works by the day or on piece work, contract work, or under any of the ordinary systems, who does not devote a considerable part of his time to studying just how slow he can work and still convince his employer that he is going at a good pace."[25]

Time-management studies led Taylor to recommend that business adopt scientific practices that emphasized harmony, not discord; cooperation, not individualism; maximum output, not restricted output; and the development of each worker to his or her efficiency and prosperity.[26]

Taylorism, as it became known, confined to the economic sphere of civil society, was an important development. But the ideas associated with Taylorism escaped the confines of the workplace. Corporations were enjoying increasing prominence in all facets of American life, and it did not take long for Taylor's principles to move out of business into other realms of society. As Daniel Nelson notes, Taylor became a spokesman "for the redemptive possibilities of systematic organization and technical expertise in economic and political life."[27]

The influence of scientific management styles can be seen in the mechanization of the workplace—sometimes referred to as Fordism—but also in how the values of that form of industrial organization escaped the workplace. David Harvey has written that what makes Fordism special and ultimately separates it from Taylorism is Ford's "explicit recognition that mass production meant mass consumption" as well as a new kind of social democracy.[28] Ford's goal, according to Harvey, was to "provide workers with sufficient income and leisure time to consume the mass-produced products the corporations were about to turn out in ever vaster quantities."[29]

Here can be seen not only the distinctions between Taylorism and Fordism but also the ability of corporate America to adapt to critique. Despite corporate America's increasing fascination with scientific management skills, Taylor remained no fan of large corporations, though he offered no solutions to their growth. As Nelson writes of Taylor, "He was hostile to big business, critical of politicians, and skeptical of humanitarian gestures, particularly those that involved workers. His labor 'reforms' were premised on the assumption that men worked for money and would improve themselves if offered appropriate financial incentives."[30] Taylor's hostility toward big business led to his alliance with Progressive reformers. In 1910, for example, he joined Louis Brandeis, a prominent Progressive lawyer and future Supreme Court justice, and used his scientific principles to oppose railroad rate increases before the Interstate Commerce Commission, combining in one moment, as Nelson recounts, Taylor's scientific principles and Progressive idealism. The result was a "scientific" solution to the problem that would benefit all parties—the consumer, the shipper, the workers, and the railroads. The Taylor-Brandeis alliance would spark an "efficiency craze" and make Taylor a public figure.[31]

But more importantly, as Fordism subsumed and adopted Taylorism, it produced a new form of democracy. As Antonio Gramsci noted long ago, Fordism changed the worker's life both inside and outside the factory. As wages increased, it became necessary for the state and industry to make sure those wages were used in responsible ways. As Gramsci wrote, "It is in their interests to have a stable, skilled labour force, a permanently well-adjusted complex, because the human complex (the collective workers) of an enterprise is also a machine which cannot, without considerable loss, be taken to pieces too often and renewed with single new parts."[32] The ultimate lesson to be learned from Taylorism and Fordism is that democracy can—and ought to—be managed. And it is here that the Progressive movement made its greatest contribution.

The Progressive Influence

The influence of Progressive thought on the development of a corporate-liberal ideology is large. The Progressive movement, running from the late 1800s through the 1920s, is generally portrayed as an effort to put experts in control of the decisions that need to be made in a democratic society—or in Wiebe's phrase, "a search for order."[33] The Progressive movement was a middle-class reform movement.[34] That is, the people who benefited the most from the reforms put forward during the Progressive Era were members of the middle class. In that same way, the Progressive movement tinkered with changing capitalism but never called into question the legitimacy of capitalism itself.

Wiebe argues that the important point is not that the Progressives were class-bound but that their version of reform tolerated the exclusion of the lower class.[35] As one example of that exclusion, Wiebe notes that during the Progressive Era, discussion about elections in the United States changed from trying to attract the largest number of voters to trying to attract the most intelligent voters. Wiebe argues that by eliminating the importance of "the people," society is damaged.[36]

But the Progressive movement also changed relationships between people, corporations, and the expertise that should be used to guide society. As Wiebe writes, "The heart of progressivism was the ambition of the new middle class to fulfill its destiny through bureaucratic means."[37] The place to find that bureaucratic structure was in the developing corporation. As Martin J. Sklar has noted, the corporation for many people in the United States became the new frontier, offering opportunities that had not been available to large numbers of Americans. But it is wrong to view this corporate reconstruction of America as displacing all class structure: "The corporate reconstruction, accordingly, was less a process of displacement of one bourgeois stratum by another than of an evolving adaptation of older prominent families and the continuous accretion of newer families, in both metropolis and province, to the corporate overhaul of market and property relations."[38]

With the rise of this new corporate power came a new way of viewing knowledge. While Progressives placed an increased emphasis on science, their definition of science did not emphasize results so much as methodology.[39] "Science," as Wiebe explains, "had become a procedure, or an orientation, rather than a body of results."[40]

This fascination with science and its democratic potential is evident in the intellectual ideas at the heart of Progressivism—the pragmatist movement. Charles Peirce argued that because knowledge is social, no one individual can ever know reality. While on its face Peirce's pragmatisim seems to directly undermine any notion of control, Thomas L. Haskell argues that what he constructed was a "bulwark against skepticism": "Even though Peirce ruled out for all practical purposes the very possibility of absolute certainty, he also promised an escape from radical uncertainty in the here and now. . . . [T]he very existence of a community of inquiry was a guarantee against intellectual chaos, because the community's current best opinion was the closest approach to the truth that mankind could ever hope to achieve in practice."[41]

Peirce and other pragmatists were fascinated with the possibility of statistics to allow society to make predictions. As Louis Menand writes in his account of the intellectual ideas that grounded pragmatism, "For people who believed—as most nineteenth-century scientists did believe—that understanding something was synonymous with being able to measure it, the appeal of statistics was plain. It permitted observations of phenomena—not just orbits and molecules, but risks, genes, suicides, nose size, almost anything— to be expressed in mathematical language."[42]

As R. Jeffrey Lustig notes, the theory that grounded pragmatism in science also said something about citizens—who they were and what role they played in democracy. It reduced "knowing" to an institutionalized epistemology where "the knower began to be seen as a person guided in his or her judgments by the verdicts of institutional experimental procedures."[43]

Science was in turn used to form and massage the body politic. Social science techniques could now be used to discover, with scientific validity, what "the people" really wanted. And, of course, it was no longer necessary to rely on the votes of the entire population; policy could be based on a scientific, statistical sample of that population. As Stuart Ewen has demonstrated in his social history of the public relations industry, the goal of Progressive-Era reformers became finding a way to use social science to manage public opinion, not as a way to necessarily increase public information. That perspective is perhaps best reflected in Walter Lippmann's *Drift and Mastery*,[44] where he argues for social science to direct a wide variety of social policy concerns. The most important thing, however, was the connection between social science and social control. As Ewen writes, "To some extent, this instrumental association between social science and social management had been brewing since the late nineteenth century. Accompanying a democratic current of social analysis that sought to educate the public at large, another—more cabalistic—tradition of social-scientific thought was emerging, one that saw the study of society as a tool by which a technocratic elite could help serve the interests of vested power."[45]

The rise of consumerism coincided with this movement. Increasingly in American society, "consumers" were replacing "citizens". The Progressive movement and its accompanying ideology thus not only influenced workers and their relation to industry but rather all social relationships. In the late 1800s and early 1900s, reformers realized that to change worker-industry relationships, they needed to redefine "the arenas in which workers might commit themselves to the industrial process."[46] Following Fordism, there was a rise in industry-sponsored theatrical performances, safety programs, and recreational programs. Consumerism arose in response to the alienating nature of industrializing society—as a way to give citizens something to do, something to achieve, and something to look forward to. As Ewen notes, "The commercial culture strove to leave corporate domination of the productive process intact and at the same time speak to the demand for a richer social life for those who worked and lived within the industrial context."[47]

Wiebe captures the irony of what he calls the "new individualism," where Americans participate in their own marginalization by adopting the "values of the atomized consumer": "As an activity common to all, modern consumerism offered a new understanding of citizenship, one that gathered people into a society without demanding anything in particular either of them or of their society."[48]

Having secured legal standing as people under the Constitution by the mid 1800s, corporations began looking for other ways to establish their humanness. In the 1900s, corporations began focusing on social welfare issues and public relations to convince people they had a soul. As Roland Marchand notes, corporate publicity went far beyond the legal boundaries and has "ensured corporate imagery a prominent role in public dialogues on family, class, community, and politics."[49]

The most damaging aspect of all of this might be what it means for democracy. The rise of a corporate culture isn't only an economic movement but a movement that fundamentally changes how people function and relate to other people within a democratic society. Ewen's work, for example, has demonstrated that underlying advertising is a message about the centralization of the political process: "Democracy was never treated as something that flowed out of people's needs or desires, but was rather an expression of people's ability to participate in and emulate the 'pluralism of values' which were paraded before people and which filtered downward from the directors of business enterprise."[50]

The business elite became someone or something to look up to. In much the same way that Thorstein Veblen argued for his idea of social emulation, where members of social classes routinely look to the next highest class for guidance, the business elite became not only the creators of consciousness but something to be emulated and admired.[51]

Conclusion

This brief historical account does not account for all of the movements that have influenced today's corporate power. Rather, the intent was to provide a link with some important ideas that have been used in unique ways to build that power. Buried within Taylorism, Fordism, and Progressivism can be seen the uneasy tension between democracy and the corporate form. While one can easily identify the link between Fordism and corporate power, that link is less secure between Taylorism and the Progressive movement. Both, at some level, opposed corporate power yet today can be identified as important building blocks in corporate rationalization. As T. J. Jackson Lears notes, cultural hegemony is a "continual process" not a "static superstructure": "As older values become less fashionable, they are widely discarded but persist in residual forms. Newer values, which sometimes seem potentially subversive at first, are frequently sanitized and incorporated into the mainstream of enlightened opinion."[52]

Some of the process identified by Lears can be seen in the establishment of corporate rationalization. While perhaps never direct advocates of corporate power, Taylorism and Progressivism contributed to the growth of corporate power in at least two important ways. First of all, they provided the intellectual tools that allowed corporations to increase their domination over public life. Such concepts as efficiency and methodologies for "discovering" public opinion have only grown in importance since the 1920s.

Secondly, both legitimized corporate values in the eyes of the public. The Progressives are often viewed as being strong advocates of open, honest government that is more protective of the average person. Kevin Mattson has eloquently defended the Progressive movement from criticism, noting that efficiency was central to democratic reforms: "Democracy was efficient because it did away with the corrupt influence of big business and the meddling of special interests in the political process."[53] Mattson argues that it is wrong to examine the Progressive movement through the modern-day lens that has grown to question efficiency as a democratic standard.[54]

Much of this is true. To criticize the Progressive movement using today's values, however, is not to assign evil intent. There is little doubt that Progressives, in all of their many forms, truly sought to improve democratic life. The question is not their intentions but the results. Today we are living, at least to some degree, with the legacy of the Progressive movement. The Progressives perhaps unwittingly laid the foundation for the rise of the corporate domination of public life. While political cronyism was limited, we also must understand that the bureaucratic form introduced and given political legitimacy by Progressivism has proven to be just as damaging to public life. To understand how that has happened, we turn to the concept of corporate rationalization.

2

Corporate Rationalization and Discourse Democracy: Seeking Alternatives

The history of corporate liberalism helps us understand the dominant political landscape that we live in today, but it does not explain how it became dominant and how citizens might critique that form. In an attempt to provide a framework for addressing those weaknesses, this chapter explores two ideas: rationalization and discourse democracy. The rationalization process, as put forward by Max Weber and applied to the modern welfare state by Jürgen Habermas, explains how bureaucratic logic has come to dominate the public sphere. Weber, while identifying the process, saw little that could be done to escape the problem. Habermas and a number of other scholars have suggested that the way out of the problem is through communication, allowing diverse communities and individuals to resolve differences among themselves. This broad project is often labeled discourse democracy, and the first part of this chapter will offer a brief overview of Habermas's relevance to this project.

The second part of this chapter will look at the implications of discourse democracy for revitalizing the public sphere, especially by offering a discursive interpretation of First Amendment rights. It will be argued that the First Amendment rights of free speech, press, and assembly are at the heart of revitalizing the public sphere. However, the public sphere will not be empowered unless it breaks free of the liberal interpretation of rights that has allowed corporations to use those rights to their advantage. Only through a discursive interpretation of the First Amendment will citizens be able to carve out public space free from corporate interference. The goal of this chapter is not to lay out a complete theory of the First Amendment but rather to identify several areas where discourse theory might be used to oppose corporate rationalization. Those differences—the public meaning of speech, the role of public fora, freedom of association, and the role of institutions—will serve as the foundation of the critique of the press and the law in subsequent chapters.

Formal Rationalization and Corporations

While Weber put forward at least four versions of rationalization, his idea of formal rationalization best describes the problem addressed in this book.[1] For Weber, society's development led to an increase in bureaucratic structures. And while he perceived a good side to the development of formal rules, he feared total control by bureaucratic structures. Known as the Weberian paradox, the increasing rationalization of society freed citizens from ties to the limits of traditional society but exposed them to increasingly controlling bureaucratic structures.

Formal rationality, in the words of Stephen Kalberg, "relates to spheres of life and a structure of domination that acquired specific and delineated boundaries only with industrialization."[2] Formal rationalization encompasses the means-end calculations that have become so important to modern-day capitalism, nicely captured in the phrase of the sociologist George Ritzer, "the McDonaldization" of society.[3] As Kalberg explains formal rationalization, "the most 'rational' type of domination is found in the bureaucracy simply because it aims to do nothing more than calculate the most precise and efficient means for the resolution of problems by ordering them under universal and abstract regulations."[4] This means-end calculation has negative consequences for the practice of democracy. It eliminates the personal element and thus moves ethical considerations to the margins. Ethics is seen increasingly as subjective— something that cannot be calculated or controlled. Policy and business questions are reduced to questions of profitability and efficiency. The trade-off is that while increased rationality tends to dehumanize society, it also leads to increased efficiency, a more predictable output, a greater ability to calculate or quantify parts of society, and a greater control over people, often through the use of technology.[5]

Weber feared that the domination of rules would lead to an iron cage from which citizens would be unable to escape. And his basic belief about the Enlightenment path leading to increasing bureaucratization of society had a profound effect on other writers, most notably critical theorists such as Max Horkheimer, Theodor Adorno, and Herbert Marcuse. For them, modern society was faced with hopelessness—there was no real chance of escape from the iron cage that Weber described. The best that could be accomplished was to criticize the condition, but escape was not really an option. As Seyla Benhabib has written, these Frankfurt School theorists believed that rationalization generated an "epistemic illusion"—"the more efficient, planned, scientific, and direct administrative control became, the more general, impersonal, and anonymous" it seemed.[6] In other words, the more domination increased, the less it was seen as direct domination. As Benhabib writes, "They agreed with Weber that by increasingly diminishing the cognitive as well as the practical capacities of individuals to defy orders and regulations, and to define for themselves a meaningful and right course of action, societal rationalization generated an irretrievable 'loss of freedom.'"[7]

It is easy to find connections between the process Weber describes and the industrialization that has accompanied the rise of corporate ownership. Taylorism, when coupled with Fordism and a growing bureaucracy encouraged by Progressivism, emphasized the very concepts central to formal rationalization. As Ritzer points out, everything from fast food to shopping malls have been influenced by the rationalization process.[8] Eric Nelson, in his examination of the largest mall in the United States, the Mall of America in Bloomington, Minnesota, notes how the development of shopping malls is linked to discovering a new way to invent community. Malls were envisioned by their "inventor," the architect Victor Gruen, as creating a new Main Street to bring people together. Nelson points out, however, that Gruen overlooked the fact that malls are about creating consumers, not citizens.[9] As Nelson writes, "Some things, however, cannot be purchased at any price. A community of consumers may have stores, restaurants, nightclubs, theaters, a school, an amusement park, a medical clinic, even a post office. What it does not have is a soul."[10]

It is often hard for people to understand the destructive force of modern corporate structures such as shopping malls on society. As we gain consumer culture, we have a difficult time realizing what we are losing in terms of civic culture. As places like shopping malls become more ingrained in the democratic culture, spending time there seems second nature. It *is* easy, convenient, and efficient. By choosing the mall, however, we tend to lose public places. This does not mean that as a society those public places no longer physically exist. In most places, they still do, but our interaction—or rather, lack of interaction—with them changes that public space. In fact, when public officials attempt to find ways to bring people back to public areas, they turn towards the commercial sector for help—to find businesses that will help revitalize areas. We journey to the mall or similar retreats, allowing our public and private lives to be structured around the needs of the corporation. As Herbert Schiller noted in 1989, "Enclosure is the appropriate description for what has been happening in the United States in the last twenty-five years, not to farmlands—most of that has long since been bought up by corporate agri-business—but to the sites and channels of public expression and creativity."[11]

Malls, then, are representative of how corporate logic has rationalized the nature and structure of public space. However, malls are simply reflective of the larger problem that faces public life today.

Rethinking the Iron Cage

Habermas, working in the tradition of early critical theorists, attempts to break free of the limitations of Weber's view of rationalization. Where Weber sees an iron cage, Habermas see roads not taken and opportunities lost. In the words of Richard Bernstein, Habermas's work allows people to "confront honestly the challenges, critiques, the unmasking of illusions; to work through these, and still responsibly reconstruct an informed comprehensive perspective on modernity and its pathologies."[12] Habermas's views on rationalization can be seen in his wider project, an attempt to recast democratic theory to allow discursive democracy to flourish.

Whereas Habermas's early work makes no distinction between society and the systems that functionally organize it, his theory of communicative action provides a more complex structural model. Essentially, he divides the modern welfare state into two parts: system and lifeworld.[13]

The lifeworld is where communicative action takes place. It is in the lifeworld that tradition, culture, and language are "intersubjectively shared" and communication is made possible.[14] As James Bohman describes Habermas's concept, the lifeworld "is the stock of consensual, background knowledge which makes processes of further mutual understanding possible."[15] The public sphere, where private people come together to form something we can call public opinion,[16] is part of the lifeworld. While action, understanding, and meaning are embedded in the lifeworld, they are functionally organized in the system. It is in the system, the area of strategic action controlled by the market and the bureaucratic state, that the material needs of the lifeworld are sustained.[17] Habermas argues that the system is organized through money or power, while the lifeworld values communication through language. The ultimate goal of the lifeworld is understanding, attempting to ascertain what other members of society are trying to communicate. As Habermas notes, communicative action serves the function of reaching understanding, coordinating action, and socializing actors.[18] Its basic goal is agreement.[19] The goal of the system, however, is vastly different. Its goal is not communicative action but strategic action. The end result is success but not necessarily understanding.

Habermas takes seriously the participatory nature of democracy. Yet, rather than restructure society entirely, he works to cordon off areas of society to enable the formation of political will absent interference from state and economic forces.[20] One of the reasons for the decline of public life, according to Habermas, is that values that govern the administrative and economic spheres have come to replace the value of communicative action.[21] Habermas argues that public life has been "colonized" by bureaucratic institutions.[22] This colonization has had a devastating impact on democratic society. Individuals within society have become less citizens than consumers—people whose primary reason for being has more to do with the markets they serve than the democratic functions they perform.[23]

Following Weber, Habermas sees the consequences of modernity—bureaucratization, professionalism, the loss of meaning—as damaging to society as a whole. The result of modernity, for Habermas, has been the rationalization of the lifeworld; that is, "the lifeworld is both uncoupled from and made dependent upon increasingly complex, formally organized domains of action, like the economy and state administration."[24] The lifeworld, in effect, is no longer necessary for coordinating action in society. Instead, the organizing function has been taken over by the system, and the knowledge to coordinate society has been transformed from practical knowledge that can be comprehended by the public to technical knowledge that can be understood only by experts.[25] The "technicizing of the lifeworld" robs citizens "of the meaning of their own actions."[26]

The result for Habermas "is the monetarization and bureaucratization of everyday practices both in the private and public spheres."[27] Bohman, in explicating Habermas's arguments, offers specific examples of this phenomenon: "[M]arkets and the defense bureaucracy have come to determine, more and more, the questions and methods of scientific research; universities are increasingly becoming integrated into the occupational system; and finally, the insurance industry is increasingly dictating the nature of medical practice."[28]

This rationalization process has had dire consequences for the public sphere. The exact contours of what Habermas means by the "public sphere" remain difficult to pin down. It is not an institution or an organization, but more properly it is conceived of as "a network for communicating information and points of view."[29] Habermas notes that the idea of a public sphere refers neither to its functions nor to the content of the discussions that it enables. Instead it refers to the "social space generated in communicative action."[30]

The public sphere is envisioned as a social space where private people come together to form something that might be called public opinion. That opinion, however, does not rule. According to Habermas, "the communication structures of the public sphere relieve the public of the burden of decision making; the postponed decisions are reserved for the institutionalized political process."[31]

Habermas's portrayal has been criticized on a number of fronts. First of all, critics have claimed, and Habermas has admitted, that his idea of a public sphere confuses the empirical and the normative. That is, his study is both an historical examination of events and a theoretical construction of an unrealized, and perhaps unrealizable, future. Critics contend that Habermas cannot have it both ways.[32] And secondly, Habermas's portrayal of the public sphere has been criticized for supporting access for all people to the public sphere but ignoring the historical reality that not all people have been included in the public sphere. Various writers have argued that women,[33] as well as workers, servants, and people supporting certain social issues, have historically been excluded.[34] Habermas has attempted to address those concerns in his more recent work, where he explains the communicative practices and principles that are at the heart of the public sphere.

Habermas attempts to reconcile the ideas of democracy and individual autonomy.[35] He hopes to find a way to allow individuals to bring their particular interests into the discussion about how society ought to be organized. Laws, for Habermas, are vital for this process: "By their very structure, laws are defined by the question of which norms citizens want to adopt for regulating their common life."[36] In this way, law and morality are intertwined in the law: "The law of a concrete legal community must, if it is to be legitimate, at least be compatible with moral standards that claim universal validity beyond the legal community."[37]

It is important to understand that Habermas does not see universal rights as natural or preexisting. Instead, individuals constitute rights through discourse.[38] He has identified some basic rights central to achieving a discursive society. These rights focus on the status of individuals (such as freedom against the state) as well as associational rights that allow citizens to come together.[39] Habermas's goal is to identify a system of rights that "consists neither in spontaneous market forces nor in the deliberate measures of the welfare state."[40] Rather, it exists "in the currents of communication and public opinion" that are central to civil society.[41] Beyond that, however, Habermas also seeks a mediating space between liberal and communitarian thought. The paradigm of law that he puts forward does not favor a "particular vision of the good life" but instead "states the necessary conditions under which legal subjects in their role of enfranchised citizens can reach an understanding with one another."[42] In the end, Habermas hopes to identify "structural similarities" between law and communicative action and a "conceptual and internal relation" between law and democracy.[43]

Habermas has claimed that the only force that can serve as a check on the growth of illegitimate power is "a suspicious, mobile, alert, and informed public sphere from which legitimate law can arise."[44] Central to this is how communicative action is converted into democratic procedures.[45]

The Foundation of Discourse Theory:
From Active to Informed Citizens

The central question for discourse theories of democracy is how to reverse the colonization of the public sphere and restore an active public. Jean L. Cohen and Andrew Arato have argued that the public sphere needs both positive and negative rights:[46] positive rights that enable participation in democratic will formation, and negative rights and liberties that assure independence from state and corporate interference.[47] Discourse theory sees the problem as larger than the implementation of rights: it seeks to change the culture of democracy.

One of the central cultural problems facing democracy is the confusion between two types of publics: an informed public and an active public. Both relate directly to the constitution of the public sphere as well as to issues of freedom of speech and press. The confusion between the two has had dire consequences for American democracy.

In most current discourse about these ideas, the two terms are used interchangeably. An informed public gathers information and uses it in some way. It is my argument, however, that today we are heavy on encouraging the collection of information and light on the idea of promoting action. In fact, much of today's information is intended to discourage—or at the very least not encourage—action.[48] Before we turn to the problem the distinction presents for democracy, I will address the ideas underlying these types of publics.

Much of the discourse about contemporary public life centers around ideas of an informed public, a group of people who are isolated and inactive but nonetheless informed about political life by society's institutions. Individualism, not community, is at the core of an informed public. It is concerned with protecting the rights of individuals to receive information. The citizen in an informed public achieves his or her goals in relative isolation, requiring only the aid of information-providing institutions.

A classic link to the idea of an informed public can be found in the writings of Paul F. Lazarsfeld and Robert K. Merton.[49] They describe the narcotizing dysfunction of the media, where members of society have substituted "knowledge about" a situation for action. Part of this is due to the vast amount of information that confronts citizens on a daily basis. Deciding what and what not to act on is difficult. However, information-providing institutions rarely encourage action.[50] And perhaps this should not surprise us. As Walter Benjamin pointed out long ago, the idea of "information" as a form of communication developed out of capitalism. Benjamin noted the authoritative nature of communication as information that comes to the audience fully explained.[51] In that sense, the idea of communication as information devalues the role of the audience and deliberation.

The idea of an informed public goes far beyond information-providing institutions such as the press, however. The Supreme Court often grounds its decisions in the idea of an informed public. For example, the Court has recognized the right of citizens to receive information from other countries, an idea closely linked to an informed public, but has refused to recognize a more active right of citizens to travel to other countries to gather that information for themselves.[52]

An active public, however, assumes a very different type of citizen. At its center is the creation of community. An active public requires or is constituted by citizens who are active in political life and who possess a shared sense of community; it has developed or is in the process of developing avenues that will make that sense of community a reality. Acting is primarily a social activity and a central part of political life, requiring other members of society to make that action relevant. As Hannah Arendt has noted, a life without speech and action "is literally dead to the world; it has ceased to be a human life" because it no longer has ties to the community.[53]

This distinction between an informed and active public is expressed in many ways in our culture. One of the more prominent ways is through the discourse about the meaning of the First Amendment. Broadly speaking, First Amendment theory revolves around two basic ideas: It articulates a way to protect an individual's right to speak or publish, or, failing that, it grants broad protections to an institution, such as the press, that serves as a stand-in for individuals. Mainstream First Amendment theory fails to recognize the importance of action, preferring to focus on speech.

The desire to separate speech from action in First Amendment theory has a long history. As early as 1911, the Supreme Court was attempting to draw a distinction between "normal speech" and "verbal acts."[54] In that vein, the Supreme Court has concentrated on attempting to determine when speech crosses the magical line and becomes conduct that government has the right to prohibit. Much of First Amendment theory is based on the idea that expression but not conduct is protected. As Thomas I. Emerson puts it, "A majority of one has the right to control action, but a minority of one has the right to talk."[55]

Where the line is drawn between expression and conduct, of course, varies from theorist to theorist and court to court. However, the expression-conduct heuristic provides the parameters for the discussion. When questions are raised about whether to allow some type of activity, be it closer to speech or action, theorists and judges attempt to fit it into that expression-conduct framework. In short, the expression-conduct debate has become part of the ideology of the First Amendment.

The problem with the expression-conduct dichotomy is that over time it ceases to be a guide to thinking about problems of expression and instead becomes a method of categorizing difficult cases. It reduces speech to the "objective" categorization of expressive acts—a categorization that masks the political content of those decisions. Action is cast as something that is not to be valued or, at the very least, that is of less value to society than expression. Those theorists who do find some value in action often elect to label that action as expression. For example, Emerson, an influential theorist in the expression-conduct formulation, has argued that burning a draft card is expression, but blocking a street or building is unprotected action.[56] To label one as expression and the other as action ignores the fact that both are physical, not verbal, acts. In effect, when Emerson elects to grant burning a draft card expression status, he is making a political choice. Perhaps it is the correct choice, but it is a political choice nonetheless.

There is good expression and bad expression, just as there is good action and bad action. There is expression that is central to the formation of the public sphere, and there is action that is central to that formation. Action can include anything from setting a house on fire to attending a city council meeting. One is to be valued and protected, the other clearly is not.

If the goal is an informed public, the expression-conduct heuristic might be a workable option. It protects the individual's right to speak and to receive information from institutional sources such as the press or governmental bodies. In that regard, the metaphor of the "free flow of information" provides an apt image of an informed public—messages flow downstream to consumers. However, rivers only flow in one direction, providing few outlets for citizens to convert those messages into action.

If the goal is an active public, the expression-conduct heuristic falls short. Using the model of an active public, the focus is placed on the exchange of information between equal members of a community. Citizens are encouraged to collect information and share it and their opinion with other citizens. Under mainstream First Amendment theory, however, the individual collection of information is often viewed as unprotected conduct. In a democracy that takes seriously the desire to create an active public sphere, the right to gather information should be protected. In that regard, the ultimate choice is not between expression and conduct but rather between an informed public and an active public.

Unfortunately, much of democratic theory is not an attempt to increase citizen action but rather to find a way to accommodate an informed public. Theorists are faced with the problem of either admitting that the United States is not a democracy because of an apathetic public or finding a way to account for that apathetic public in their theories.[57] The latter option is more frequently used, as institutions are treated as proxies for an inactive public. Often lost in that struggle, however, is the very question of the value of political action to democratic life—a question that for many seems irrelevant or hopelessly idealistic in a country as large and diverse as the United States.

To dismiss the possibility of an active public, however, is to give up on what some believe to be a central component of democratic life. Arendt, for one, argues for the importance of political action. In her classic work *The Human Condition*, she admits to the loss of community in modern society but struggles to hold on to its relevance for society. "What makes mass society so difficult to bear is not the number of people involved, or at least not primarily, but the fact that the world between them has lost its power to gather them together, to relate and to separate them."[58]

First Amendment Implications of Discourse Theory

If we begin from the point of discourse theory, the structure and rights that are needed to attain an active public change. The following is an attempt to articulate how discourse theory might affect our understanding of the First Amendment and the role it plays in constituting public life. It will be argued that discourse theory leads to substantial breaks from current understandings of the First Amendment in the United States and that this interpretation might be used to oppose corporate rationalization. I will identify several areas where discourse theory departs from traditional understandings of the First Amendment, particularly focusing on four areas that are of particular importance to the idea of the corporate rationalization of public life: the public meaning of private speech, the regulation of public fora, the concept of freedom of association, and the role of institutions.

Underlying Principles

In addition to making a distinction between an informed and active public, discourse theory also breaks from the liberal understanding of free speech. In attempting to put limits on government's control of speech, liberal theorists have tended to overvalue individual freedom and idealize the marketplace.[59] While liberalism's ideas of individual freedom and the marketplace of ideas emerged separately and exist in an uneasy tension, they are nonetheless influential.

It could be argued that discourse theory is simply another term for a marketplace of ideas—that Habermas's public sphere is nothing more than a marketplace where people come together to exchange ideas. To do so misses Habermas's point, however. In his early work, he drew a distinction between what he called a culture-debating public and a culture-consuming public.[60] As the rule of the market enters the public realm, it distorts dialogue, making it into something that can be bought and sold. Discourse theory struggles to remove the market from public discourse, believing that unequal economic forces lead to coercive dialogue.

Jon Elster has defined this distinction as the difference between the market and the forum. Democratic theory that follows a market model, such as the theory of Joseph Schumpeter and more recently social choice theory, builds on economic terms and aggregates individual decisions. Democracy that functions as a forum is less about individual decisions and more about collective action for a common purpose.[61]

Perhaps more importantly, however, the merging of liberal thought and the marketplace creates an instrumental approach to freedom of expression. Liberal theory, with its connections to the marketplace metaphor, creates avenues in which individuals are to fight to achieve expressive victory. Free speech in our modern understanding of the concept deemphasizes the exchange of ideas and emphasizes individual expression and winning the debate in the marketplace of ideas. The goal is not understanding, as in Habermas's idea of communicative action, but winning, or strategic action. The power of this instrumental understanding of free speech is illustrated in numerous writings by free speech proponents, from John Milton's famous challenge, "who ever knew truth put to the worse in a free and open encounter?"[62] to Justice Oliver Wendell Holmes's classic articulation of the marketplace of ideas, "the best test of truth is the power of the thought to get itself accepted in the competition of the market."[63]

Put another way, the difference between an instrumental and a discourse approach to free speech is: In liberal thought, discourse serves as a means to an end (achieving truth, individual freedom, justice, and so on),[64] while in discursive thought the discourse is an end in itself.[65] The marketplace in liberal free speech thought is not a place where ideas are exchanged for the sake of deliberation but a way to assure that an idea becomes dominant.

This becomes obvious when analyzing the ideas that underlie Holmes's vision of a marketplace and its role in democratic life. Seeing combinations as a fact of modern life, he attempted to create the space for them (be they workers or businesses) to establish what would pass as truth. As R. Jeffrey Lustig notes, "He was not pro-labor; he was pro-combination. And he was content that modern society was dominated by capitalist combinations."[66] Holmes was content to allow the status quo to dominate and determine what was considered true. And so in his *Abrams* decision, he grants protection to the protesters only because there is little threat that they will achieve their objectives.[67] The marketplace of ideas, in Holmes's worldview, does not serve a discursive function but rather helps establish order in the chaos of democratic life. Lustig sums up Holmes's views as follows: "He may truly have been a friend of the common man, but only to the extent that such men and women would benefit by life in a society where order flowed from the needs of objective institutions rather than from subjective rights."[68]

It has already been noted that in modern western society, administrative and economic systems have become uncoupled from the public sphere. Free speech then becomes instrumental in that it is less about deliberation on how we ought to live than about "marketing" an idea to an audience. This is nowhere more evident than in today's political dialogue[69] and in the increasing protection given by the Supreme Court to commercial speech in the United States.[70]

Another important distinction between discourse theory and current American interpretations of the First Amendment lies in their different conceptions of state action. While discourse theory remains suspicious of government, it does not view government as the sole or even necessarily the most important impediment to a just society. Important restrictions on free speech come from the private sector. For discourse theorists, a real threat to public life exists when private concerns receive power and legitimacy through governmental action. Following Cass Sunstein, discourse theory envisions state action as a much broader concept than its current interpretation provides. Rather than denying or limiting government's role in a system of freedom of expression, common in traditional liberal interpretations, Sunstein argues for an active governmental role. Building on arguments first put forward by New Deal reformers in relation to property rights, he argues that freedom of expression cannot be "prepolitical."[71] In this sense, freedom of expression is a construct of the state, much like property rights. As Sunstein notes, "The fact that markets are creatures of law meant not that they were impermissible, but that they would be assessed in terms of what they did on behalf of the human beings subject to them. Markets would not be identified with liberty in an *a priori* way; they would have to be evaluated through an examination of whether they served liberty or not."[72]

Sunstein does not attack the idea of markets[73] but rather suggests that markets are a creation of government and therefore subject to review by government. Therefore, in his opinion, shopping center owners are allowed to exclude protestors only because the government has given them the power to do so;[74] broadcast owners can exclude speakers because the government has provided them with exclusive ownership rights.[75]

The critique of state action, then, is twofold: state action is used by courts either to avoid making difficult decisions or to protect certain empowered groups. Discourse theory calls for a broader interpretation of state action, recognizing the vital role government plays in the creation of a system of freedom of expression and arguing that that system is only legitimate if it enables citizens to exercise discursive rights.

Having provided some background assumptions, I will now explain how discourse theory differs from liberal First Amendment theory in several areas.

The Public Meaning of Speech

Scholars from various disciplines have challenged the simplistic idea that meaning exists only in the author or speaker. In fact, some communication scholars, such as John Fiske, argue that meaning exists primarily in the audience.[76] Critics of that approach, such as Douglas Kellner, argue for a broader understanding of meaning.[77] Kellner refuses to "truncate" cultural studies and recognizes the need for understanding the role social relations and institutions play in constructing meaning for the audience.[78]

While discourse theory is closer to Kellner's ideas than those of Fiske, there are important differences between Kellner's views and discourse theory. Meaning, which is the product of the lifeworld for Habermas, is produced through the free and independent exchange of ideas. In what has come to be called his linguistic turn, Habermas argues that meaning is derived from "linguistic expressions rather than from speakers' intentions."[79] Meaning is derived from the linguistic relationships in which citizens find themselves and is a product of understanding that arises from the interaction between two individuals who agree to seek that understanding. For Habermas, "Speakers and hearers understand the meaning of a sentence when they know under what conditions it is true. Correspondingly, they understand the meaning of a word when they know what contribution it makes to the capacity for truth of a sentence formed with its help. Thus . . . the meaning of a sentence is determined by its truth conditions."[80]

Meaning, under discourse theory, is discursively redeemed; it does not exist solely in the author's intent but in the complex linguistic relationship between speaker and hearer. The key to creating that ethical discourse is allowing all citizens who want to participate to do so.

In the law as well as journalism, intent plays a critical role in the discovery of meaning. Through the attempt to discover the original intent of some speaker or text, both institutions seek to fix meaning in space and time. The discovery of the original intent of a speaker or a text is an authoritative act that is often used to block challenges and to claim a higher status for an idea. The interpretation is no longer the opinion of one isolated individual but rather an agreed upon meaning that has historical and cultural power. Discovering meaning is reduced to methodology.

This becomes apparent in the writings of U.S. Supreme Court Justice Antonin Scalia, who has termed himself a "faint-hearted originalist." He recognizes that the discovery of meaning is difficult, if not impossible, and that judges need to be cautious. Yet, he explains, "Originalism does not aggravate the principal weakness of the system, for it establishes a historical criterion that is conceptually quite separate from the preferences of the judge himself. And the principal defect of that approach—that historical research is always difficult and sometimes inconclusive—will, unlike nonoriginalism, lead to a more moderate rather than a more extreme result."[81]

As can be seen from Scalia's comments, if we begin from the idea that intent can be fixed in time and space, then the discovery of that intent becomes a question of methodology. But more than anything else, the search for original intent makes the individual speaker or text the focus of attention rather than the public sphere.

Recent free speech doctrine puts the control of meaning securely in the hands of the speaker (or, perhaps more accurately, in the hands of the owner). The meaning of a public event, such as a parade or public demonstration, is what the speaker or owner wants it to be. In that way, free speech doctrine endorses an authoritarian approach to the establishment of meaning. When the U.S. Supreme Court allowed a state-owned television network to hold political debates from which minority-party candidates were excluded,[82] it ignored the discursive needs of the public sphere. The Court allowed the network, the speaker, to decide the meaning of the debate. Viewing meaning as residing in the speaker results in an informed public. The only role for the audience is listening.

The importance of authorial intent is so powerful in the eyes of the Supreme Court that it plays a significant role in deciding whether conduct is deserving of protection as expression. In 1974, the Court ruled that the First Amendment protects a student's right to display an American flag with a peace symbol taped on it. In a *per curiam* opinion, the Court wrote, "A flag bearing a peace symbol and displayed upside down by a student today might be interpreted as nothing more than bizarre behavior, but it would have been difficult for the great majority of citizens to miss the drift of appellant's point at the time that he made it."[83]

At least in the eyes of the Court, the intent and successful communication of the message helps move the flag from unprotected conduct to protected expression. As the Court noted, "An intent to convey a particularized message was present, and in the surrounding circumstances the likelihood was great that the message would be understood by those who viewed it."[84] At least some of the protection provided to expression, then, is linked to the successful transmission of meaning from author to audience. Might the speech not have been protected if the message was not clear? The Court does not, however, create any space for the idea that the audience might be able to create its own meaning or to interpret the message in a new, different way. One cannot help but conclude that if conduct is interpreted in a way that differs from the actor's intent, that conduct would not receive First Amendment protection.

It is interesting to note that the Court has not always relied on this interpretation of meaning. In 1943, the Supreme Court through Justice Jackson defined meaning in a very different way. In deciding that public schools cannot force students to pledge their allegiance to the American flag, Justice Jackson wrote, "A person gets from a symbol the meaning he puts into it, and what is one man's comfort and inspiration is another's jest and scorn."[85] While that definition still falls short of recognizing the discursive nature of meaning creation, it does acknowledge that meaning can and often does differ from the creator's intent. The Court recently seems to have broken from Justice Jackson's idea and more firmly placed meaning in the hands of the speaker. In many ways, this move coincides with the idea of corporate rationalization.

If we recognize the creation of meaning as a process, the focus of protection changes. No longer is protection predicated on the intentions or clarity of the individual speaker but on the creation of meaning through the interaction of the speaker and audience. Discourse theory clearly values the process of the creation of meaning and the needs of the public sphere.

Regulation of Public Fora

Discourse theory rests on the notion that expressive liberty for the individual does not automatically trump equality of access. Regulations that would provide more equality in the political process, whether in the area of media access[86] or campaign financing,[87] are as important, if not more important, than individual speech. The goal of discourse theory is to provide avenues so that all citizens may enter the public sphere.

Public areas—including those that are government-owned and those that are privately owned but generally open to the public—need to be regulated to promote discursive principles. In government-owned fora, where courts have looked at the traditional use of property and/or examined the rules that have been put in place to govern speech at the locations,[88] discourse theory takes a more functional approach. Discourse theory accepts, in the words of Joshua Cohen, a "presumption that any location with dense public interaction ought to be treated as a public forum that must be kept open to the public."[89] While discourse theory allows access to public facilities or facilities that have been made public, it does not give speakers the right to interfere with, disrupt, or block another speaker's expressive activity, which would allow coercion to enter the public sphere. Discourse theory creates an opportunity for citizens to speak, but it does not assure effective discourse; it merely allows speakers to enter the public sphere and use it for discursive purposes.

As for privately owned areas that have been made public, discourse theory would endorse the rule in *Pruneyard Shopping Center v. Robins*,[90] where the U.S. Supreme Court upheld a discursive interpretation of the California state constitution by the California Supreme Court. The decision opened privately owned shopping malls to public expression in California. The Court recognized that state courts may interpret their constitutions freely as long as their decisions expand, rather than negate, federal rights.[91]

Deciding what types of speech will be allowed in public spaces is perhaps the most difficult issue in discourse theory. For example, Sunstein would protect speech that contributes to political deliberation:

> [T]here is a distinction between a misogynist tract, which is entitled to full protection, and pornographic movies, some of which are in essence masturbatory aids and not entitled to such protection. Personal, face-to-face racial harassment by an employer of an employee is not entitled to full protection, while a racist speech to a crowd is. There is a distinction between a racial epithet and a tract in favor of white supremacy. An essay about the value of unregulated markets in oil production should be treated quite differently from an advertisement for Texaco—even if an oil company writes and publishes both.[92]

While Sunstein seeks to protect the deliberative nature of speech, the discourse theory presented here breaks from Sunstein's approach in some respects. Although Sunstein would protect a racist speaker delivering a message to a crowd, apparently because it is not addressed to an individual, discourse theory would not provide automatic protection. The level of protection would depend on the speaker's intent and the context in which the speech takes place.

To provide one example, in discourse theory there is a fundamental difference between a student shouting racial epithets at passing students and a student advocating white supremacy while engaging others in a discussion about the topic. The former is an example of instrumental speech, while the latter is discursive. The former is about intimidation and winning expressive (or some other kind of) victory, while the latter is about understanding. Perhaps this idealizes public discourse in our society; it is true that few public discussions take this form. The question that follows, of course, is why is this so. Is this simply the way that citizens naturally discuss public issues? Or is this a style of argumentation that we have learned? First Amendment doctrine should nonetheless recognize the intrinsic value of this type of discourse and protect it. The attitude, actions, and intent of the speaker are as important in discourse theory as what the speaker says.

Expressive Association

Freedom of association is vital to discursive democracy. Habermas sees a close link between the freedoms of assembly, association, and expression. The ability to express oneself is vital but not greater than the "right of parties to collaborate in the political will-formation of the people."[93] For Habermas, the value of expression is not simply what is said but the fact that citizens are engaging in discourse. In choosing to express themselves, citizens reinforce and actualize the value of a political public sphere.[94] For Habermas, "[A]ctors who support the public sphere are distinguished by the dual orientation of their political engagement: with their programs, they directly influence the political system, but at the same time they are also reflexively concerned with revitalizing and enlarging civil society and the public sphere as well as with confirming their own identities and capacities to act."[95]

And while association is not a recognized constitutional right, the U.S. Supreme Court has long protected associational rights. Not surprisingly, however, the Court has tended to see freedom of association through a liberal framework that is not protective of discursive rights. Generally speaking, there are two ways that the Supreme Court justifies freedom of association. The first is linked to the idea that freedom of association is an individual right. It allows the individual to come together with other members of society to give that citizen a stronger voice in democracy. As Justice William Brennan once wrote, "[T]he constitutional shelter afforded such relationships reflects the realization that individuals draw much of their emotional enrichment from close ties with others. Protecting these relationship from unwarranted state interference therefore safeguards the ability independently to define one's identity that is central to any concept of liberty."[96] Brennan saw freedom of association not as an intrinsic discursive right but as an instrumental right that serves the free speech needs of individuals.[97]

The other line of reasoning stems from protecting organizational autonomy. Association is less important as a way of protecting individual freedoms than as a way of allowing organizations to exist absent governmental interference. As Chief Justice William Rehnquist put it in defending the right of the Boy Scouts of America to exclude homosexuals, the right of association is "crucial in preventing the majority from imposing its views on groups that would rather express other, perhaps unpopular ideas."[98] In that way, it is not the right of individual members to express themselves that is paramount but rather the right of the organization's official position to dominate. The Court seems to have moved away from viewing freedom of association as an individual right towards the idea that it is an organizational right.[99]

Both interpretations fail to aid in the formation of a discursive public because of their emphasis on autonomy rather than the creation of community. There is no doubt that the ability to protect the right of individuals to join associations is important to democracy, as well as the right of associations to be free from government-sanctioned beliefs. It is often through those associations that public life is played out. However, too much associational freedom—either for individuals or for organizations—is bad for democracy. It fragments society, creating private interest groups that tend to speak only to themselves. Associations are not simply about communicating within groups but communicating between groups. As the public sphere splinters into discrete associations, the public sphere as a whole loses its vitality. Citizens begin preaching to the choir. Therefore, how the Supreme Court has chosen to look at associations merely reflects different sides of the same coin. Both have direct connections to liberal ideas of free speech and association, however Justice Rehnquist's ideas seem to directly reflect the growing expansion of corporate rights. The disagreement between Brennan and Rehnquist is not over the role that associations play in a democratic society but rather who gets to control the meaning of an association. Brennan would allow individuals to control the meaning; Rehnquist would allow the organization itself to make that determination. The Court fails to recognize that the democratic value of associations is not granting freedom to simply create an association or to control meaning but rather the freedom to use the association to communicate ideas or thoughts to other members of society. Associations play a valuable role in the creation of public meaning. As such, discourse theory would urge the Court to protect those actions by associations that are discursive in nature.

Reflecting traditional liberal thought, the Court also protects association only from governmental interference. The majority is often silent on the issue of corporate influence at the associational level. One justice who deviates from this standard is Justice Sandra Day O'Connor, who sees less protection for commercial associations than for expressive associations.[100]

Actions of associations that promote discourse across groups should be valued and encouraged; actions of associations that disrupt discourse should not enjoy as much constitutional protection.

The Role of Institutions

A discourse model of democracy does not restructure society to eliminate the role of institutions. Institutions are seen as playing a fundamental role, albeit not the role many political theories see them playing. Habermas has repeatedly recognized and wrestled with one of the most difficult dilemmas in modern society: how to maintain the organizing and communicative functions of organizations without allowing their bureaucratic structures to dominate democratic will-formation.

Habermas, like other theorists, has recognized the importance of institutions to democratic life.[101] To achieve the goal of expanded citizen participation in public life, he advocates stronger constitutional controls on the power of the mass media in society. While American media today are free to forge relationships with powerful members of society, Habermas apparently would support some limits on that freedom. He argues, "The mass media must be kept free from the pressure of political and other functional elites; they must be capable of raising and maintaining the discursive level of public opinion–critical audiences."[102]

Habermas views the mass media as similar to the judiciary,[103] serving as a tutor to the public sphere.[104] The media, in Habermas's eyes, ought to understand themselves as being "mandatary of an enlightened public" and "presuppose, demand, and reinforce" a capacity for criticism.[105] Based on this idea, political and social actors, including the mass media, would only be allowed to use the public sphere "insofar as they make convincing contributions to the solution of problems that have been perceived by the public or have been put on the public agenda with the public's consent."[106]

Clearly, Habermas sees the media as being entitled to constitutional protections only when fulfilling a discursive mission. In fact, the media's mission should be to promote discourse, to allow voices to be heard that have previously been silenced by the "administrative and social power."[107]

In Habermas's earlier work, too often ignored by some scholars, he advocates opening up existing corporate structures within society as a way to halt the decline of the public sphere. He calls for "private organizations of society that exercise public functions" to reveal their inner structure and linkages with other organizations as a matter of public record and debate. For Habermas, this would include "requiring that organizations provide the public with information concerning the source and deployment of their financial means."[108]

Habermas is equally concerned about the growth of expert cultures, which are often tied directly to dominant institutions. As Stephen K. White explains, for Habermas, as the insulation of expert cultures grow, so does the inability of average individuals to participate in democracy. Citizens are bombarded with information but are able to do little with it because consciousness remains fragmented. For Habermas, "'The conditions for a colonization of the lifeworld are thereby fulfilled; as soon as it is stripped of its ideological veil, the imperative of independent subsystems press in from the outside on the lifeworld and compel assimilation, like colonial masters in a tribal society."[109]

Institutions play a vital role in discourse democracy. That role, however, is different from the one played in the corporate-liberal world. Institutions do not serve as a stand-in for an inactive public but rather as an avenue that allows the public sphere's wishes to be adequately expressed. Institutions must fight to find ways to remain part of the public sphere, being vigilant in their protection of rights for the public sphere. Public institutions, such as the press and law, must struggle to make sure that the interests they serve are not their own but rather those of public life. In some instances, this might force them to make decisions that are contrary to their own best interests. However, if they are to play a vital role in the structuring and realization of an active public sphere, that obligation must be taken seriously. In discourse democracy, institutions that do take that public tutor role are clearly entitled to more freedom than institutions that do not.

Conclusion

One of the greatest problems facing democracies is the transparency of corporation rationalization. As early critical theorists noted, corporate influence on the factors that guide public life appear to us as natural. Discourse democracy is valuable to this project for two reasons: (1) It provides a framework for citizens to recognize the forces that structure democracy, and (2) To suggest alternatives to the current structure of the public sphere.

The pages that follow will have more in common with the first reason than the second. Through the framework provided by discourse democracy, the following chapters will identify how corporate values have come to dominate the public sphere.

PART 2

Corporate
Rationalization
and Democratic
Institutions

3

Professionalization of the Press and Law: Routinization and Management

In 1922, Walter Lippmann clearly put forward the Progressive view: "[E]very complicated community has sought the assistance of special men, of augurs, priests, elders. Our own democracy, based though it was on a theory of universal competence, sought lawyers to manage its government, and to help manage its industry. It was recognized that the specially trained man was in some dim way oriented to a wider system of truth than that which arises spontaneously in the amateur's mind."[1]

For Lippmann, it is not so much that citizens are inept but rather that the world has become far too complicated for the "amateur" citizen to grasp. The answer to the problem could be found in expert knowledge. His hope was for, as James W. Carey puts it, a "science of society," a new "high priesthood."[2] This new priesthood of social scientists would not be limited to the traditional professions; it would transcend all levels of society. Lippmann's hope was that the benefits of expert knowledge would be realized by other occupations, especially journalism. He wonders, for example, why journalists have been unable to achieve the professional status of doctors, engineers, or lawyers even though the "intrinsic power of the reporter appears to be so great, the number of very able men who pass through reporting is so large."[3]

In many ways, Lippmann was advocating turning democracy over to experts, what Jürgen Habermas might call the technicizing of the lifeworld. Democracy is no longer something citizens can comprehend by themselves; they need the technical knowledge produced by scientists to interpret, guide, and mediate their decisions. In a phrase that has gained a great deal of popularity, Lippmann called for the depoliticalization of the public sphere, where, as Carey notes, "[i]ntellectual-political activity had to be professionalized if truth was to be produced."[4]

Reliance on expert knowledge does not come without a cost, however. Not only does it devalue the role of the public in democracy, it also leads to the formation of powerful occupational groups that attempt to secure for themselves an area of knowledge that will insure their power.

This chapter explores the relationship between professionalization and corporate rationalization. It will be argued that, contrary to writers such as Lippmann, professionalization of public occupations such as journalism and the law has damaged democracy by creating an avenue for corporate values to enter the public sphere. It begins with a review of the concept of professionalization and then applies it to journalism and law. In the end, it will be argued that the professionalization of the press and the law have not only separated those occupations from the public sphere; professionalization has brought with it assumptions about what role public life should play in a democracy. Professionalization helps establish the legitimacy of corporate values such as efficiency, clearing the way for the management of the public sphere.

The Professions in Public Life

The history of the professions is a long one. Although the modern idea of a profession did not emerge until the nineteenth century, Eliot Freidson shows in his study of the semantic history of the term that its meaning has changed over the years. Used as a verb (to profess), it originally had a dual meaning, one positive and one pejorative. In the positive sense, it was linked to the implication of "religious and moral motives to dedicate oneself to a good end."[5] However, it also carried a negative meaning, connected to the idea of insincerity and lying. Freidson noted that the phrase, "He professes to know nothing about it," was in use as early as the sixteenth century.[6] As a noun, it referred to the university-educated occupations. During the sixteenth century, the word began to be used not only to refer to a few occupations "but rather the whole range of occupations by which people were identified and made their living."[7] Today's usage carries dual meanings as well. A professional is an "accomplished expert, a full-time specialist cultivating a particular kind of skill and activity."[8] But *profession* can be a disparaging term, for example when someone is referred to as a "professional politician."[9]

Attempts by sociologists to define what constitutes a profession have been fraught with similar difficulties. At the beginning of the nineteenth century, there were three recognized professions: divinity and its related university teaching, law, and medicine.[10] By the end of the century, however, professional associations had expanded impressively.[11] But while professional associations were growing, the study of professions did not begin until the twentieth century. That early work on the professions tended to focus on two main areas: the "natural" progression professions followed, and the typologies of a true profession.[12] More recently, sociologists have turned from trying to identify the common traits of a profession towards focusing on the function of professions in society. Scholars began to recognize that professional growth was not a natural progression but rather an attempt to accumulate power. Andrew Abbott describes the conclusion of these studies: "Ethics codes came late in professionalization not because they were a culmination of natural growth, but because they served the function of excluding outsiders, a function that became important only after the professional community had been generated and consolidated."[13]

Magali Sarfatti Larson attempts to provide a history of the rise of professionalism and to link it to its capitalistic roots. For Larson, professionalism becomes an attempt by an occupation to obtain monopolistic control over an area of work, often with the sanction of the political and economic elites in society.[14] Concentrating on professionalization in the United States, Larson shows how closely the movement was connected to political and economic forces. She traces the rise of the professions from the earliest years of the movement, through the Jacksonian era, to modern times. The Jacksonian period, 1829–41, is often seen as the "Era of the Common Man and the Age of Egalitarianism."[15] But for Larson, the period represents a puzzling paradox. While she recognizes the rapid economic development and democratization of the electoral process during that age, she also notes "profound social dislocations."[16] Jacksonian democracy attacked "the forms, but not the substance, of inequality."[17] The changes did not open the traditional professions to the common people. They remained locked away among the elite: "[T]he enlargement of the professions brought about by the Jacksonian movement, and above all, by laissez-fare economic development, did not mean democratization. On the contrary, if the established professionals did not always resist democratic encroachments, it was because they did not threaten the *internal stratification* of the professions."[18]

The Progressive Era was, for Larson, an attempt by professionals to apply a corporate model to the management of public affairs in America.[19] Efficiency became the goal, with science being the means to achieve it. The reliance on science assigns the "trained and credentialed" expert an important role in society, but also "emancipates them from class allegiances and class interests."[20] The result of the Progressive Era was the rise of the bureaucracy, which in its own way has become a new profession while feeding and supporting new and old professions by providing "models, sponsorship, equipment, and resources."[21] This internal support allies professionals not with their clients, in accord with the traditional view, but rather with their colleagues or the political economy. For Larson, "a profession is always defined by its elites."[22]

The importance of professionalism can be seen in the passivity it has created within the body politic. Individuals began to regard professional judgments, often supported by scientific data, as unquestionable, "discouraging independent evaluation."[23] Burton Bledstein argues that the power granted to professions to handle the "dangers to the public" clears the way for the ordinary citizen "to go about the absorbing business of making a living."[24] Bledstein finds a suitable example of this in modern journalism, where reporters and editors gain attention "by exaggerating the importance of the daily news, especially its apocalyptic and menacing overtones."[25] He notes, "Professionals not only lived in an irrational world, they cultivated that irrationality by uncovering abnormality and perversity everywhere: in diseased bodies, criminal minds, political conspiracies, threats to the national security. An irrational world, an amoral one in a state of constant crisis, made the professional person who possessed his special knowledge indispensable to the victimized client, who was reduced to a condition of desperate trust."[26]

Abbott attempts to move beyond the traditional studies of professionalization and their focus on the structure of professionalism. A profession's task is tied directly to its ability to establish jurisdiction over an area of expertise. Performing a skill for society is not the same as holding jurisdiction, however. For Abbott, a profession claimed jurisdiction when it asked society "to recognize its cognitive structure through exclusive rights; jurisdiction has not only a culture, but also a social structure."[27] Jurisdictional claims generally are made in three areas of social life: the legal system, public opinion, and the workplace. In the legal system, the profession attempts to get official state sanction of its occupational control of an area of work. In the United States, this battle occurs in three areas: legislatures, courts, and the administrative and planning structure. Abbott notes that in the United States, "legislatures have traditionally dominated in the legal establishment of professional rights."[28] State-sanctioned professional power is not usually the first action, however. Abbott found that in most cases, official authorization is usually preceded by a victory in the sector of public opinion.[29]

Public opinion is the most common way for professions in America to gain legitimacy.[30] Abbott notes, "Along with the right to perform the work as it wishes, a profession normally also claims rights to exclude other works as deemed necessary, to dominate public definitions of the tasks concerned, and indeed to impose professional definitions of the tasks on competing professions. Public jurisdiction, in short, is a claim of both social and cultural authority."[31]

For Abbott, every profession "aims for a heartland of work over which it has complete, legally established control."[32] That heartland may or may not already be in the hands of another profession. In the extreme, this takes a strong form: "one profession, one jurisdiction."[33] The goal is not only to win approval through public opinion but through the legal system as well.[34] According to Abbott, "a profession with legislated privileges is more likely to gain further privileges than is another profession to overthrow them."[35]

There are many connections, then, between professionalization and corporate rationalization. First of all, professions and corporations share many of the same values: efficiency, expertise, and profitability. Secondly, professionalization becomes a way for corporations to not only dominate an area of work but to move beyond the economic sector. Operating behind a professional cover of public service and impartiality, professionals pass on ideology to other parts of society. Along with that ideology comes many assumptions about the public sphere and how best to structure and manage democracy. That impact can be seen in both the press and law.

Press Professionalization and Corporate Rationalization

In many ways, the American press is a unique institution. Operating with perhaps the most political freedom in the world, the mainstream American press continues to present a very narrow range of ideas and opinions.[36] Watching the nightly network television news and quickly changing channels to observe what stories are being covered, a citizen will find that not only are the networks often covering the same stories, but often they are presented in exactly the same order. How can completely independent news programs, operating free of political influence, come to exactly the same conclusions night after night about what constitutes news? Recognizing that news is a human creation—something that is made rather than simply discovered—this lack of diversity becomes an even more complex problem. The professionalization process, which brings with it notions of routine practices and norms of conduct, helps us understand not only the lack of diversity but also what press professionalization means for public life.

Journalism organizations have been engaged in the professionalization process for a long time. Stephen A. Banning has noted the Missouri Press Association's discussions of the moral standards of journalism as early as the 1870s.[37] Hazel Dicken-Garcia has identified the Minnesota Editorial Association discussing ethical principles in 1888.[38] National press associations began to form in the 1920s. The first was the American Society of Newspaper Editors (ASNE), which ratified its first code of ethics in 1923.[39]

Perhaps the most common point from which to begin the study of press professionalization is the development of the penny press, the movement often identified as changing the face of American journalism from one based on partisan politics to one based on the interests of the commercial marketplace. More often than not, such studies focus on the rise of the penny press in New York City in the 1830s. For these scholars, evidence of professionalization can be found in the penny press's increased reliance on the methodology of objectivity as well as other precursors to so-called modern journalism.[40] For example, Dan Schiller argues that objectivity combined with commercialism to give the press a new political function: the surveillance of the public good. "In one jump the newspaper moved from the self-interested concerns of partisan political warfare to the apparently omniscient status of protecting the people as a whole."[41]

Other scholars tend to view the journalistic techniques associated with the professionalization process as not arriving on the scene in a sudden, cataclysmic burst, but rather as the result of a slow development over a lengthy period of time. John Nerone, for example, argues against what he calls the "mythology" of the penny press, claiming that changes in the American press are best understood not by looking at the innovations of a few entrepreneurs in one city but rather "shifts in the social and cultural environment."[42] These shifts can be traced back to the American Revolution and the rise of partisan politics and a market economy, which becomes clear if historians look at the "typical" rather than "the notorious or dramatic."[43]

Some, while not neglecting the penny press, have argued that the beginnings of the professionalization of journalism are more accurately traced to the end of the Progressive Era, or around the 1920s. The penny press, rather than recognizing professionalism, is better seen as the beginning of the move towards professionalism. Michael Schudson sees the rise of objectivity as a professional methodology coming into play after World War I. The result was that while science played a central role up to World War I, objectivity did not become its chief methodology until after the war. According to Schudson, objectivity arose "not so much as an extension of naive empiricism and the belief in facts but as a reaction against skepticism; it was not a straight-line extrapolation but a dialectical response to the culture of a democratic market society. It was not the final expression of a belief in facts but the assertion of a method designed for a world in which even facts could not be trusted."[44]

Evidence of professionalization can be found in other areas as well. Douglas Birkhead has argued that in these early years of professional development, the press was engaged in a "social project of reinterpretation," trying to transform its image.[45] Journalism thus turned to another established institution, the university. The creation of journalism schools in the early 1900s gave the press an opportunity to shape and refine itself. As Joseph Pulitzer, whose endowment created one of the first journalism schools, wrote: "'It is not too much to say that the press is the only great organized force which is actively and as a body upholding the standard of civic righteousness.'"[46] Birkhead suggests that the professionalization movement was an ideological attempt to convince workers and the public of journalism's new professional mission, though the structure of the industry and its function were essentially left unchanged.[47]

The Rationalization of the Press

Links to the corporate rationalization of the press can be seen in the increased reliance on methodology and the routines that dominate the press. Habermas has identified some of these changes in connection with the decline of the public sphere. He notes that professionalization changed journalism from a literary practice to a technical activity with accepted styles and formats.[48] Journalists increasingly became specialists, with the creation of work rules and codes of ethics. People who wrote for newspapers were no longer strictly members of the public; they were members of a profession, a distinct class of workers with emerging professional standards.

Objectivity has become one of the guiding methodologies of professional journalism, even though journalists often use other terms to describe it. To cite two recent examples, Jim Lehrer, the anchor of PBS's "Newshour," noted that his show has had to reject stories from foreign news organizations because they "do not meet our standards for objectivity and fairness."[49] And when Bob Garfield of National Public Radio's "On the Media" questioned Ibrahim Halal, the chief editor of Al-Jazeera, about his objectivity, Halal responded by asking Garfield to explain what he meant. Garfield responded, "Well, I mean . . . keeping balance, fairness, trying to keep your personal viewpoint away from your coverage."[50]

Objectivity is thus an epistemology that has become the methodology for turning everyday occurrences into news. The sociologist Gaye Tuchman has termed objectivity a "strategic ritual" that journalists use to turn facts into truth. The methodology of objectivity—presenting conflicting possibilities, use of supporting evidence, use of direct quotes, and constructing the story in an appropriate sequence—helps disguise the fact that it presents a constructed reality. Stories that appear value-free are filled with political choices such as who to interview and what events to cover. Objectivity has become the accepted ideology to the extent that even as journalists discover the limits of the methodology for reporting the news, the public insists that they live up to their goals. In many ways, objectivity has become an ideological trap. As W. Lance Bennett has noted, "American journalism may have become trapped within an unworkable set of professional standards, with the result that the more objective or fair reporters try to be, the more official (and other) biases they introduce into the news."[51] In that way, the methodology of journalism limits the kinds and amount of information citizens receive.

Just as important is the concept of journalistic routines. Mark Fishman has argued that faced with daily deadlines, journalists seek to expose themselves to the most reliable flow of material they can find. That secure, reliable, and efficient source of material is the government, and most news organizations organize their "beats" around the structure of government.[52] It is not a coincidence that Sunday is known in the United States as a slow news day, not, of course, because things don't happen on Sunday, but because it is the day that government is shut down.

The consequence of this organizational strategy, according to Fishman, is that the role of news in a democratic society is greatly restricted. The need for a reliable source of material means that the government will always be "news"; people outside of government will have a difficult time attracting the attention of the news media. But perhaps more importantly, Fishman notes that the world comes to the journalist "bureaucratically organized."[53] That is, the news is already filtered through governmental structures and interests.

This routinization of the news, where journalists report on what government tells them rather than what they witness, has changed the role of the reporter. James W. Carey has argued that the creation of the "professional communicator" has had important consequences for the press. The professional communicator not only links the elites with general audiences, it also links together the different communities that comprise the audience.[54] The message the professional communicator produces is not marked by that person's thoughts and beliefs but rather "operates under the constraints or demands imposed on one side by the ultimate audience and, on the other side, by the ultimate source."[55] In that way, the news is shaped less by individual action than by the constraints placed on and the information provided to the journalist.[56] Professionalization of the press brings corporate values to the public through its routinization of the news process and its valuing of the scientific methodology of objectivity—a methodology that serves to reinforce dominant values within society.

For Carey, professionalization of the press has consequences not only for the reporter and the production of news; it also influences the role of the citizen in public affairs. And while professionalization, with its emphasis on routine and efficiency, has created a sameness about the news, it has also served to disempower citizens by envisioning them as an informed public.

Creating a Watchdog Press

Corporate rationalization has influenced democracy not only by its reliance on scientific methodology and its influence on the methodology of journalism; it also changed the way institutions relate to citizens. As Lippmann suggests, the Progressives put forward a paternalistic view of the citizenry. That view is reflected in the developing professional ideology of the press as a watchdog on government.

While the Progressives and their followers embraced the watchdog function of the press, it was not an invention of the Progressive Era. Elements of the watchdog function can be traced to the earliest years of the country. Jeffery A. Smith notes that the earliest printers argued that "the press should serve as a check on" the use of state power.[57] He chronicles what he calls the development of a "professional pride and mission" among eighteenth-century printers as the press became the "eyes, ears, and voice of the electorate and its parties."[58] Yet, despite those ties, there are some important distinctions to be made. Printers of the era had often overt ties with political leaders, something that modern-day journalists would see as a violation of ethical norms. Thomas C. Leonard recounts how the editor of the *New York Evening Post*, William Coleman, looked forward to the visits of Alexander Hamilton to dictate articles for the paper: "'When he stops, my article is complete,' Coleman said. 'I have no pride of authorship,' the editor told Hamilton, with the wish that nothing in an article should inadvertently offend the patron. '. . . [A]lter or suppress it as with your views,' Coleman said."[59]

This does not mean that the printers had no connection with today's journalism. Leonard notes that even in prerevolutionary times, printers of weekly publications increasingly realized that their stories required some investigative work, thorough enough not to make readers "incredulous or bored." Attempting to draw readers by promising to unearth new information, the printers took "on the role of stewards to the community."[60]

That stewardship would greatly increase in the nineteenth century. Many trace this development directly to the changes brought about by the penny press. Schudson views the rise of the middle class during the Jacksonian era as being of utmost importance to the development of the penny press. But perhaps more important than the democratization of all walks of life during this period, Schudson sees the rise of the "culture of the market" as playing a large role in transforming society. Self-interest became the driving force, and one individual was as good as the next.[61] The penny press became the public's representative of that egalitarian ideal.[62]

Schiller, however, sees more to the relationship between the press and its audience during the penny press era. He claims that the press was far more than the "paeans" of the middle class. The penny press instead became the defender of the public order.[63] By giving citizens equal access to knowledge, it changed the public sphere.[64] The new role that reporters were starting to play in this public sphere, as well as their rising social status,[65] is illustrated by the discretion given to James Gordon Bennett, the editor of the *New York Herald*. Bennett, attempting to enter a brothel where a murder had been committed, pushed his way through the crowd. When someone asked a police officer why Bennett was allowed to enter, the officer replied, "He is an editor—he is on public duty."[66] Focusing on the abuse of state power and criminal activities, "the commercial press cultivated a new social role."[67] As Schiller notes, "In the eyes of many readers the cheap papers turned to defend the rights of man, through crime news especially, at a time when those rights seemed to be threatened by changing social relations, and when other institutions only turned their backs on cardinal republican values."[68]

The change in the press between 1830 and 1850 from an emphasis on groups to an emphasis on information initiated the growth of its watchdog function and a concern for the public's right to know. As Dicken-Garcia writes of this period, "If the press was to serve individuals and protect them from the abuses of institutions, then it must watch institutions and expose abuses. Correlated with this function, the public had a right to know about such abuses in order to be able to correct them and protect individuals from powerful institutions."[69]

The Progressive Era has many links with the development of journalism.[70] Lippmann, in 1920, issued a call for the professionalization of the newspaper industry to correct the information being collected by "anonymous and untrained and prejudiced witnesses."[71] He wrote that "there is everywhere an increasingly angry disillusionment with the press" and warned journalists that if they do not control themselves, "the next generation will attempt to bring the publishing business under greater social control."[72] Lippmann's call for professionalization of the press was shared by others in the industry, but his criticism was unique in that the press did not have to be saved from big business, but rather from itself.[73]

It also brought with it a new, paternalistic view of the press's role in society. Schudson associates this development to the changing notion of public opinion. Whereas it had been linked with the middle class in nineteenth-century America, by the early twentieth century public opinion had no claim to representing the middle class and therefore was not rational.[74] According to Schudson, "The professional classes now took public opinion to be irrational and therefore something to study, direct, manipulate, and control. The professions developed a proprietary attitude toward 'reason' and a paternalistic attitude toward the public."[75]

Schudson contends that the rise of the profession of public relations in the early part of the twentieth century can be seen as an attempt to help shape public opinion.[76] But the rise of public relations in many ways posed a direct challenge to the power of the press, raising questions about what was illusion and what was truth. Schudson argues that the press placed its faith in objectivity—"a faith in 'facts,' a distrust of 'values,' and a commitment to their segregation"—as a way to separate their work from that of publicity agents.[77]

Christopher P. Wilson sees this move towards scientific thought as a move towards realism, where writers tried to "mirror the common life."[78] It was a move from telling a story to providing information. Schudson notes that the move brought with it a change in the audience, where "[i]nformation is a genre of self-denial, the story one of self-indulgence."[79]

During the Progressive Era, literature ceased to be a romantic endeavor and became a "product of labor."[80] No longer did writers and editors rely on an "inner calling," but their value was in their "responsibility to the American public."[81] As Wilson notes, "Writers and editors now spoke not of an author's 'inner muse' or 'vocation,' but of the value of ritualized routines, careful sounding of the market, and hard work."[82]

Perhaps even more than increasing the scientification of journalism, the Progressive Era helped further establish the watchdog role of the press. Thomas C. Leonard, in his study of the history of political reporting in America, notes that the Progressive Era presents a paradox: at the same time that muckraking journalism grew—a movement intended to excite citizens about public life— political participation declined.[83] Leonard argues that Progressivism and the journalism of that period undermined "the ritual" of political participation, turning people away from parties to which they commonly turned for "indoctrination, social pressure, and, if need be, the payoff."[84] Some journals of the day deplored mass democracy, and their message found elites who were willing to listen.[85] Leonard notes that the muckrakers saw it as wrong to use politics to protect "parochial interests" and hoped to create a new citizen by getting rid of "ethnic and religious loyalties."[86] The end result was one that today is all too familiar. "A profession that loved politics increasingly followed reporting conventions that made the public turn away," Leonard writes. "Gains in drawing attention to politics were often a loss in comprehension about how the political system worked. That easy vernacular of politics had broken down because the stories that the press now told meant less to those listening."[87]

Reporters became active players in the political process. In the words of Wilson, they became mired "deep in the muck of American life."[88] As a result, journalism increasingly relied on groups, scientific methodology, routines, and managing public life, all central elements of the corporately rationalized watchdog function of the press. The watchdog theory is an important element in the guiding rhetoric of contemporary American journalism. Today's press justifies its existence and its place in society through the public, arguing that it serves the public's right to know.[89] As Carey notes, modern journalism "is above all a journalism that justifies itself in the public's name but in which the public plays no role except as an audience: a receptacle to be informed by experts and an excuse for the practice of publicity."[90]

The Press and an Inactive Public

The watchdog concept of the press, where, in the words of the First Amendment lawyer Floyd Abrams, the press is "guarding against abuse of governmental power,"[91] is often linked with another so-called right, the public's right to know.[92] In fact, the press's right to know is often equated with the public's right to know. As U.S. Supreme Court Justice William O. Douglas wrote, "The press has a privileged position in our constitutional system, not to enable it to make money, not to set newsmen apart as a favored class, but to bring fulfillment to the people's right to know."[93]

While the idea of a popular right to know has a long history,[94] the professionalization of the phrase can be traced to a 1945 speech by the executive director of the Associated Press, Kent Cooper.[95] Eleven years later, Cooper wrote that journalists had adopted the phrase "as a slogan in the cause of conserving and broadening the right which has commonly been called 'press freedom.'"[96] The press's ties to the concept were furthered in 1953 when ASNE commissioned Harold Cross to study the issue. Cross's study trumpeted not so much a public right, but rather a press right. He suggested that newspapers fight for the public's right to know because it is through newspapers that the public will benefit. Cross argued that while justifications for denying access to information to the general public can be defended, those justifications cannot hold for the news media. "The newspaper does not act out of mere or idle curiosity. It is not in the competition with the fee status of records custodians. . . . In a manner of speaking, when made by a newspaper, application of the right to inspect tends to circumvent, or at least dilute, the fear that if one citizen or other person be granted such right the rest of the community will march in upon the records, not as single spies but in battalions."[97]

Several things are important to note about Cross's comments. First of all, acting out of curiosity is cast as a bad thing. Citizens who are seeking information simply to enlighten themselves is not to be protected, while people or institutions acting for instrumental reasons is to be valued. And second, the public is envisioned not as citizens but as spies. A public interest in obtaining information is seen as a threat to the stability of government. The press can thus help subvert that threat by being the professional collector of information and protecting government from hordes of citizen-spies.

While some have viewed the watchdog concept as dangerous to a free press,[98] it is often viewed as a way to insure the realization of a good society. One of the clearest accounts of this version can be found in what has been called the social responsibility theory of the press, which can be traced to the work of the Commission on Freedom of the Press in 1947.[99] In social responsibility theory, the press found a "philosophical paradigm"[100] to institutionalize the watchdog concept as a way to address the problems of modern democracy. Following in the steps of Progressive reformers, social responsibility theory puts its faith in educated, enlightened individuals to lead society. The development of that elite can be achieved through the professionalization of journalism.[101]

This view of society is evident in the writings of some of the members of the Commission on Freedom of the Press. For example, Zechariah Chafee Jr. at one point concluded that "'the public will never live up to the kind of newspaper which this commission would like to have.'"[102] William E. Hocking, perhaps the philosophical guiding force of the commission, noted that liberalism was built on certain apparently erroneous assumptions: "'[T]hat man by nature knows what he wants, and consistently wants the right. The fact that we appear to face today—and one that closely concerns the responsibilities of the press—is that men do not know what they want in any socially reliable way.'"[103]

Hocking clung to the idea that the answer to the problem could be found in the press. Since the public might not know what to expect from its press, it is up to the press to "educate demand."[104] As Theodore Peterson summarizes social responsibility theory, it is not so much that people are no longer rational but rather that they are "lethargic." Peterson notes, "[Man] is capable of using his reason, but he is loath to do so. Consequently, he is easy prey for demagogues, advertising pitchmen, and other who would manipulate him for their selfish ends. Because of his mental sloth, man has fallen into a state of unthinking conformity, to which his inertia binds him."[105]

Social responsibility theory puts forward a vision of the public in which citizens need to be educated and watched over. Or, as one journalist of the day wrote: "The public prefers not to think."[106]

The influence of these views can be found in the writings of more recent press theorists. The Columbia law professor Vincent Blasi's "checking value" theory of the First Amendment provides the consummate watchdog definition of the press.[107] For Blasi, the core meaning of the First Amendment for eighteenth-century theorists was the role free expression "performs in checking the abuse of official power."[108] The rise of big government has necessitated "well-organized, well-financed, professional critics" to counter government.[109] For Blasi, "[T]he role of the ordinary citizen is not so much to contribute on a continuing basis to the formation of public policy as to retain a veto power to be employed when the decisions of officials pass certain bounds."[110] Blasi favors a strong institutional, professionalized press endowed with special privileges to watch over government. He sought a "highly protective reporter's privilege" to enable journalists to carry out their function.[111]

In the end, the watchdog concept undervalues the role of the public sphere and removes the press from the public sphere. Seeing the watchdog theory of the press as the only realistic option, its advocates are only too willing to put the press in a privileged position in an attempt to check government. But by granting the press institutional status, they effectively remove it from the public sphere. The press moves closer to state authority, to the elites, and towards representing the governors rather than the governed.

But while they are criticized for placing the press under the heavy thumb of the collective, watchdog proponents cannot be called communitarians in the traditional sense of the word. As Blasi suggests, their faith rests not in the community of citizens but rather the elite.[112] The watchdog function reduces the press to the instrumental role of checking government and, in effect, ties the press to government.[113] The public exists as an audience for the official press-government battle—an audience that is expected to observe rather than participate.[114] Instrumental reasoning does not come without a price. It turns questions about what is good and right into technical questions that cannot be addressed by the general citizenry.[115] Under the watchdog theory, the press plays a technical, not a social, role. In the press's social role, it functions to help in the formation of consensual norms with the ultimate goal being understanding.[116] In other words, the press's role, according to watchdog theorists, is not aiding in the creation of community but merely informing the community.

Professionalization of Law and American Legal Thought

Just as the professionalization process has played an important role in transforming the way the press relates to the public sphere, the professionalization of the law has changed its relationship with the public. There are numerous ways to examine the professionalization of the law. The traditional way is to review how professionalization has changed the way lawyers work. This section argues that to understand the law's impact on public life, we need to move beyond the work of lawyers and examine the intellectual ideas that structure the law. Through an examination of these ideas, we can understand the methodology that is used to legitimate the law in a democratic society and how the law sees itself in relation to the public sphere.

This section will highlight some of those developments by broadly tracing changes in the intellectual development of the law. And while those intellectual debates often appear as little more than internal squabbles to non-lawyers, they have proven to be very powerful in shaping the role law plays in society. I will argue that these developments have increased the corporate rationalization of the law and, following the advice of Kim Lane Scheppele, demonstrate that law is "embedded in a larger institutional framework that routinizes solutions to unusual events and that values regularity and predict-ability."[117] In that way, law shares more in common with journalism and corporate rationalization than many might want to admit.

To highlight the impact of corporate rationalization, this section will tell law's story from the end. The law-and-economics movement, which empha-sizes that the best law is the most efficient law, has greatly influenced the current structure of American law. In many ways, it is the real-world articu-lation of the concept of corporate rationalization. The law-and-economics movement represents the culmination of a long series of developments and influences that are often seen as distinct. This chapter argues, however, that movements such as legal formalism, sociological jurisprudence, and legal realism established the foundation for the law-and-economics movement. Much as Taylorism and the Progressives made Fordism possible, sociologi-cal jurisprudence and legal realism made law-and-economics possible. And while those earlier movements were often critical of corporate influence on the law, law-and-economics has been able to subsume critical portions to increase the corporate rationalization of the law.

The Law-and-Economics Movement

Perhaps no development in legal thinking so completely captures the idea of corporate rationalization as the law-and-economics movement. Most identify the writings of Ronald H. Coase[118] and Guido Calabresi[119] as provid-ing the intellectual foundation for the movement. However, the writings of Richard Posner, a federal circuit judge on the U.S. Seventh Circuit Court of Appeals, provided the spark. Spurred by Posner's multitude of writings, fol-lowers have applied economic principles to deciding cases in ever-expand-ing areas of the law. To illuminate the connections between the law-and-eco-nomics movement and corporate rationalization, this section will explore some of Posner's writings, with a special emphasis on their application to First Amendment issues.

Posner believed that the underlying idea that should guide the law is wealth maximization, a concept that has ties to traditional utilitarian thought but differs in significant ways. Posner merged libertarian and utilitarian values, which many consider to be opposed, to provide more protection for indi-vidual rights: "The ethics of wealth maximization can be viewed as a blend of these rival philosophical traditions. Wealth is positively correlated, al-though imperfectly so, with utility, but the pursuit of wealth, based as it is on the model of the voluntary market transaction, involves greater respect for individual choice than in classical utilitarianism."[120]

Following that lead, Posner has interpreted a wide range of issues through his economic lens. It has led him, for example, to argue that social responsibility on the part of corporations is inefficient. The primary goal of any corporation, in Posner's view, is profit maximization. A corporation that tries to be socially responsible by reducing emissions that pollute the water will hurt profit maximization. And profit maximization will increase the wealth of shareholders, which will allow them to individually exercise social responsibility through political and charitable donations.[121]

The result for Posner is that the legal course that produces the greatest wealth maximization is the correct choice for judges to follow. In true economic form, Posner employs formulas to aid judges in deciding how to determine what will produce the greatest wealth maximization. And, of course, those formulas and their application have produced the greatest controversy surrounding the law-and-economics movement. As Peter J. Hammer has written, all attempts at modeling require some degree of abstraction—a fact that is often obscured by law-and-economics advocates. "Too little attention is paid to identifying the implicit assumptions behind the economics and asking whether those assumptions are justified by the legal setting to which they are being applied."[122]

Posner has applied his ideas to free speech and when government might be justified in curtailing speech. The writings of Learned Hand, an influential federal judge from 1909 through 1951, figure prominently in Posner's thinking. Hand was one of the first federal judges to try and develop a more systematic approach to understanding free speech by breaking it into its component parts.[123]

Posner leaned on Hand's writings to develop an economic model of free speech. He reduced free speech to this formula: $V + E < P \times L/(1+I)<n>$.[124] V is the social loss from suppressing valuable information; E is the legal-error costs from implementing the regulation; P is the probability that the speech will cause harm; L is the magnitude of the social cost of the speech, and I is the rate of time that discounts the future cost of harmful speech. N is the number of periods between the time the speech occurs and the manifestation of the harm.

While such a formula raises many questions, the point here is not to critique Posner's model—criticism has been leveled at it from many angles. Rather, we can see in it, and his attempts to justify it, important ties to the concept of corporate rationalization.

For Posner, efficiency is central to determining wealth maximization. "'Efficiency' means exploiting economic resources in such a way that 'value'—human satisfaction as measured by aggregate consumer willingness to pay for goods and services—is maximized."[125] In Posner's view, the focus on efficiency and wealth maximization makes efficiency easier to compute than when compared to the utilitarian standard of greatest good for the greatest number.

Some critics of law-and-economics argue that the movement favors the market, which tends to shift protection away from the individual in favor of "socially aggregated sums" or societal needs. As a result, individual freedoms are diluted in the name of societal benefits. Such criticisms miss the real impact of the movement. Law-and-economics does not simply threaten individual freedoms or favor certain social causes over others: It leads citizens to look at problems of democracy through the lens of the market. It is not that the movement favors societal interests at the expense of individual interests but that it inherently favors the market. Individual and societal interests are irrelevant to the needs of the market; they are fine and valuable if they further the market, and they might well be relevant factors for the market to consider. But to say that the market favors societal over individual interests is to misunderstand the logic of markets, which are inherently neutral to such concerns.

As can be seen in professionalization movements in general, political neutrality is valued not because of concerns over individuals or communities, and definitely not because of shared political values. Rather, it is a way of assuring market dominance over a particular area of work. The law-and-economics movement is another step toward the bureaucratization and professionalization of legal practice. In short, it has reduced the practice of law to a formula—a formula with efficiency as its foundations—that only those with expert knowledge can apply.

Within the movement lies perhaps the clearest example of corporately rationalized law. Posner has argued that law has not professionalized enough—it has not become sufficiently rational.[126] For Posner, the law has yet to tie itself directly to the sciences and social sciences and particularly lacks an established sociology. "The law is still in the process of building a body of knowledge of the kind that has enabled other professions to move decisively in the direction of genuine professionalism."[127]

It is telling that Posner singles out for praise not conservative Supreme Court justices like Justice Antonin Scalia but more moderate justices such as Justice Stephan Breyer.[128] He clearly sees his approach as the best way to enable judges to implement an economic approach to the law—a law that is driven less by ideology (which seems to be central to Scalia's writings) than by efficiency and calculation (as representative of many of the current moderates on today's court). In that way, law-and-economics does not favor judges who are moved by ideology; it attracts judges who are technicians who have learned to apply a methodology to facts.

While it has been argued that the law-and-economics movement represents the high point of the corporate rationalization of the law, it is wrong to suggest that there is not an intellectual history to the development of these ideas. How did we get to the point where questions of efficiency drive out understanding of law? The answer lies in the historical and intellectual development of U.S. law.

The Early Years of American Legal Thought

The story of American legal thought begins with English common law. But while some have argued that American law is nothing but English common law transferred to the colonies, that is far too simple. The early American colonies selected which parts of the English common law they wanted to adopt, and each colony selected different parts. As Lawrence M. Friedman notes, "Throughout the colonial period, the colonists borrowed as much English law as they wanted to take or were forced to take. Their appetite was determined by requirement of the moment, by ignorance or knowledge of what was happening abroad, and by general obstinacy. Mapping out how far colonial law fit English law is almost a hopeless job."[129]

Nevertheless, the United States in its early years did rely a great deal on England's common law system. The highest source of law was not the enactment of a legislative code but rather a custom that was reflected in the decisions of judges.[130] It is important to remember that the earlier practitioners of common law did not see law as human-made. Rather, law just existed, waiting for the judges to discover it.[131]

Until the mid 1800s, the lawyers and judges in the United States who were expected to "discover" the law were primarily laymen. Not formally trained in law schools, these early lawyers learned their craft through apprenticeships.[132] For example, in seventeenth-century New Jersey, justices of the peace, sheriffs, and clerks acted as lawyers.[133]

First-generation lawyers in the United States often followed the tradition laid out by England's Inns of Court and English barristers. As Colin Croft has noted, these barristers viewed legal practice as an "honorable calling for gentlemen" with an overriding sense of public service.[134] When combined with the American sense of civic republicanism, Croft found that these early American lawyers served as mediators between the propertied classes and the democratic majority.[135]

By the mid 1850s, American law began to change. Following the lead of reformers such as David Dudley Field, the American legal system began to codify the common law.[136] The codes were intended to streamline the legal process and eliminate the uncertainty that existed in common law. As Field summed up the problem, "Justice is entangled in the net of forms."[137] As Friedman notes, the reformers saw the common law as an "amorphous entity, a ghost, scattered in little bits and pieces among hundreds of case-reports, in hundreds of different books. Nobody knows what was and was not law."[138]

The codification movement can be directly tied to a change toward a more modern society. As business became more dependent on the courts, because of more complex social and economic relationships, law needed to become more efficient. In that regard, the codes that were developed favored expansion, growth, and a dynamic economy. Some codes even went so far as to make the law so simple and clear that the average citizen would not need a lawyer, though that idea was never adopted.[139] Field clearly saw codification as a way to open the law to the public and give the law determinacy as well.

Field's code, which was published in 1865 and was intended to open the secrets of the law to the public, was being widely used by 1900 in modified forms.[140] The codes were particularly popular in the western states, where the bar association was weaker.[141] Still, the reformers had only a superficial impact on law in the United States. The changes were, in Friedman's words, mainly "paper changes" put forth by the bar as a public service that mainly served to improve the "tarnished image" of the legal profession.[142]

While the codification movement is often viewed as an attempt to democratize the law, it also has ties to rationalization. As much as Field sought to open the law to citizens, he also sought to make the common law more efficient. A common criticism of Field's code was that by writing down the common law, the law would be less flexible—less able to change to meet to the needs of society. Field, however, argued that the common law was inefficient, forcing judges to "make the rule at the same time that they apply it."[143] Perhaps more than that, however, Field argued that his code would "lessen the labor of judges and lawyers," save resources and "capital" because law libraries will not be required to purchase as many materials, and that it is the most efficient way for the people to "know the law."[144] He thus brought together what might seem to be two unrelated concepts—the democratization of the law and efficiency.

And even if his justifications for his code were little more than rhetorical flourishes, it is telling that Field felt the need to sell his ideas through an argument from efficiency.

The codification movement was the precursor to a much stronger movement that began at about the same time—legal formalism. But while codification's effects were limited, the impact of legal formalism can still be seen today.

Legal Formalism

In many ways, the rise of legal formalism was a reaction to the claims of the radical codification movement. For the legal formalists, law is not dominated by politics and indeterminacy, as the radical codification movement claimed, but rather by rationality. As Morton J. Horwitz notes, legal formalism became a new way to justify the power of common law judges. "The new and defensive emphasis in orthodox legal theory on the 'scientific' nature of the law arose simultaneously as a reaction to the claim of the radical codifiers that the common law was political. . . . What does seem extremely clear, nevertheless, is that the attempt to place law under the banner of 'science' was designed to separate politics from law, subjectivity from objectivity and layman's reasoning from professional reasoning."[145]

This movement from claims of indeterminacy to claims of certainty was exemplified by those who attempted to turn law into a science—a movement that coincided with legal professionalization. Christopher Columbus Langdell, appointed dean of the Harvard Law School in 1870, while not the first to suggest that law is best seen as a science, was perhaps the movement's most influential spokesperson. Members of the codification movement, especially Field, had also described law as a science, hoping that science would make law more certain and less subject to the whims of the judges.[146]

One of Langdell's first moves was to introduce the case-study method of teaching law, where law is discovered inductively through a reading of primary sources.[147] For Langdell, law is at its base a formal discipline. If properly practiced, it could not easily be manipulated through political maneuvers or rhetorical practices. There are several assumptions built into this idea, in addition to the fundamental claim that politics and rhetoric are bad and can be limited through scientific methodologies. Other assumptions that guided Langdell's reasoning on the law were: (1) Only through an analysis of the original cases could lawyers learn the fundamental doctrines that govern the law; (2) Once those fundamental doctrines were discovered, the will of the law would be known—there is no need, for example, for historical analysis, as Langdell "severed the cords" that tied law to American scholarship and life;[148] (3) And finally, the most important part of law is process. Langdell argued that it is more important that the law be consistent than right, turning the law from questions of justice to questions of methodology.

Langdell's new science of the law was particularly attractive to the profession. Horwitz argues that formalism invested more power in the hands of the legal profession, brought together the elite of the legal profession with the "newly powerful commercial and entrepreneurial interests," and helped those commercial interests "freeze" legal doctrine for their benefit.[149]

Whatever the reasons for the rise of formalism, it had important and long-lasting effects on legal thought. Law-as-science reflected a turn away from the importance of politics to the law. Law was, at its base, hard and fast if only the lawyers engaged in the proper methodology. But as Friedman notes, law-as-science was not viewed an experiment or experience as much as the one true source of empirical data as recognized in the reported cases. "If law is at all the product of society, then Langdell's science of law was a geology without rocks, an astronomy without stars," Friedman notes. "Lawyers and judges raised on the method, if they took their training at all seriously, came to speak of law mainly in terms of a dry, arid logic, divorced from society and life."[150]

But perhaps more importantly, legal formalism was the search for an efficient, consistent, and predictable form of law. It can be argued that formalism had a beneficial impact on society. For example, by making the law consistent, it created a sense of fairness and increased the legitimacy of the law in the public's mind. It also might have allowed people to understand the rules that govern society—what a person can do and how a person can act. But along with those positive attributes come important questions. Does the desire for consistency and legitimacy avoid more difficult question of what is right or fair?

The desire to make law an objective science was obviously tied closely to the role of law and lawyers in society. Max Weber has noted that legal formalism and the bureaucratic administration of the law increased its rationalization and the appearance of objectivity.[151] Coupled with the desire to make law a science, legal formalism (and the professionalization movement that accompanied it) increased law's ties to corporate rationalization.

During the late 1800s, corporations not only helped change the structure but also the practice of the law. At about the same time that law schools emerged in the United States, corporate clients began needing their services.

The expansion of government rules and regulations, especially those impacting on corporations, called for corporations to rely on the expertise of lawyers. The American Bar Association was founded in 1878 by a small group of lawyers from prominent East Coast law firms.[152] As Larson has noted, with the growth of corporate clients, lawyers began to specialize. The emergence of elite lawyers, mainly from prestigious law schools, led a move away from litigation and towards behind-the-scenes settlements and negotiations. As Larson puts it, "The emergent business corporation was drawing to itself new forms of legal talent, providing a structural support for a new type of legal elite, which had not yet moved to translate its de facto advantages into educational superiority."[153]

Legal formalism advanced the idea of corporate rationalization by reducing the question of justice to the scientific pursuit of consistency and predictability, but also by changing the nature of the practice of the law. It moved the practice of law away from individual practice to the large law firm, with its corporate clients and corporate organization. And as Larson observes, the rationalization of the law "increases the power and prestige of an elite of jurists and adds to the appearance of autonomy and impartiality of the legal profession as a whole."[154]

The Challenge to Legal Formalism

The historian Thomas L. Haskell has written, "The market teaches us not one but many lessons."[155] The Progressive movement brought serious challenges to legal formalism, and while those challenges are often viewed as attacks on the corporate domination of society, the Progressive challenge to formalism was more an attempt to redraw the boundaries than to break away from established ideology. The Progressive movement called on legal professionals to stop playing with the law and start playing with public policy as a way to manage society. Two legal-reform movements grew out of the Progressive Era: sociological jurisprudence and legal realism.

Herbert Hovencamp has called the Progressive legal movement the first law-and-economics movement for its attempt to bring Progressivism together with a theory of economics. Two intellectual ideas were central to Progressive legal thought: the theory of evolution by natural selection, or what Hovencamp calls Reform Darwinists, and the economic theory of marginalism. Reform Darwinists believed that while all species continue to evolve, only humans possess the unique ability to control or "manage" that evolutionary process.[156] And it is through the state that this management of evolution can take place.

Closely linked to these ideas was the economic theory of marginalism, or the idea that willingness to pay is the ultimate determinant of value to individuals and society. If a person craves apple pie, marginalism suggests that he or she will pay more for the first apple pie than the second, and even less for the third, because the craving has been satisfied. The demand for, or the utility of, the apple pie is far greater for the first pie than subsequent pies. Marginalism thus had strong connections to utilitarian thought.[157]

Through this combination, Progressives believed that society could be managed, that people desire goods but that desire diminishes as they accumulate more goods, and that policy can control people's conduct by "metering rewards and penalties."[158] This social engineering, so important to Progressive thought, is reflected throughout the intellectual challenges to legal formalism.

Sociological Jurisprudence

Hovencamp has noted that not all Progressives advocated all principles associated with Progressive legal thought. Oliver Wendell Holmes was a Progressive and a marginalist, but he rarely bought into state programs to improve the conditions of the poor and working classes.[159] Influenced by the pragmatism of John Dewey and William James,[160] Holmes argued that Langdell was missing the point about law's importance to society. In an oft quoted phrase, Holmes remarked that "[t]he life of the law has not been logic; it has been experience."[161] Holmes added, "More than that, he must remember that as it embodies the story of a nation's development through many centuries, the law finds its philosophy not in self-consistency, which it must always fail in so long as it continues to grow, but in history and the nature of human needs."[162]

Holmes's cry that the science of law is more than only logic and consistency was the beginning of what has been called sociological jurisprudence. The backers of sociological jurisprudence, especially Holmes, Louis Brandeis, and Roscoe Pound, hoped to bring law back into the experience of American life. They sought to improve society through the law. To achieve that end, law must be pragmatic, capable of changing and adjusting to the needs of society. For example, in 1908 Brandeis compiled a hundred-page brief attempting to demonstrate the reasonableness of a fifty-hour work week for women.[163] People who believed in sociological jurisprudence hoped to move law away from laissez-faire individualism and toward a concern for social justice; it was a reaction against a law based on property rights and in favor of a law based on human rights.

These ideas were reflected in the proposals put forward by Pound, a former dean of the Harvard Law School. Relying on the methods of social science, he hoped to reclaim law from what he called the "legal monks."[164] First, Pound wanted more data on the impact of law on society. And second, he wanted to free judges from formal rules so they could use social scientific data to arrive at decisions that would improve society. For Pound, the ultimate end for the law is not consistency but a just result:[165] "The sociological movement in jurisprudence, the movement for pragmatism as a philosophy of law, the movement for the adjustment of principles and doctrines to the human conditions they are to govern rather than to assumed first principles, the movement for putting the human factor in the central place and relegating logic to its true position as an instrument, has scarcely shown itself as yet in America."[166]

For the purposes of this exploration of legal thought, sociological jurisprudence represents an important step in the corporate rationalization of the law. While legal formalism tried to turn law into a science separate from the public sphere, sociological jurisprudence started using science to influence the law as a way to manage society. Law became an instrumental weapon to be used to achieve the good, which was determined by social science methodology. While sociological jurisprudence was perhaps a more humane type of law, it also created the conditions for the increased management of the public sphere.

Legal Realism

The ideas put forward by advocates of sociological jurisprudence were taken up by a group of lawyers and judges in the 1920s that was to become known as the legal realists. These lawyers attempted to take the ideas of Pound, Holmes, and Brandeis a step further in their attempt to reform the practice of law in the United States. As one study of that movement observes, "Emphasizing personal psychological factors in the mind of the judge rather than adjustment of the law to social change, legal realists all but abandoned the traditional idea of the rule of law as the basis of the constitutional state. Instead of a body of fixed rules and controlling precedents, law for the legal realists became a kind of ad hoc method of arbitration."[167]

Legal realism was less a philosophy than a way of practicing law; there was no truly unified school of legal realism.[168] As Karl Llewellyn pointed out, there was some general agreement among the people who practiced legal realism, but generally their versions of realism engulfed a wide range of ideas.[169] As Wilfrid Rumble notes, "The legal realists were a heterodox lot."[170] And Jerome Frank, a federal judge and a leading realist writer, wrote in 1970 that realists have only one thing in common: "[S]kepticism as to some of the conventional legal theories, a skepticism stimulated by a zeal to reform, in the interest of justice, some court-house ways."[171]

Two of the leading realists were Frank and Llewellyn. Each represented one of the many branches of legal realism. Frank wrote in the preface to the sixth printing of *Law and the Modern Mind* that the realists could be divided into two groups. The first was what he called "rule skeptics." Led by Llewellyn, this group argued that judicial rules are too unreliable to allow lawyers to predict to their clients how a case will turn out. The "rule skeptics" sought "real rules" that would serve as reliable predictors of events.[172] The second group, of which Frank considered himself a member, can be called "fact skeptics." They argued that rules, in whatever form, are of no help to lower courts in predicting the outcome of cases because of the elusiveness on which judges' decisions turn. "Fact skeptics" sought more judicial justice.[173] As Frank described the ideas that separated the two groups, the rule skeptics were "the left-wing adherents of a tradition," but the fact skeptics wanted to break from the tradition itself.[174]

While realists sought to break with formalist rules, they never were able to completely achieve that goal. As James Boyle sums up the realist movement, "The two central legal realist arguments depended upon a critique of essentialist rationality in linguistic interpretation and a defense of the essential rationality of science. Thus the judge was supposed to give up playing with words and to begin playing with policy science."[175] As noted in chapter 1, the pragmatic vision of the realists was not a way of surrendering management of society but rather a different way of theorizing it.

Legal realists, like their forebearers who advocated sociological jurisprudence, were empiricists but not really social theorists. They enjoyed strong connections to sociology and social science research in general but stayed away from the theoretical sciences such as economics. In important ways, some of the legal realists were ahead of their time. Many advocated the ideas associated with economic institutionalism, which sees institutions (groups of individuals that form rules for the allocation of resources) as an effective substitute for conventional markets.[176] For example, Llewellyn would argue that because law is a scarce resource, economic decisions must be continually made about how to allocate the law.[177]

In addition to changing the way people thought about the practice of law, legal realism also changed the way law interacted with society. Fundamental to this belief was the idea that law is not prepolitical. That is, law did not exist prior to the creation of a nation-state, and thus it is inherently political. Flowing from that belief, the legal realists fundamentally changed how we think about issues such as contracts and property. As J. M. Balkin notes, "No regime of contract, property, and tort was unregulated or free of governmental policy or government intervention—there was only different possible regimes and different choices about which persons to benefit at the expense of others."[178]

We can see the importance of this shift in thinking through an examination of New Deal legislation. As Balkin notes, the legal realists were not arguing for "the wholesale restructuring of the American economy" but instead were creating the foundation for a new form of corporate liberal state that would become a reality in the New Deal.[179] By arguing that many economic issues, including property, are human creations, the New Deal built an argument for active government involvement in areas that had previously been considered off-limits. They were building a foundation for the idea that government not only has a right to make value choices in the name of society but that it is obligated to do so.

The result was the creation of a large number of governmental agencies that directly influenced rights that many believed had been cordoned off from government involvement. For example, in the area of free speech alone, Sunstein notes that the New Deal spawned the Securities and Exchange Commission (speech involving stocks and bonds), the Federal Communications Commission (the broadcast industry), the Food and Drug Administration and Federal Trade Commission (advertising), and the National Labor Relations Board (exchanges between employers and employees). Sunstein observes one common thread running through the creation of all of these agencies: They were a "response to the perception that in light of the existing distribution of rights and entitlements, legal controls on speech may actually turn out to promote a well-functioning system of free expression."[180]

The legal realists, through a rethinking of property, created a system that allowed policy makers to rethink the distribution of resources within society, especially those controlled by corporations, and refused to break away from scientific methodology. The realists, by increasing the governmental role and ignoring the government-corporation connection that is central to corporate liberal beliefs, aided the rationalization process. The realists then substituted one form of control (the law) for another (large government).

In the end, sociological jurisprudence and legal realism, while identifying legal formalism as the opponent, failed to recognize their real opponent and how their opposition was being shaped by the culture of the market. Haskell notes that the market doesn't favor formalism or antiformalism but does favor the battle for dominance between the two.[181] And Haskell asks, "[C]ould it be that in adapting the posture of antiformalism they have unwittingly been riding in the swift central current of cultural transformation, echoing and even amplifying the very market forces they set out to master, occupying as it were an attributive niche that the market itself carved out for them?"[182]

Professionalization and American Law

At their base, the debates about law and its role in society contribute to the corporate rationalization of the law. Legal formalism tied the law closely to prominent research universities that would then be applied to exert control over entry into the field. But perhaps even more importantly, legal formalism began envisioning law as a science. To legal formalists, law is something that a privileged few are allowed to do—an occupation for elites.

Sociological jurisprudence and legal realism encouraged those elites to start using their power, and science, to manage society. Sociological jurisprudence, with its ties to the Progressive movement, is often viewed romantically as a movement to aid democracy. However, much like the Progressive movement in general, sociological jurisprudence was less about democratizing the law than about allowing the educated elite to govern policy using social scientific methods. Sociological jurisprudence didn't break with the elitist notions of formalism but rather attempted to channel those notions in a different direction. In the process, the Progressive movement tied law even more closely to at least one element of corporate rationalization—social scientific methodology. And while those directions might be "better" from a social welfare standpoint, they did little to help the public sphere.

Legal realism would appear to present the biggest challenge to the threat of corporate rationalization, but in many ways realists also refused to break away from the professional powers associated with the law. While it is true that the realists, with their suspicion of rules and facts, challenged the basic epistemological foundation of the law, they, too, refused to break free from professionalization. Realists often admitted that the law was not a science, but that admission was made more in the name of pragmatics than methodologies. The realist challenge poked holes in law as a science yet yearned to find a way to make law more scientific. In the end, they often argued that the best that could be done was to empower professional judges—judges who would not act on their emotions and biases but would bring a scientific detachment to their work. And the realist challenge created the foundation for the corporate liberal state that increasingly manages more and more areas of public life.

These intellectual movements within the law laid the foundation for the law-and-economics movement and its current popularity. The influence of corporate rationalization on the law far exceeds the boundaries of the law-and-economics movement, however. It takes the professionalization of the law, inside and outside the legal profession, to a new level through an emphasis on efficiency and procedure, framing how we think about problems that face our society.

Consider a news report by National Public Radio on the question of whether racial profiling is a constitutional way to identify potential terrorists following the September 11, 2001, attacks on the World Trade Center and the Pentagon. The story centered on an Iranian-born American citizen who was removed from an airline flight because the pilot was uncomfortable flying with him aboard the plane. He was put on a later flight. When a George Washington University law professor attempted to explain why racial profiling of this type ought to be allowable when dealing with possible terrorists as opposed to the war on drugs, he fell back on the language of the law-and-economics movement: "Quite frankly, we can let a nickel bag get by or even some cocaine get by in order to avoid the social costs of having racial profiling. The costs are a little different at an airport. There are forty million people that travel by air in this country. We cannot stop each one of them and make an individualized determination of risk. We have to develop some type of profile. The fact is, profiling is a legitimate statistical device. And it's a device that we may have to use if we're going to have a meaningful security process at these airports."[183]

The impact within the legal profession is just as significant. Larson has noted that power within the bar association has moved from individual lawyers to the state, corporation, and university.[184] For some, the result is that older ideas of professionalism (noblesse oblige, public service, and so on) have come to be redefined. Being a professional today is less about public service than about being efficient. Balkin argues that in the postmodern era, these older ideas of professionalism have been replaced by "an industrial model where service is defined in terms of discrete units of production that can be duplicated and evaluated on a mass scale."[185] Balkin notes that these ideas are already central to American legal practice in a postmodern society—"We already have mass-produced litigation and mass-produced judicial administration to deal with it. Already most federal judicial opinions are written by twenty-five-year olds, so that the language of opinions does not really mean what it says, because it was not said by the persons whose meaning really counts."[186]

The professionalization of the law has real consequences for the public sphere. Through the concept of professionalization we can see the corporate rationalization of the law and begin to understand its consequences for public life. Those consequences can be observed on a number of levels. It changes how those who practice law relate to the rest of society. Law increasingly becomes something that is done outside of the public sphere rather than a part of the public sphere. The dominant way that law is done today is through the corporate model using corporate values.

Professions and the Public Sphere

If the public sphere is to survive and flourish in a democratic society, it needs supportive institutions. The press is capable of providing the information and expressive avenues that are vital to an effective public sphere, while the law is capable of providing the legal freedom to make the public sphere effective. Professionalization, as it has played out in both occupations, fails to meet the needs of public life. Because of an emphasis on routines and methodology, the information that the press provides lacks the needed diversity. By focusing on establishing its own professional standing, the press has elected to view the public as a body to be informed and managed rather than activated.

The professionalization of the law has had a similar impact on the public sphere. Rather than providing the legal cover needed for public life, the legal profession has attempted to make the law more scientific, to tie it up in methodological questions that effectively remove citizens from the discussion. Law has come to be more concerned about the role it plays in assuring elite management of society than in enabling the public sphere to exercise its influence. Much as it has removed journalists from the public sphere, professionalization has served to separate judges and lawyers from the public sphere. While this chapter has examined the ideas that ground this development, it does not answer the question of how this move occurred. The next chapter will begin that investigation by looking at how the press and the law have used professional practices to limit public life and, perhaps more importantly, how the two institutions sometimes act in concert to effectively limit an active public sphere.

4

Defining a Professional Mission: The Law and the Question of Public Representation

Vanessa Leggett is an odd poster child for American journalism's professionalization movement, but in 2001 and 2002 she became just that. A freelance book author with only one published article to her credit, no book contract, and no representation from a major media firm, she is not what generally comes to mind when we speak of a professional journalist. Her ambition in life was to write true-crime books, to explore, as she told one reporter, "the duality of human nature, our ability to be imbued with such goodness and yet have a capacity for such evil."[1]

She began collecting material for a book on the murder of a Houston, Texas, socialite. Along the way, she had cooperated with law enforcement officials, willingly exchanged information, and even appeared before a federal grand jury to answer questions. She balked, however, when the FBI asked her to become a paid informant.[2] When a prosecutor asked her to turn over all of her notes for her book, she refused and was jailed for 168 days, the longest incarceration of a journalist in the history of the United States. Leggett's case, and the reaction of the journalistic community to it, tells us something about the debate over the professionalization of public institutions and the role those institutions play in modern democracies.

Despite her tenuous connection to what might be called institutional journalism, professional journalists rushed to Leggett's defense. Four influential groups, the Reporters' Committee for Freedom of the Press, the American Society of Newspaper Editors, the Radio-Television News Directors Association, and the Society of Professional Journalists, joined by twenty media organizations, including the *New York Times,* the *Washington Post,* the *Wall*

Street Journal, ABC, CBS, and NBC, filed a friend of the court brief with the U.S. Court of Appeals, Fifth Circuit, asking the court to free Leggett. The brief provides an interesting glimpse into how professionalization shapes a public institution. It is clear that the groups are less concerned about Leggett as an individual than about what the disposition of her case means for the profession of journalism and the group it represents, the public. As the groups say in the brief, the impact for journalists is "real and immediate." The brief continues: "Reasonable journalists will fear that the use of similar subpoenas will allow prosecutors and civil litigants to use journalists as private investigators, thereby restricting the free flow of information to the public."[3]

For these groups, Leggett deserves her freedom not so that she can express herself or earn a living writing true-crime books but rather because of what her case means to the institution of the press and its role in democracy. While the brief argues that "[i]t is the public need for information that should be at the center of this debate, particularly with respect to confidential sources and information,"[4] nowhere does it tell us what the public is actually missing because of Leggett's incarceration. It seems that the fight for an institutional right is far more important than understanding what the public gains in information.

Leggett's story, and the profession's reaction to it, demonstrates the uneasy tension prompted by press professionalization in the United States. As we have seen, the the press is often viewed as a stand-in for the public, a role that is closely tied to its professionalization movement. In that regard, the press is viewed as an institution *of* the public. But as the press attempts to stake its claim to professional status, it is forced to separate itself from the public and demonstrate why it alone should be vested with certain rights and responsibilities.[5] Individual rights become institutional rights that are justified because they serve the public good, but the individual becomes secondary to the profession. Leggett should be freed not because of what she is actually reporting, nor because she has any inherent individual rights. Rather, her jailing is wrong because she is in some sense a part of an occupational group that is vital to the survival of democracy. The Fifth Circuit refused to buy the argument, however. In an unpublished opinion, the court ruled that "the journalist privilege is ineffectual against a grand jury subpoena, absent evidence of governmental harassment or oppression."[6]

Cases such as Leggett's provide a glimpse into how the press and courts theorize democracy. In that battle for professional status, the press and the courts struggle to figure out their role in democratic life. This chapter examines appellate-level cases involving the issue of journalist's privilege between

1897 and 2003.[7] Only criminal cases were examined for this study. Admittedly, the question of journalist's privilege pertains to civil cases as well. For example, a First Amendment–based privilege was explored in a 1958 libel case, *Garland v. Torre*.[8] However, criminal cases are arguably at the heart of the privilege because it is here that the government becomes directly involved in how the press operates. And appellate courts often deal directly with policy issues. In short, appellate-level courts articulate ideology through their interpretation of common law and statutes.[9]

While the courts were shaping the concept of journalist's privilege, they also were shaping the way institutions relate to the public sphere. In other words, contained within the judicial decisions are narratives—judicial stories—that shape public life in the United States. This chapter argues that this legal battle offers evidence of the corporate rationalization of public life, the press, and the law. Within these decisions we not only see how a public institutional mission is crafted but also how the press and the courts envision the public sphere as something to be managed and watched over.

While evidence of corporate rationalization can be found in privilege cases, privilege cases are not the primary agent of professionalization. Rather, they are best viewed as reflecting similar movements that were occurring within the public sphere, the press, and the law at the same time. The privilege cases are a window that allows us to see how corporate rationalization has been played out in one small arena of public life. Researchers who study professionalization of the press, however, rarely look at press law.[10] This oversight is surprising because in journalist's privilege cases the press perhaps comes the closest to achieving the status of the traditional professions of law and medicine.[11] It is through this privilege, either statute or common law, where the press is granted a protection of evidentiary or documentary information.

The judicial story of journalist's privilege in the United States revolves around the U.S. Supreme Court case *Branzburg v. Hayes*.[12] Since the Court, prior to 1972, had never directly addressed the issue, the judges that adjudicated cases prior to that period were operating with little guidance from the country's highest court.[13] Judges who ruled on cases after 1972, however, struggled with the *Branzburg* ruling in an attempt to square their decisions with the facts of the cases. The result is that the *Branzburg* decision plays an important role in judicial narratives themselves. The cases for this study will therefore be examined in three periods: pre-*Branzburg*, the *Branzburg* decision itself, and post-*Branzburg*.

More importantly, evidence of corporate rationalization is embedded within the *Branzburg* decision and its interpretation. At one level, the decision and its progeny are about the privileges enjoyed by journalists. At another, often unexamined level, the case brings to the forefront assumptions about an inactive public sphere and the role dominant institutions play in managing public life.

The Path toward *Branzburg:* An Emerging Professional Status

In 1848, a reporter for the *New York Herald* refused to identify his source after obtaining a copy of a confidential draft of a treaty to end the Mexican-American War. In the first reported privilege case, the reporter refused to answer questions from a U.S. Senate committee and was subsequently jailed for contempt of Congress.[14] In other early privilege cases to reach appellate courts, primarily libel cases,[15] courts refused to recognize a privilege for members of the press. These early cases helped set the scene for the question of journalist's privilege prior to the *Branzburg* decision.[16] Prior to 1900, only two privilege cases outside the libel area reached appellate courts, with the press losing both.[17] As the twentieth century progressed, the number of privilege cases increased.[18] As the frequency of the privilege claims increased, the arguments used to protect journalists changed. This is most obvious in two areas. First of all, the arguments that journalists used to seek a privilege changed from an individual right to a professional, institutional right. And second, as the cases moved towards the 1970s, the press articulated a clear public mission— a mission that puts the institutional press at the center of the structure of modern democracy.

Claiming Professional Status

While the number of privilege cases prior to the *Branzburg* decision is limited in number, they do provide some evidence of a change in professional ideology among journalists. In the earliest cases, journalists portrayed themselves as individuals—individuals with whom government has no right to intervene. The argument in defense of a privilege is not based on a professional standard of protecting the public or on organizational affiliation but rather on a claim of the rights and liberties of individuals.

When a board of police commissioners attempted in 1911 to force T. J. Hamilton, a reporter for the *Augusta (Ga.) Herald,* to reveal his source of information for a story on a murder, Hamilton refused. He told the court that the questions asked of him "were questions which he, as a citizen, had a legal right to refuse to answer" because they could cost him his means of livelihood. Hamilton told the court that he viewed his promise not to reveal the name of the source as being as "sacred as the obligation to tell the truth after being sworn by the commission." Revealing the name of the source would hurt his standing in the community, Hamilton argued. "It would ruin me in my business," he told the court. "It would cause me to lose my position as a newspaper reporter for the *Augusta Herald*, and would prevent my ever engaging in the occupation of the newspaper reporter again."[19]

A similar argument was used in 1917, when a Missouri grand jury sought the name of Robert E. Holliway's sources for a story on indictments handed down by a grand jury. Holliway, a reporter for the *St. Louis Republic*, refused to cooperate, "standing on my constitutional rights."[20] He did not cite the First Amendment in his constitutional defense but rather refused to answer "because the answer thereto tended or might tend to incriminate him."[21]

Much the same line of argument was followed in 1921 by a reporter for the *Chicago Evening American*, Hector H. Elwell. When called before a grand jury and asked to reveal the source of his information for a story about graft and U.S. officials, Elwell refused and said, "'If newspapers do not protect people who furnish them news, it would be impossible for them to get news.'"[22]

Concerns about revealing information and its implications for the business of the press continued into the 1950s. When Reubin J. Clein, the editor of *Miami Life*, printed a story on a grand jury investigation and the grand jury asked him to reveal his informant, Clein refused, claiming he had broken no law. "If I was to reveal the source of my information I may as well go out of business," Clein told the grand jury.[23]

But Clein also reflected the press's growing professionalization movement and its changing conception of its role in society when he claimed that such a professional right had existed for years. Clein argued that "it is more or less an unwritten law" that journalists, unless they break the law, would be granted a privilege to protect their sources. "Newspaper men have more or less taken it for granted through the years that they would be accorded that courtesy," he said.[24]

Claims of professional status and public duty were, until this point, generally absent from the arguments made by journalists seeking special protection before appellate courts. In the 1960s, they began to ground their arguments more firmly on the press clause of the First Amendment. In 1963, editors from *The Bulletin* in Philadelphia argued that the source of newspaper-obtained information is "encompassed within, and protected by," the constitutional protections of freedom of the press.[25] And in 1968, a journalist for a student newspaper at the University of Oregon argued that the sources for her story on marijuana use were protected on "constitutional and professional-ethics grounds."[26]

In the end, the early privilege cases show that as case law moved towards *Branzburg*, journalists based their defense less on individual rights and more on institutional protections. It is difficult to say with certainty that this change is due to journalists thinking about their work in a different, more institutional context. It could be entirely a pragmatic response—once courts accepted the institutional status of reporters, they began relying more on that argument as a way of securing rights. However, even if this is the case, it tells us something about how occupations secure professional status in a democratic society. Viewing work through an institutional context is central to the idea of corporate rationalization. The institution routinizes not only work products but also its guiding ideals. By the 1950s, journalists were referring to an "unwritten law," an institutional professional code that would grant them special status before the law. Becoming a professional institution cannot be achieved absent a public mission, however. And in the privilege cases, we can see the emergence of that mission.

The Law and the Creation of a Public Mission

Just as the arguments that journalists used to support their privilege claims changed, how the judges viewed those claims changed as well. Prior to *Branzburg*, appellate judges moved from never recognizing a privilege claim to the development of a rationale for why the press should be entitled to greater privileges than the average citizen.

In the early years of the claim, appellate judges were steadfast in their refusal to recognize a privilege for journalists. The courts relied on the lack of precedent[27] and the belief that the search for truth is more important than reporters' rights not to incriminate themselves or to protect their livelihoods.[28] Judges believed that granting reporters the ability to protect information would hinder the state's ability to punish wrongdoing. As the New Jersey Supreme Court noted in 1913 when a reporter refused a grand jury's request to identify his source because he was a newspaper reporter, "In effect he pleaded a privilege which finds no countenance in the law. Such an immunity, as claimed by the defendant, would be far-reaching in its effect, and detrimental to the due administration of law. To admit of any such privilege would be to shield the real transgressor and permit him to go unwhipped of justice."[29]

In 1917, the Missouri Supreme Court labeled Holliway's privilege claim "poor patriotism and worse citizenship." It added, "[I]t is at best a vicious sort of harmful intermeddling with the enforcement of the law, or the conservation of the public welfare."[30]

By 1936, some courts were starting to wrestle with the question of who had the power to grant a privilege—courts or legislatures. In 1936, a New York appeals court said that the power to approve a privilege rests in the hands of the legislature, not the court.[31] Courts did, however, continue to play a crucial role in the interpretation of privilege legislation. For example, a New Jersey court provided a strict interpretation of that state's shield law in 1943. When editors of the Hudson County newspapers were asked to identify who delivered press releases to their offices, in an attempt to determine the author of the releases, the editors refused to cooperate based on the New Jersey shield law. The court, however, ruled that the shield law protects only the source of the information, not the messenger.[32]

In the 1960s, courts began to look more favorably on reporters' claims. Along with the more favorable view came more explicit examinations of the role of the press. In 1963, the Pennsylvania Supreme Court described the press as society's "principal watch-dogs and protectors of honest, as well as good, Government." Giving a broad reading to the state's shield law, the court noted, "They are, more than anyone else, the principal guardians of the general welfare of the Community and, with few exceptions, they serve their City, State or Nation with high principles, a zeal and fearlessness. They are, in the best sense of the maxim, '*pro bono publico.*'"[33]

The Pennsylvania Supreme Court viewed the press's mission as prescribed under the state's shield law as primarily being a check on big government, a way of exposing the wrongdoings of governmental officials. The Court viewed the public welfare as being better served by protecting sources than by forcing their disclosure: "It is vitally important that this public shield against governmental inefficiency, corruption and crime be preserved against piercing and erosion."[34]

Much the same argument is put forward by the Ninth Circuit Court of Appeals in 1972. When two staff members of a Black Panther newspaper were questioned about threats by other party members to kill President Richard Nixon, the court ruled that government was infringing on their First and Fifth Amendment rights. The court held that the press's rights did not belong to the staff members but to the public at large. "The larger purpose was to protect public access to information," the court wrote.[35]

Writers have long worried that by allowing press rights to be justified by public rights, the courts are weakening press protections. Such arguments, the reasoning goes, invite judges to decide the public's interest, and some fear that the ruling might not always favor the press. That fear was realized when the Wisconsin Supreme Court grounded its decision in the principle that the 1960s were a time of "disorderly society." Because of that disorder, curtailment of fundamental freedoms can be used to restore order to society. In the end, the court recognized a reporter's privilege but argued that if there is an overriding public interest, such as returning tranquility to society, "it must yield to the interest of justice."[36]

Prior to 1972, then, we can find in the journalist's privilege cases an emerging sense of professional status for the press. That status is reflected not only in the justifications that journalists used to defend themselves but also in the role that judges see the press playing in society. By the early 1970s a tension was already developing about who is the proper protector of the public welfare—the government or the press. But perhaps more importantly, we can see that prior to 1972, journalists and judges were talking about how First Amendment rights were less individual freedoms than institutional rights.

As it developed a public professional mission, accepted by the courts, the press itself became a way to manage society. The press was seen as a way to make government more responsible and responsive to the public. The idea of a privilege for journalists, originally seen as destructive to social order, became a potential way to tap into the public mood. And while not all courts embraced that logic, at least some were willing to experiment with the idea the press might be a potential partner in the management of disorder. The unclear status of privilege claims by journalists, as well as the recognition of its professional standing and mission, led the U.S. Supreme Court to consider its first case in the area in 1972.

The *Branzburg* Decision

The *Branzburg* case was a product of the civil unrest of the 1960s.[37] The first privilege case to be heard before the U.S. Supreme Court, it brought together three separate cases that all touched on the issue of journalist's privilege. The first case involved Paul Branzburg, a reporter for the *Louisville Courier-Journal* who wrote two stories, one in 1969 and one in 1970, about drug use in the area. His first story involved two area residents who synthesized hashish. In exchange for the information, Branzburg promised not to identify his sources. Two grand juries subpoenaed him, and he refused to testify, citing the Kentucky reporter's privilege statute and the First Amendment. Appellate courts ruled that the Kentucky privilege statute protected only information provided to him by sources and not what he personally witnessed.[38]

The second case, *In re Pappas,* involved a television reporter named Paul Pappas, a newsman-photographer working in Providence, Rhode Island. In 1970, he was assigned to cover civil disorders in New Bedford, Massachusetts. Pappas gained access to a conference held by the Black Panthers, recording and photographing the reading of a prepared statement. He was allowed to remain inside the headquarters as long as he did not disclose anything he heard or saw other than an anticipated police raid. The raid never materialized, and Pappas never reported on what went on inside the headquarters. Following a grand jury subpoena, Pappas refused to testify, claiming a First Amendment privilege. An appeals court rejected his claim, stating that the responsibility of a reporter is the same as that of any other citizen—to provide evidence when called about potentially criminal activities.[39]

United States v. Caldwell stands alone as the one case in the *Branzburg* trilogy that the press won at the lower level. Caldwell, a reporter for the *New York Times,* had been assigned to cover the Black Panther party and other groups. In 1970, he was called to testify before a grand jury and ordered to bring with him his notes and tape recordings of interviews with Black Panther leaders. Caldwell argued that meeting with the grand jury in secret would damage his relationship with party leaders and that the First Amendment protects the collection of information. When Caldwell failed to appear before the grand jury, he was held in contempt. An appeals court reversed the contempt charge, claiming that Caldwell enjoyed a qualified First Amendment privilege as a reporter.[40]

The meaning of the U.S. Supreme Court's often confusing five-to-four *Branzburg* decision is difficult to capture. Of particular importance was the divisive nature of the Court. While Justice Byron R. White's opinion was able to attract a majority, Justice Lewis F. Powell Jr. also authored a short concurring opinion that has grown in importance. (For example, the court relied heavily on Powell's opinion in the Leggett case.) Justice Potter Stewart, joined by Justices William J. Brennan Jr. and Thurgood Marshall, wrote an influential dissenting opinion, and Justice Douglas authored a separate dissenting opinion.[41] The result is a confusing decision where, for many, Justice Stewart's dissenting opinion has proved to be the most important element.[42]

The following is an examination of the leading opinions, attempting to discover where they differ but also trying to pull from the opinions the justices' views of the press and the public.

Justice White: Writing Is Not the Same as Doing

The Court's majority opinion, written by Justice White, defines the general contours of its views on the idea of journalist's privilege and public life. White sought to minimize the damage done by his opinion to press freedom from the beginning. By narrowing the legal topic to the question of whether journalists can refuse to testify before grand juries, White was able to still claim that news gathering enjoys some First Amendment protection: "[W]ithout some protection for seeking out the news, freedom of the press could be eviscerated."[43]

His strategy not only takes away some of the sting for the press; it also allows him to frame the issue as a confrontation between the press and the judicial system, a framework that is vital to the success of his argument. In effect, Justice White constructs a story not about the press's importance to society but rather its confrontation with the judicial system in the administration of society. In White's scenario, the only way for the press to successfully argue its case is by resorting to elitist and antidemocratic arguments— that it is above the law and different from other members of society. The important question is not how the public is best served but rather who has the power to best protect the public.[44]

For White, at least when it comes to criminal investigations, the public is best represented by grand juries, not the press. The press, by writing stories about crime, does not operate in the public interest. The press's claim is based "on the theory that it is better to write about crime than to do something about it."[45] And for White, that is an uncertain proposition at best.

White chastises the press for seeking a privilege for itself and not for the source, who it allegedly is trying to protect.[46] Still, White apparently would not look favorably on a plan to protect those sources any more than one to protect the press. A privilege is not needed because, White argues, any "whistleblower" who is sincerely interested in improving public life would willingly deal with public authorities "charged with the duty to protect the public interest."[47]

White was not seeking a system that is accountable to the public but rather a system accountable to a governmental bureaucracy, where "[t]he public through its elected and appointed law enforcement officers" will deal with crime in society.[48] White saw no First Amendment right for journalists to refuse to testify before grand juries, but he was willing to grant that idea constitutional legitimacy if legislative bodies perceived the need.[49] Yes, White admits, grand juries can abuse their role, but when that happens the judiciary will step in and correct the problem. For White, there is little role for the press and public to play in the criminal justice system.

In the end, White turns the question of journalist's privilege into a battle between values: the value to society of press reports from undisclosed, unverified sources versus the value to society of government pursuing and prosecuting criminal actions. In White's view, there is no question that constitutional and legal history favors the government's prosecution of criminal actions.

Justice Powell: Balancing Society's Interests

In many respects, Justice Powell tried to find some agreement between the majority opinion and the dissenting opinions. He notes in his short concurring opinion that the Court's holding is of a "limited nature" and that First Amendment protections remain in place "even if one seriously believed that the media . . . were not able to protect themselves."[50] Powell advocates a case-by-case balancing test to be used by courts in which the goal is to protect freedom of the press and the obligation of citizens to provide information about criminal conduct.[51] Still, his sympathies clearly rest with maintaining the judiciary's power over questions of privilege. Powell criticizes claims by journalists that they should be allowed to refuse to appear before a grand jury unless a court has found that their testimony is relevant and needed. To allow journalists to refuse to appear would "defeat such a fair balancing and the essential societal interest in the detection and prosecution of crime would be heavily subordinated."[52] Under Powell's balancing test, journalists would be required to appear and then seek a remedy if they believe the investigation were not being conducted in good faith.[53]

Justice Stewart: The Press and Its Democratic Function

Justice Stewart tells much the same story about public life in the United States as the other members of the Court, but he comes to a very different conclusion about who is the public's representative. Justice Stewart preferred to put his faith in the press. In fact, he accuses the Court's majority of attempting to annex the press "as an investigative arm of government."[54] In the long run, Stewart argues, the Court's actions will hamper rather than help the administration of justice.[55] Journalists, fearing that they will be forced to reveal the identity of their sources, "will cease to investigate and publish information about issues of public import."[56]

Justice Stewart put forward a constitutional right for reporters to maintain confidential relationships with their sources. Society's interest in protecting this relationship stems from its interest in "a full and free flow of information to the public."[57] The goal for society, according to Stewart, is an "informed citizenry," and the press plays a vital role in achieving that end: "Not only does the press enhance personal self-fulfillment by providing the people with the widest possible range of fact and opinion, but it also is an incontestable precondition of self-government."[58]

For Stewart, the press does much more than print "public statements" or "prepared handouts." Unless journalists are free to enter into confidential relationships, not all of the information needed for public discourse will be obtained.[59]

Stewart points out that the press's privilege claim does not exist for purely individual reasons, nor for First Amendment reasons for either party. "Rather," Stewart argues, "it functions to insure nothing less than democratic decisionmaking through the free flow of information to the public."[60]

Stewart sees the press as an occupation with accepted professional standards and a clear public mission. In fact, he claims that the majority's decision puts journalists in a difficult position: either be punished by the government for contempt or violate their own "professional ethics."[61]

Stewart's answer to the competing standards of free press and the investigation of criminal activities is to support a method of "circumscribing investigative powers" by placing "a heavy burden of justification on government officials when First Amendment rights are impaired."[62] Stewart advocated a three-part test, put forward by the lower court in *Caldwell*, that makes the government prove (1) that the information being sought is relevant to the government's case; (2) that the journalist has the information being sought; and (3) that there are no other ways of obtaining the information that would be less invasive of First Amendment rights.

Interpreting *Branzburg:* The Management of Public Life

The *Branzburg* decision is often interpreted as a blow to the press's professionalization. It is difficult to escape the surface argument made by Justice White that the press is no different than the ordinary citizen. But White fails to capture the fact that the press and the public do not begin from the same point. The press enters the question with special rights and privileges already accorded to it. The real meaning of *Branzburg* is not that the Court endorsed an active citizenry by refusing to grant the press professional status, but rather the opposite. Promoting an active citizenry would have been to recognize a press privilege *and* a privilege for citizens who are involved in discursive activities. Justice White starts by assuming an inactive public sphere and then lowers the press to the same level as citizens. The difference between White and the other justices in *Branzburg* is that others favored an active press as the best alternative to an active public. No justice was endorsing an active public. In fact, White seems to actively endorse an inactive press *and* an inactive public. By saying that the press is no different than the average citizen, he is not making a case for a more participatory form of democracy. Instead, he is making an authoritarian, bureaucratic argument. Perhaps he is right in not wanting to separate the press from the public sphere, but he chooses to bring the two of them together by disempowering both.

The Supreme Court justices tell different stories about the role of the press in society, even if they share similar conclusions. In a sense, these stories contain descriptions that serve as ideal types, models around which society constructs its press and public sphere. The one definition that is shared by all justices is that of the inactive private citizen. Modern democracy is not achieved through the actions of private citizens who have voluntarily come together to form themselves into a public, but rather through the actions of the elites in society. The only real difference between the justices becomes whether the press is to be considered a member of that elite.

The uncertainty of the Court's decision has left lower-court judges free to pick which opinion to follow. More often than not, that choice seems to reflect a judge's view of the press's role in society. Generally, the cases examined for this section can be divided into two categories: a management model favored by Justices White and Powell, which often tends to favor the administration of justice and the needs of government, and a press model, which recognizes news-media protections through Justice Stewart's three-part test but also brings with it a notion of an inactive public.

The Management Model: Balancing Society's Interests

The management model, formulated out of the opinions by Justices White and Powell, is most often the guiding rationale in cases that are decided against the press. Lower-court judges find in the White-Powell approach a justification for limiting the press's power: issues of press freedom rarely outweigh the state's power to punish criminals. State courts give strict interpretations to state shield laws.

In interpreting legislative decisions regarding privilege claims, appellate courts have used the management model widely, as they attempt to determine which right takes precedent—the right of freedom of the press, or the right of a defendant to a fair trial and the power that gives to the judiciary. Appellate courts have occasionally found that the competing rights are equal,[63] but more frequently they have found that a defendant's right to a fair trial is greater than the press's rights.[64] Courts that use the management model tend to see the press's privilege claims as stripping courts of their power and taking the investigatory authority away from grand juries. As a state appellate court wrote in interpreting New York's shield law, "[T]he Shield Law privilege cannot be honored if invoking it significantly lessens the Grand Jury's investigative power. It seems to us inarguable that the Shield Law was ever intended to serve as a shield for, or to conceal the commission of, a crime."[65]

Courts that follow the management model tend to take a narrow view of who qualifies as a professional journalist and what information is protected, all in an attempt to protect the court's power. In 1979, a New York court refused to grant a privilege to the author of a book about an alleged crime family, saying that the state's shield law protected only "professional journalists" and "newscasters." The court wrote that it should not grant a "strained interpretation" to "encompass those engaged in a different field of writing and research."[66] The court argued that confidential sources are vital to the work of professional journalists but not to the work of authors, who tend to rely on documents and background interviews. The court concluded, "Thus, his contacts with confidential sources, being minimal vis-à-vis those of an investigative journalist, would be far less likely to have any impact on the free flow of information which the First Amendment is designed to protect."[67]

The court found that protecting the integrity of the courts was more important than expanding the protection of journalist's privilege: "More important than any inhibiting effect on the right to gather news is the public interest in the fair administration of justice. . . . The very integrity of the judicial system and public confidence in the system depend on full disclosure of all the facts, within the framework of the rules of evidence."[68]

Absent legislative actions, such as shield laws, the results under the management model are often the same. In a 1978 case where a federal court allowed the government to review the long-distance telephone records of reporters, the court wrote: "Good faith investigation interests always override a journalist's interest in protecting his source."[69] Even in courts that recognize a qualified common law privilege, the balance is often tilted towards the court.[70]

Courts that adopt the management model tend to provide their own readings of *Branzburg*. A Maryland court noted in 1983 that *Branzburg* meant that even if there is an "incidental burden" on the free flow of information, "it is surely outweighed by the vital, historic role played by the grand jury investigation of criminal conduct."[71] In that same vein, a Maine court held that even though the First Amendment protects news gathering and the editorial process, Powell's method provides protection only to confidential sources and not to sources "who voluntarily responded to a news reporter's questions."[72]

Not all of the readings are limited to the narrow question contained in *Branzburg*, however. Courts that use the model have been willing to take that approach outside of the narrow question of grand juries. As a New York court wrote in 1980 about the *Branzburg* decision, "there is little doubt that its reasoning applies to subpoenas served by criminal defendants for testimony or the production of documents at trial."[73]

In the end, the management model that is used to resolve the question of journalist's privilege can be reduced to a jurisdictional battle between the press and the courts over who will manage public life. The result is not surprising: The courts cast themselves in the role of the public's protector. In the words of a federal court, "if a balance must be struck, then it must be struck in favor of the general public's interest in effective law enforcement investigation."[74]

The Press Model: Public Surrogates

Justice Stewart's approach to questions of privilege is generally used by courts that issue decisions favoring the press. Courts using Stewart's rationale often give broad interpretations to shield laws, finding that the state has either not exhausted alternative sources for the information or that the information possessed by the press is not directly relevant to the case.[75] This is not to say that the press wins all cases in front of courts that use Stewart's approach. However, the press won a majority of the cases examined for this study.

Whereas the management model views the courts as the public's representative, the courts that adopt the press model tend to see journalists as "surrogates for the public."[76] They argue for a special role for the press, to transmit information to the general public[77] and to act as an aid to public policy.[78] Using the argument that the press is instrumental to democracy, they claim that by not granting a privilege to the press, judges not only hurt the press but the public as well. As a member of the New Jersey Supreme Court wrote, "The process helps people learn what they need to know. To hamper it is to hamper ourselves."[79] And the California Supreme Court noted, "Unfortunately, if this right is not protected, the real losers will be all Californians who rely on the unrestrained dissemination of information by the news media. . . . A free press protects our basic liberties by serving as the watchdog of our nation."[80]

As such, press-model advocates tend to give a liberal construction to shield laws, recognizing, as one court writes, that the judicial function is "to add force and life to the cure and remedy according to the true intent of the makers of the act, for the public good."[81] Shield laws are not viewed as "irritations" but rather as rational legislative judgments that a free press is more important to society than access to confidential information. By building on Stewart's dissent, a New Jersey court recognized a privilege for eyewitness information collected by journalists,[82] an Ohio court recognized an absolute privilege to protect the names of confidential sources,[83] and a Tennessee appeals court rejected a lower court's request for an *in camera* inspection, labeling it a "fishing expedition."[84]

Judges who advocate the press model also tend to view the *Branzburg* decision as limited in reach, often arguing that it only limits testimony before grand juries.[85] Its advocates find more value in the opinions of the *Branzburg* court's dissenters than in the majority.[86] J. Skelly Wright, chief judge of the District of Columbia court of appeals, wrote in 1978, "While reporters have, since *Branzburg*, been required on some occasions to disclose confidential sources in grand jury investigations and at trials, the courts have consistently read *Branzburg* as recognizing the First Amendment interests of reporters in confidentiality and as requiring a judicial balancing before disclosure is ordered."[87]

More importantly, judges who adopt the press model also tend to have a more favorable view of the press's role in society than the balancers. In the battle to represent the public, judges who side with Stewart are likely to view the press as the true representative of the public. They tend to see the gathering of news as "essential to the preservation of liberty."[88] The Idaho Supreme Court argued that the "needs of present-day society" can only be met through a qualified journalistic privilege.[89] "Today's world of democracy demands information as never before," the court said. "It is that fact that leads to the inescapable conclusion that a common law journalist privilege does exist."[90]

In the end, Stewart's press model often results in decisions that are favorable to the press. Because of the inherent importance to society that judges who use Stewart's test assign to the press, and by placing the burden of proof on the government to demonstrate that it needs the information, judges are able to find support for the privilege claims of press. However, along with Stewart's view of the press comes his view of the public. The press is not a part of the public but stands outside and above it, feeding it information and opinion, acting as a stand-in for a public that no longer has an interest in participation.

Journalist's Privilege as Corporate Rationalization

The story of journalist's privilege, as told by appellate-level judges, supports the idea that the press is continuing its professionalization movement. That movement, and what it means for society, is reflected in a number of elements that are present in the legal texts. First of all, the claims for privilege have changed over the years. In the early privilege cases, journalists based their claims not on their professional status or their representation of the public good but on their rights as individuals. Government, it was argued, has no right to interfere with their right to make a living. As the courts moved toward *Branzburg,* journalists began relying less on their rights as individuals and more on the powers of the institutional, professional press. Grounded in the First Amendment's press clause, reporters began to argue that the privilege is not theirs as individuals but theirs as a representative of an inactive public. As we see in stances such as Leggett's, institutionalizing a right can hinder public life. Who is entitled to protection depends greatly on whether the institution wants to protect them and, more importantly, whether the courts want to recognize them as a part of the institution.

And secondly, the cases tell us that the press's professional mission helps formulate an inactive public. This becomes particularly evident in the two dominant opinions that arise out of the Supreme Court's *Branzburg* decision. Justices White and Stewart differ not over their definition of the public but rather what institution best represents an inactive, uninterested public. For White, government or the courts are the public's best representative, while Stewart would prefer to put his faith in the press. Neither opinion provides any role for the public sphere other than that of spectator.

In important ways, the privilege cases demonstrate the professionalization struggle engaged in by the press and the judicial system's reaction to it. Within journalist's privilege, the press and law work together to limit the public sphere. They disagree on who will be the public's representative but agree that the public is inactive. If Andrew Abbott is correct in claiming that one sign of professionalization is jurisdictional battles, then the opposing narratives found in *Branzburg* and subsequent privilege cases indicate the importance of that professionalization movement to the public sphere. As the press battles the government for the title of public representative, the role of the public in a democracy is forgotten. The press, supported to some degree by the legal system, constructs a professional mission that separates it from the public sphere. The professional press is not of the public but rather stands apart from the public sphere and provides citizens with information. The end result is that there is little room for an active public within the story surrounding journalist's privilege.

These cases indicate the impact of corporate rationalization not only on the press but also on the judicial system itself. In the years prior to and following *Branzburg*, courts came to rely increasingly on multipronged tests to decide privilege cases. In fact, many recent privilege cases rely to a large extent on some variation of the three-part test articulated by Justice Stewart. That development—the reliance upon an objective methodology—has important links with the concept of corporate rationalization. As the legal historian Morton J. Horwitz wrote about the Supreme Court in 1993, "[M]ost of this Court's opinions are surrounded by a thick undergrowth of technicality. With three or four 'prong' tests everywhere and for everything; with an almost medieval earnestness about classification and categorization; with a theological attachment to the determinate power of various 'levels of scrutiny'; with amazingly fine distinctions that produce multiple opinions designed in Parts, sub-parts, and sub-sub-parts, this is a Court whose Justices appear caught in the throes of various methodological obsessions."[91]

The decisions in the privilege cases reflect Horwitz's observations. But perhaps more importantly, the search for an objective methodology reflects what Horwitz calls a "fear of change"[92] or what Robert M. Cover has called the "violence of administration."[93] As judges search for better ways to separate their opinions from the curse of subjectivity by creating general terms and concepts that can be applied across a wide range of cases, it reduces the law to a technical practice.[94] As numerous legal scholars have argued, objective principles fail to escape subjectivism because they attempt to freeze a concept in time, accepting as a baseline existing conditions.[95]

These objective principles are not used to guide public life but rather to manage it. Questions of free press and speech are reduced to public policy questions, such as who will be considered a reporter, whether forcing disclosure will aid prosecution, and whether there's a need for the information.

These are questions answered not by the public sphere but by government and are, in the end, attempts to make the administration of justice more routine and efficient as seen through bureaucratic eyes.

The point of this chapter is not to argue that granting journalists a special privilege is always wrong. A strong journalist's privilege might be beneficial to public life, given the right public environment. If American democracy currently enjoyed an active, vital public sphere, a strong press privilege might greatly aid public life. Without that active public sphere, the privilege serves to increase citizen reliance on dominant institutions for information and guidance. The professionalization of the press and law damages the public sphere because it replaces public oversight of a process with rules and procedures that are applied by professionals. Journalist's privilege, then, becomes an exercise in bureaucratic control of public life and a debate over how to manage the public sphere. Having said that, however, the way to fight corporate rationalization is not by hindering the flow of information to the public sector by eliminating a privilege for journalists but rather by finding ways to activate the public sphere. It is this last problem that continues to be the most vexing for the press and the law. As the journalist's privilege cases indicate, the press and law are not serving as institutions of the public sphere but rather as institutions that occasionally use the public sphere. As will be demonstrated in the following chapters, this becomes increasingly obvious in other areas of the law where both institutions fail to grasp the fundamental issue: The problem facing modern democracy is not a press problem or legal problem but a public problem.

PART 3

The First Amendment and Public Life

5

Corporate Ownership and the Press: Collapsing Distinctions

The uneasy relationship between corporations and the press reflects the problems corporations present for American democracy. Corporations have changed how journalism is done and where it focuses its attention. Journalists have long railed against corporate ownership—if not ownership in general—yet they continue to work within a system that fails to take their concerns seriously. While many journalists openly express their contempt for large media corporations such as Gannett, Knight-Ridder, and others, they also realize that these corporations are their source of financial security. Journalists who received stock options and large bonuses from corporately owned media have benefited when those media properties were sold.[1] And while only a relatively small number of journalists have profited from the corporate control of the press, there seems to be little question among the profession that corporate control has forever changed news institutions. As Leonard Downie Jr. and Robert G. Kaiser of the *Washington Post* bluntly note, "[M]ost of the corporations that own newspapers are focused on profits, not journalism."[2] Just as professional status imposes constraints that often seem inescapable, corporate ownership of the press has become a nagging reality for journalists.

While journalists write books and articles complaining about the decline of good journalism in the name of profits and corporate ownership, greater questions go unaddressed: What has corporate ownership of the press meant for public life? What happens when one of the public sphere's dominant institutions becomes a vehicle for the accumulation of profits rather than a way of activating citizens? Of course, it is debatable whether today's corporate press represents a fundamental change in the political-economic structure of the industry, or whether it is simply a change in the flow of the money (that is, from owner to stockholder). Few, however, see the corporately owned press as providing a better journalistic product for citizens.

One aspect is certainly new. As corporations have increasingly come to dominate public life, the U.S. Supreme Court has been forced to wrestle with their place in civil society. And while the Court has long grappled with the question of corporations and their place in democracy, only recently has it visited the question of what corporate ownership of the press means for a democratic society. Despite the dissents of various justices, most notably Justices Hugo Black and William Douglas,[3] the Court has moved in recent decades to steadily expand the First Amendment rights of corporations. Objections have been raised that corporations are not entitled to protection under the Bill of Rights because they are artificial entities. However, as the Court noted in 1978, it is now widely accepted that "corporations are persons," an idea often referred to as corporate personhood theory.[4]

The legal fiction that corporations are people has been widely studied and debated.[5] However, the protection granted to media corporations under the press clause of the First Amendment has been the subject of little examination. Often when examining the history of corporate personhood theory, scholars ignore much of its application to the press, arguing that the press "has a greater claim to constitutional protections than do other corporations" because of the press clause of the First Amendment.[6]

This claim is problematic for several reasons. First, it ignores the fact that the argument that the First Amendment protects the institutional press is far from settled legally.[7] Second, and perhaps more importantly, such a claim makes the constitutional status of the press, rather than the press's role in public life, the central element of the debate. Put another way, the focus of the debate is not about what role the press plays in a democratic society but rather about whether it is to be considered a person under the Bill of Rights. Without answering the first question, it is difficult to answer the second.

Through an examination of recent Supreme Court cases, this chapter argues that bright-line distinctions between "the press" and corporations are no longer sustainable. And while this damages the press as a public institution, it also removes the press as a buffer between corporations and the public sphere. As a result, the public sphere is more vulnerable to corporate influences.

Corporations as People

The rights of corporations, particularly in the areas of the Bill of Rights and the Fourteenth Amendment, have been developing since the early 1800s. Sanford A. Schane traces the idea of corporate personhood back to nineteenth-century jurists in Germany and France and the development of at least three competing theories. Creature theory viewed human beings as "conscious and willing entit[ies]" with "inalienable rights" but failed to see the groups formed by those human beings as possessing any preexisting rights.[8] Since corporations are the creations of the state, they only possess those rights that states endow to those entities.

In opposition to creature theory was group theory and person theory. Group theory held that "persons conducting business under a corporate name are entitled to the same protection of the law that is guaranteed to them as individuals."[9] Corporations enjoy rights not because of their corporate status but because they are composed of individuals who enjoy rights. Person theory, however, made that final leap in recognizing corporations as people. Groups were seen as being as real as people. As Schane notes, for person-theory advocates, a group acquires "a common will and pursues its own goals, and its life continues regardless of changes in membership."[10]

Creature theory dominated American law at the beginning of the nine-teenth century.[11] Schane argues that new economic needs, as well as a mistrust of governmental special charters, led to free incorporation. It was less clear whether group or person theory would dominate a new way of regulating corporations. Schane suggests that group theory was rejected primarily because it could not accommodate features such as corporate immortality and limited liability. As a result, person theory, or what some refer to as "natural entity theory," emerged victorious because it best met the "evolving needs of American corporations."[12]

The U.S. Supreme Court began wrestling with the question of corporate rights as early as 1809.[13] Most writers trace the development of the Supreme Court's recognition of corporations as people to its 1886 decision in *Santa Clara v. Southern Pacific Railroad*,[14] where the Court granted corporations Fourteenth Amendment protection.

While the Court was willing to grant corporations protection under the Fourteenth Amendment, protection under the Bill of Rights came much later. As Carl J. Mayer notes, up to 1960, corporations only enjoyed Fifth Amendment protection.[15] Corporations apparently were in no hurry to fight for protection under the Bill of Rights, primarily because those protections were not needed throughout most of the early twentieth century. Mayer has argued that the combination of Fourteenth Amendment protection and substantive due process (giving courts authority to invalidate laws that limited property rights), which grew out of the Court's decision in *Lochner v. New York*,[16] was a powerful tool in the hands of American corporations. In the *Lochner* decision, the Supreme Court threw out a New York state statute limiting the number of hours employees could work. A bakery owner had maintained that the statute interfered with his freedom of contract and was therefore unconstitutional under the Fourteenth Amendment. Substantive due process, the general limitation upon the police power of the state, evolved out of the *Lochner* decision. As Alfred H. Kelly, Winfred A. Harbison, and Herman Belz comment on substantive due process prior to the 1930s, "Any state statute, ordinance, or administrative act which imposed any kind of litigation upon the right of private property or free contract immediately raised the question of due process law. And since a majority of statutes of a general public character imposed some limitations upon private property or contractual right, the ramifications of due process were endless."[17] In short, the combination of the *Lochner* decision and substantive due process allowed the property rights to be sovereign. It also allowed corporations to challenge and invalidate many state regulations.[18] With the end of the *Lochner* era in 1937, substantive due process ceased to be a protection for corporations, and they needed to find other ways to protect their interests.[19]

Mayer has argued that corporate requests for Bill of Rights protections increased after 1960 because of changes in corporate regulations. According to Mayer, modern corporate regulation is social (environmental, women's rights, and so on), not simply economic; primarily federal, not state; more intrusive, systematic and routinized than New Deal or Progressive regulation; and covers more industrial sectors as opposed to being focused on a single industry.[20] In addition to changes in regulation, there was also a rethinking of the concept of property. Property was no longer limited to tangible items but now included intangible items such as knowledge and information.[21]

To confront these new regulatory challenges to corporate rights, the battle shifted from the Fourteenth Amendment to the Bill of Rights, with its more expansive protections. And along with that movement came a rise in a new kind of substantive due process. Mayer notes, "When the Supreme Court pronounces on the nature of the corporation (for constitutional purposes) it imposes its own economic views, as it did during the substantive due process era. The question: What is the nature of the corporation? is similar to the economic questions that the Supreme Court was criticized for asking in the *Lochner* era. In fact, theorizing about the nature of the corporation ends up as an inquiry into the propriety of regulation."[22]

Historical Development of Corporations and the First Amendment

Many historians dismiss the study of corporate theory as it applies to the press because of the press's special status under the First Amendment. Ignoring for the moment the complexity of that interpretation of the First Amendment, corporations other than the press have also been claiming First Amendment protection since the 1970s. Two types of corporate speech have been the primary focus of that attention: commercial and political.

In the area of commercial speech, the Supreme Court broke from the commercial speech doctrine, articulated in 1942, and in the 1970s began granting more freedom to corporations to advertise their products and ideas.[23] At the heart of commercial speech is the protection of advertising, a central part of the modern understanding of property.

In *Central Hudson Gas and Electric Corp. v. Public Service Commission of New York*,[24] the Court recognized communication as a form of property. The Court applied a balancing test to determine that a state could not prohibit utility corporations from promoting the use of electricity if the state's ban was broader than necessary to achieve the stated goal.[25] Justice William Rehnquist, in dissent, argued that the Court's action in striking down the state legislation was a decision with ties to the *Lochner* era.[26] Since that decision the Court has granted protection to a number of different forms of commercial speech, ranging from the prices of prescription medicines[27] to advertisements by lawyers.[28]

While the Court has continued to use the *Central Hudson* test as a way to decide commercial speech disputes, the Court's decisions in the area of corporate political speech are more noteworthy for this study. The Court granted corporations political speech rights in *First National Bank of Boston v. Bellotti*.[29] In the case, a group of Boston corporations challenged a Massachusetts law that prohibited corporate expenditures on an income tax referendum. The Massachusetts Supreme Judicial Court, supported by the legislation, carved out a new category of political speech. A corporation's speech on issues that might "materially affect" its property, business, or assets could be prohibited. But while the state court chose to focus on the question of whether a corporation should enjoy First Amendment rights, the majority of the U.S. Supreme Court argued that the central question was whether the legislation "abridges expression that the First Amendment was meant to protect."[30] Justice Lewis Powell argued that the First Amendment was intended to protect the discussion of governmental affairs. "If the speakers here were not corporations, no one would suggest that the State could silence their proposed speech," Powell argued. "It is the type of speech indispensable to decision making in democracy, and this is no less true because the speech comes from a corporation rather than an individual. The inherent worth of the speech in terms of its capacity for informing the public does not depend upon the identity of its source, whether corporation, association, union, or individual."[31]

Powell's decision followed a long line of legal argument. That argument, in its purest form, is that corporate speech is valuable not because it allows corporations to speak but because it allows the public to have access to a diversity of ideas. As Powell wrote: "A commercial advertisement is constitutionally protected not so much because it pertains to the seller's business as because it furthers the societal interest in the 'free flow of commercial information.'"[32] In that same vein, Powell argued that the Court's decisions granting press and media institutions special privileges are based not only on "fostering individual self-expression" but also on their "role in affording the public access to discussion, debate, and the dissemination of information and ideas."[33]

Justice Byron White's dissent centered on a slightly different interpretation of what the First Amendment protected. Following the First Amendment theorist Thomas Emerson, White argued that the Constitution's principle focus of protection is on self-expression, self-realization, and self-fulfillment.[34] As White argued, "Ideas which are not a product of individual choice are entitled to less First Amendment protection."[35]

While willing to admit that corporate speech did enjoy some protection under the First Amendment—primarily in the areas of advertising and promotional activities[36]—White was more than willing to limit a corporation's political speech. The threat that a corporation poses to the political system through its ability to economically influence the electoral process was very real to him.[37] But more importantly, the political speech of a corporation could not lead to individual self-fulfillment because the ideas are "divorced from the convictions of individual corporate shareholders."[38]

The perceived threat that corporations pose to the electoral process has led the Court to limit their ability to make political campaign contributions. Over the years, the Court has upheld distinctions between political contributions and expenditures. For example, under current law it is unconstitutional for corporations to make direct contributions to political candidates, but it is acceptable for them to make expenditures through political action committees in support of political causes. While some justices have found that distinction to be fraught with problems,[39] the majority of the Court has over the years bought into the wisdom of that distinction. Most recently, in *FEC v. Beaumont*, the Court in a seven-to-two decision ruled that a group known as North Carolina Right to Life (NCRL) could constitutionally be prohibited from making direct contributions to political candidates. NCRL had established a political action committee that made contributions to federal candidates. The Court, through the opinion of Justice David Souter, argued that limits on corporate donations to political candidates were needed to prevent corruption of the electoral process.[40] However, Souter's opinion seems to turn less on the type of speaker than the type of speech that is involved. Since *Buckley v. Valeo*[41] in 1976, the Court has held that political contributions enjoy fewer First Amendment protections because they "lie closer to the edges than to the core of political expression."[42] In a footnote to the *Beaumont* decision, Justice Souter wrote, "Within the realm of contributions generally, corporate contributions are furthest from the core of political expression, since corporations' First Amendment speech and association interests are derived largely from those of their members. A ban on direct corporate contributions leaves individual members of corporations free to make their own contirubtions, and deprives the public of little or no material information."[43]

Souter's writings are important for understanding how the Court views the First Amendment rights of corporations. Despite the Court's anticorporate rhetoric, the ban on corporate-campaign contributions is constitutional primarily because political contributions are marginal to the First Amendment, not because of who the speaker is. The fear of the impact of corporations is forgotten in favor of a more supposedly neutral way of classifying speech. The classification hides the fact that the justices are making a political choice—a choice where the majority of corporate free speech rights are maintained.

The Corporate Press as a "Natural Entity"

The *Bellotti* decision is pivotal to the story of corporate press rights for several reasons. While the majority in *Bellotti* agreed that corporations should enjoy a broad range of First Amendment protections, it was less clear where the corporate-owned press fell in that category. Justice Powell noted that while the Court has recognized the press's unique role in "educating the public, offering criticism, and providing a forum for discussion and debate," it does not have "a monopoly on either the First Amendment or the ability to enlighten."[44] Justice White would only go so far as to note that the First Amendment "does not immunize media corporations" from having to comply with restrictions on campaign contributions and expenditures.[45]

It was left to Chief Justice Warren Burger in his concurring opinion to bring questions of the press and corporate ownership directly into the discussion. As Burger wrote, due to the concentration of ownership it has become virtually impossible to distinguish media corporations from other types of corporations.[46] He went on to state that because of threats to the electoral process, "it could be argued that such media conglomerates as I describe pose a much more realistic threat to valid interests than do appellants and similar entities not regularly concerned with shaping popular opinion on public issues."[47]

Central to Burger's argument is the meaning of the press clause and whether it is distinct from the speech clause. While that issue has been the subject of much scholarship,[48] the Court has yet to clearly articulate how the speech clause is different from the press clause, if in fact they differ. Even though Chief Justice Burger claimed that "the First Amendment does not 'belong' to any definable category of persons or entities,"[49] he admitted that the Court "has not yet squarely resolved" the issue.[50]

The chief justice's concurring opinion is valuable because it foreshadows a problem that has increasingly plagued the Court and, in turn, public life in the United States: Is there a constitutional distinction between the press and corporations in modern-day democracy? The Supreme Court granted the corporate press First Amendment protection in *Grosjean v. American Press Co.*[51] In the case, newspaper publishers challenged a Louisiana state tax on newspapers and other periodicals when they exceeded a circulation of twenty thousand. While the tax was specifically linked to advertising carried by those publications, publishers convinced a unanimous Supreme Court to throw out the legislation as an unconstitutional restriction on freedom of the press. The Court held that the corporate press was a "person" within the "meaning of the equal protection and due process" clauses of the Fourteenth Amendment and therefore was protected by the First Amendment.[52] The Court delved into the American history on taxation of the press and concluded that special taxation on newspapers is a form of prior restraint.[53] But the Court said remarkably little about why the corporate press is entitled to First Amendment protection. This becomes particularly interesting when the Court notes that the tax is not wrong because of the limitations placed on the publishers but rather because it is a "deliberate and calculated device in the guise of a tax to limit the circulation of information to which the public is entitled in virtue of the constitutional guarantees."[54] Yet again, in the eyes of the Court, First Amendment freedoms belong to the corporate press only because of the constitutional guarantees of the public, not because of any property right endowed in the corporate press. Since citizens have free press rights under the First Amendment, those citizens have a right to receive information *from* the corporate press.

The Court's decision in *Grosjean* grounds a long debate about the meaning of the First Amendment. Some have argued that the First Amendment was meant to, or should be interpreted to, protect the institutional press. Former Justice Potter Stewart went so far as to say that if the speech and press clauses of the First Amendment meant the same thing, it would be a constitutional redundancy.[55] And while some argue that the historical evidence suggests that the framers of the Constitution intended to carve out protections for the press,[56] others have argued that privileging the institutional press under the First Amendment is neither valid constitutionally nor democratically.[57]

Without a clear legal answer to the puzzle of the meaning of the press clause, today's Court seems to have divided into two general camps. The more conservative justices argue that the corporate, institutional press does not hold a privileged position in our Constitutional framework, and because of that, the press has no First Amendment rights greater than other corporations. Opposite that school of thought, the more liberal camp tends to see the press playing a special role in society and therefore carves out a limited form of privilege, or at the very least clears the way for the creation of that privilege.[58] These competing schools of thought have become important in decisions since *Bellotti,* as the justices have puzzled over the press-corporation distinction.

FEC v. Massachusetts Citizens for Life, Inc. (1986) `

In 1978, Massachusetts Citizens for Life, Inc. (MCFL), a nonprofit, nonstock corporation, published a special edition of its newsletter. In that special edition, it urged voters to vote "pro-life" in upcoming elections, identified candidates in federal and state elections, and listed whether each candidate supported or opposed right-to-life issues. The Federal Election Commission brought action against MCFL, claiming that its actions violated Section 316 of the Federal Election Campaign Act (FECA), which prohibits corporations from using treasury funds in connection with a federal election. The Supreme Court, through Justice William Brennan, agreed with the court of appeals and found that while MCFL's newsletter did fall under the statute, the statute was unconstitutional as applied.

The MCFL case forced the Court to wrestle with the question of how to define the press. FECA exempts "any news story, commentary, or editorial distributed through the facilities of any . . . newspaper, magazine, or other periodical publication, unless such facilities are owned or controlled by any political party, political committee, or candidate." However, Justice Brennan denied that the special edition of MCFL's newsletter qualified for this exemption, although apparently its regular edition might have. Brennan noted that the special edition was not comparable to other issues of the newsletter. "It was not published through the facilities of the regular newsletter, but by a staff that prepared no previous or subsequent newsletters," Brennan noted. "It was not distributed to the newsletter's regular audience, but to a group 20 times the size of that audience, most of whom were members of the public who had never received the newsletter. No characteristic of the Edition associated it in any way the normal MCFL publication. The MCFL masthead did not appear on the flyer, and, despite an apparent belated attempt to make it appear otherwise, the Edition contained no volume and issue number identifying it as one in a continuing series of issues."[59]

Brennan offered a definition of the press that turns mostly on form. Its components are: (1) the special issue must be comparable to regularly published issues; (2) it must be prepared by staff who have done previous issues; (3) it must be distributed to the normal audience; and (4) it must contain the masthead of the regularly published issue and contain volume and issue numbers. These distinctions, for Brennan, might very well seem to be "superficial," but they were necessary so as not to grant press protections to "entities that happen to publish newsletters."[60]

Brennan was willing, however, to protect MCFL's right to publish, even though it did not qualify for the press exemption. That protection was rooted in its position as a nonprofit corporation. Nonprofit corporations do not pose the same threat to the political system as corporations that are intended to accumulate capital, Brennan argued. And while MCFL might benefit in some way from its corporate form, "those advantages . . . redound to its benefit as a political organization, not as a profit-making enterprise."[61] As such, Brennan argued that three features are needed for a corporation to be exempted under FECA: (1) the corporation was founded for the "express

purpose" of promoting political ideas and does not engage in business activities; (2) there are no shareholders who have a claim to assets or earnings;
and (3) the corporation was not established by a business corporation or
labor union and does not accept contributions from those entities. Brennan
thus hoped to cut off "corporations serving as conduits for direct spending"
that might hinder the political process.[62]

The dissenting justices, led by Chief Justice Rehnquist, opposed Brennan's
willingness to give greater protection to nonprofit corporations. Rehnquist
labeled Brennan's argument "distinctions in degree that do not amount to
differences in kind" and argued that those distinctions should only be made
by legislatures.[63]

Austin v. Michigan State Chamber of Commerce (1990)

The debate over the regulation and role of nonprofit corporations in political life continued when the Michigan State Chamber of Commerce challenged the Michigan Campaign Finance Act, which prohibited corporations
from using treasury funds to endorse candidates in state elections. The chamber had wished to use treasury funds to place newspaper ads that supported
candidates for state office. The majority of the Court ruled that the act did
not violate the First Amendment rights of the chamber.

Led by Justice Thurgood Marshall, the Court argued that the chamber did
not meet the three-part test established in *FEC v. Massachusetts Citizens for
Life:* its goals were not all political in nature, its members were similar to
shareholders, and it accepted contributions from business corporations.[64]

More important is the Court's attempt to once again define why the chamber's attempts to publish its ideas do not qualify for protection under a press
exemption. The Michigan law carries a "media exemption" that excludes
from regulation any "expenditure by a broadcasting station, newspaper,
magazine, or other periodical or publication for any news story, commentary, or editorial in support of or opposition to a candidate for elective office
. . . in the regular course of publication or broadcasting."[65] The chamber
argued that such exemptions treat "similarly situated entities unequally."[66]
Marshall dismissed the claims by arguing that any corporation that wanted similar protection was free to enter the news business and that the press
plays a unique role in American democratic life.[67] The resources of media
corporations, unlike other corporations, "are devoted to the collection of
information and its dissemination to the public."[68] Because of that, "a val-

id distinction" exists between different types of corporations. And while the Constitution might not recognize this unique role of the institutional press, Marshall argued that it was acceptable for Michigan to grant greater protection to the press.[69]

Marshall's commentary on the purpose of the media corporations in American society provoked a response from Justice Antonin Scalia. If the Court was really interested in preventing corporate wealth from influencing political debate, he argued, it should *include* rather than *exclude* media corporations from regulation. "Amassed corporate wealth that regularly sits astride the ordinary channels of information is much more likely to produce the New Corruption (too much of one point of view) than amassed corporate wealth that is generally busy making money elsewhere," Scalia wrote. "Such media corporations not only have vastly greater power to perpetrate the evil of over-informing, they also have vastly greater opportunity."[70]

He noted that media corporations "make money by making political commentary" and called the theory put forward by the majority "a dagger" at the throat of the press by making the institution dependant on the good will of legislatures.[71] "One must hope," Scalia wrote, "that Michigan will continue to provide this generous and voluntary exemption."[72]

Justice Anthony Kennedy, in dissent, went even further in noting the increasingly problematic nature of defining the press in today's society. He called the majority's definition of the press "unsatisfying," adding that "[a]ll corporations communicate with the public to some degree, whether it is their business or not; and communication is of particular importance for non-profit corporations."[73] Beyond that, he noted the "web of corporate ownership" that makes it difficult to separate media corporations from nonmedia corporations: "Newspapers, television networks, and other media may be owned by parent corporations with multiple business interests. Nothing in the statutory scheme prohibits a business corporate parent from directing its newspaper to support or oppose a particular candidate."[74]

Los Angeles Police Department v. United Reporting Publishing Corporation (1999)

In 1996, the California legislature passed a law limiting public access to the current addresses of victims of crimes and people who had been arrested by police. Addresses were available if requests were made for "a scholarly, journalistic, political, or governmental purpose, or . . . for investigation purposes by a licensed private investigator."[75] The legislation prohibited the information from being "used directly or indirectly to sell a product or service to any individual or group of individuals, and the requester shall execute a declaration to that effect under penalty of perjury."[76] United Reporting Publishing Corporation is a private business that provides names and addresses of people who had been arrested to attorneys, insurance companies, drug and alcohol counselors, and driving schools. Lower courts had invalidated the statute, claiming that it was an unconstitutional inhibition on commercial speech.

The majority of the Court, led by Chief Justice Rehnquist, ignored the fundamental issues raised in the case and instead focused on a procedural item in denying United Reporting's appeal. Rehnquist argued that United Reporting made a "facial attack" on the statute rather than an "applied to" attack.[77] As such, United Reporting attempted to rely on the effect of the statute on its potential customers. Rehnquist argued that he could not see how the customers had been harmed—"no threat of prosecution . . . hangs over their head"—and added that they were entitled to qualify for the information under the statute.[78] Following from that argument, the majority was able to find that the statute did not violate anyone's First Amendment rights but was simply "a law regulating access to information in the hands of the police department."[79] Rehnquist noted that United Reporting had not even attempted to qualify to receive the information and, since the state could refuse to provide all information without violating the First Amendment, the corporation did not meet the standard for facial invalidation.

Other justices pointed to the failure of the majority to deal with what it considered to be the main issue before the Court—how United Reporting could not qualify as a member of the press. Justice Scalia, who concurred in the decision because the "statute is nothing but a restriction upon access to government information," nevertheless pointed to the majority's refusal to address a more fundamental question.[80] He noted that a statute that "allows access to the press . . . but at the same time denies access to persons who wish to use the information for certain speech purposes, is in reality a restriction upon speech rather than upon access to government information."[81]

Justice John Paul Stevens, whose dissenting opinion was joined by Justice Kennedy, disagreed with the Court's focus on the facial challenge. Stevens viewed United Reporting as making an applied-to challenge but added that a "different, and more difficult, question is presented when the State makes information generally available, but denies access to a small disfavored class."[82] Stevens wrote that the state's attempt to justify the restriction by arguing that it would protect the privacy of victims and arrestees fell far short of what was

needed: "Although that interest would explain a total ban on access, or a statute narrowly limiting access, it is insufficient when the data can be published
in the news media and obtained by private investigators or others who meet
the Amendment's vague criteria."[83] Stevens argued that the real, unstated
reason for the statute was to prevent lawyers from soliciting business from
unrepresented defendants.[84]

Seeking Differences Where None Exist

As these cases indicate, justices have struggled in recent years to articulate
differences between the press and corporations. Various justices have put
forward several options. They include:

Form over function: Led by Justice Brennan, some have argued that the press
can be differentiated from corporations by the form of its communication.
In this test, the emphasis is on what the product looks like, who it is disseminated to, and who produces it. If the public relations staff of a corporation
puts together a newsletter, apparently it will not qualify for protection under the press clause. While Brennan's intention was to find a way to promote
and protect the integrity of the press, his test also serves as a protection primarily for the institutional or corporately owned press. Brennan's test not
only places nonmedia corporations outside of press clause protection but also
the alternative presses that might not be distributed on a regular basis or to
a large audience.

Courts in other areas of the law have addressed the problematic nature of
relying on form to define who is the press. The U.S. District Court for the District of Columbia, in ruling that the public-interest law firm Judicial Watch is
entitled to a news media exemption to waive search fees under the federal Freedom of Information Act, did so reluctantly. Judicial Watch's main venue of
publication is a website. Judge James Robertson noted that the group's website does not resemble a "'news medium' in any traditional sense" and that it
tends to be "self-serving accounts of . . . activities and transparent solicitations
for either financial support or for clients."[85] "Traditional lines separating actor and reporter, objectivity and spin, even truth and fiction, have become
blurred," Judge Robertson wrote. "At a time when the news media are frequently their own lead story, a publicity seeker may be a representative of the
news media, and vice versa. Indeed, if the regular publication or dissemination of information to the public is enough to qualify for a 'representative of

the news media' waiver, then arguably anyone with a website is entitled to demand free search services under the Freedom of Information Act."[86]

Relying on the form of a publication to separate the press from corporations seems to be increasingly problematic.

Function over form: Justice Marshall moved away from the focus on the form directly into assessing the content of the publication. In his analysis, the press is privileged because its primary mission is not to make money but to disseminate information. Of course, with the growing corporate control of the news media in the United States, that argument—if it was ever true—is certainly being challenged.[87] Many media corporations emphasize high profit margins—higher than most other major industries in the United States[88]—which calls into question the corporate press's dedication to disseminating news over making money.[89] This type of distinction becomes particularly problematic when we try to figure out how a corporation that collects information on people who have been arrested and disseminates it to subscribers differs from the function performed by a daily newspaper, which also reports on arrests and distributes the information to people who subscribe to its service. Why is one the press and the other not? If one replies that it is because the newspaper's audience is more public, then would moves by the press to tailor its product to a specific target audience more attractive to advertisers eliminate newspapers from that protection?[90] In the end, it is difficult to sustain bright-line distinctions between the press and corporations in today's media through an emphasis on function.

Corporate Leveling: A number of justices, led by Justice Scalia,[91] have argued that the press is not special and that the press clause was not intended to protect a specific institution. Corporations, being people, should all be treated the same. This, however, has not meant that these justices have sought to bring the corporate press down to the level of nonmedia corporations. Rather, they have attempted to raise nonmedia corporations to the level of press corporations by granting all corporations First Amendment rights. This argument is especially powerful in Justice Burger's opinion, when he posits the idea that nonmedia corporations can serve as a check on media corporations. Even if we concede that granting corporations First Amendment rights will serve as a check on the corporate media, that says little about what such a decision means for the freedoms of average citizens and their ability to participate in their society. Corporations, whose primary mission is making money, seek to segment society to make it easier to reach targeted groups of people. This segmentation tends to fragment the public sphere.

It turns citizens into "Soccer Moms" and "SUV drivers" with little in common other than demographic variables and buying habits. The segmentation of society builds off of how citizens are different from someone else in their community. And while those values might be a reasonable way in which to organize an economic system, they are not necessarily conducive to discourse democracy. Creating and highlighting differences rather than identifying and highlighting commonalities hinders the formation of an active public sphere. As Stuart Ewen notes, "As a precondition for other changes, we need to question demographic categories of identity that, at present, divide the public against itself and separate people who—when viewed from a critical distance—may share common interests. Demographics is a powerful tool of divide and rule. To combat it, we need to rediscover a sense of social connectedness. Beyond looking out for ourselves—as individuals or as members of a particular group—we must also learn to rediscover ourselves in others, to see our concerns and aspirations in theirs."[92]

Corporate leveling is little more than corporations trying to stop the Supreme Court from doing to them what they have already done to public life. It emphasizes the commonalities of corporations while seeking to ignore the differences.

More importantly, corporate leveling is a form of corporate rationalization. It increases the separation between the public sphere and its institutions and envisions democracy as a battle between elite organizations. To the victor goes public opinion.

Seeking Solutions

The perspectives outlined above have come to dominate the discussion about the First Amendment and corporations. The solutions advocated by the Court, however, do not adequately promote a functioning public sphere. Jürgen Habermas has suggested that corporations should only be granted certain rights if they enable the functioning of public life. As he noted in an interview in 1998, "I do not think I really harbour any illusions about the condition of a public sphere in which commercialized mass media set the tone."[93] Yet, when asked how society might redefine the media's role, he responded that that was a question "for which I have no immediate answer."[94] This section will briefly explore several options that might be starting points for addressing the corporate press dilemma.

Holding Corporations Accountable

One way to halt the encroachment of corporate values into civil society would be to break from precedent and revert to treating corporations as artificial entities. Despite dissents from various justices advocating such a move over the years, no justice has seriously suggested this since the 1940s. Rather than fighting to change precedent, some groups have begun trying to force states to hold corporations accountable for their actions. Some groups suggest that since corporations were created by the state in which they were chartered, that state also has the power to revoke the charter. As Thomas Linzey, the president of the nonprofit Community Environmental Legal Defense Fund, has written, "Harmful corporations should be put out of business, and citizens must regain control over these unelected, unaccountable entities in order to preserve human and environmental health."[95]

All states, except Alaska, have *quo warranto* statutes that allow them to revoke charters for corporations that have abused or misused their charter powers. Many of these statutes, however, give the state attorney general discretion over whether to initiate proceedings against a corporation.[96] Delaware, for example, has one of the strongest charter revocation statutes in the United States. It requires the attorney general to bring action against a corporation whenever a "proper party" presents "clear and convincing evidence" that the corporation has abused its charter.[97] In the past, states have revoked corporate charters for statutory violations, nonpayment of taxes, failing to file required disclosure forms, playing baseball on a holiday, price fixing, and other violations.[98] And while charter revocation was seen as a powerful way to control the autonomy of corporations, it has not been used of late. As Linzey notes, "The virtual disappearance of charter revocation actions by the 1920s conveniently coincides with the rise of corporate America as a primary employer of citizens and the consolidation of industrial capital through the emergence of quasi-monopolies."[99]

In recent years, the attempts to revoke corporate charters have centered on environmental issues. Those attempts have proven unsuccessful, at least in terms of actually revoking corporate charters.[100] They may have been more successful in making people aware of the opportunities that exist for change and initiating long-term agendas for reform. As Richard Grossman, the co-director of the Program on Corporations, Law, and Democracy, has observed:

We are not aspiring to bring about good corporate citizenship—corporations are fictions, not citizens. We are not looking for corporate responsibility either. As subordinate entities, corporations must do what "we the people" tell them to do. WE are the ones who must act responsibly. . . . We plan to accomplish these goals by amending state corporation codes, by rewriting corporate charters, by revoking charters, by forbidding corporations from owning other corporations, by limiting corporate capitalization and property holding; by banning corporations entirely from participating in elections, in our lawmaking, in our education, by ending the absurdity of corporate personhood.[101]

So far, no group has initiated a challenge to the corporate charter of a media corporation. The media's performance, however, has not escaped the attention of groups that work in that area. Grossman has asked whether we can have a democracy "when corporations write the news and instruct us in our history."[102]

Working from Within

If we begin from the standpoint that the Supreme Court is unlikely to turn back freedoms granted to corporations, we need to find ways within the existing case law to bring more power to the public sphere and reward those corporations that work to benefit society. A starting point could be to continue to build on Justice Brennan's argument in *FEC v. Massachusets Citizens for Life* that nonprofit corporations might enjoy more privileges than corporations that primarily function to make money. The Court has already accepted this premise. Brennan's decision has cleared the way for the granting of greater freedoms to corporations that seek to disseminate political ideas rather than make money. Of course, the Court would have to be resolute in its inquiry about each corporation's mission.

Providing privileges, whether through tax benefits, subsidized printing, or access rights to information to certain nonprofit corporations based on content, would undoubtedly be challenged from the perspective that the state is (1) making content-based decisions in an effort to (2) interfere with the private property of the press. The second argument is more easily dismissed than the first. As we have seen, as far back as the Court's decision in *Grosjean,* the press's special status has less to do with property rights than with its perceived role in society. As Owen Fiss has noted, "The property rights of newspapers . . . come from laws that apply to all businesses. However, the special status of the press and its claim for freedom derive from the function of that institution in society—to inform the public—and should not turn on the source of its property rights or the particular dynamics that gave rise to them."[103]

Even as harsh a press critic as Justice Scalia has noted that the institutional press has elected to cast its lot with the state and the emphasis on its role in democracy rather than by making property arguments. The second objection, then, seems less compelling, even though those property arguments are still recognized by the Court.[104]

More difficult to dismiss is the content argument. In long-established precedent, the Court has generally held that government is precluded from making decisions based on the content of the message. However, if we recast the media as public fora, not unlike shopping malls or public parks, then the state can play an affirmative role in the creation of democracy. Under this proposal, existing First Amendment rights would not be taken away from corporations, but those nonprofit organizations that serve the public sphere would enjoy benefits above and beyond their for-profit corporate brethren. The Court itself has noted that granting more rights to certain groups is acceptable, as long as the state does not subtract rights from the rest of society.[105]

A similar suggestion has been put forward in the broadcast arena by R. Randall Rainey and William Rehg. They have proposed the formation of what they call the Corporation for Public Interest Speech and Debate.[106] Created by Congress, this institution's primary mission would be to "design, establish, and operate a noncommercial electronic public affairs network in which the unorganized discourses originating in civil society may be presented in the public sphere in a multifaceted, decentered electronic public forum."[107] Through strict oversight and a broad-based membership, Rainey and Rehg hope that such a corporation could escape "the corrosive influence of ideology, bias, and the abuse of power."[108] Funding for the corporation would come from federal monies raised through taxes on the telecommunications industry.[109] The hope is that through the creation of better institutions, we can find ways to allow people to gather and exchange information while limiting the influence of for-profit corporations.

Conclusion

This chapter has argued that without rethinking and restructuring the Supreme Court's current understanding of a free press, democratic society will suffer. Current definitions of "the press" put forward by the Court help us little in trying to separate that institution from other corporations. In the end, perhaps some members of the Court are correct in suggesting that we cannot find differences where none exist. However, adopting that framework will hurt not only free press rights in society, but, more importantly, the vitality of public life. If, as Habermas suggests, the media are a central institution in the maintenance of a democratic society, then granting for-profit corporations another avenue of entry into the public sphere through the application of the doctrine of corporate personhood is a potentially devastating decision.

Once again, it would be wrong to see this as a press problem that can be solved by separating corporate ownership and the news media. The influence of corporate rationalization stretches beyond the press into how the law manages the use of public space. And we turn to that subject next.

6

Public Television, Parks, Parades, and Rest Areas: Managing the Property of Public Life

One of the ways that corporate rationalization dominates public life is by changing how citizens interact with space. In recent years, public life has increasingly been evaluated in corporate terms—as a form of property to be managed efficiently. Viewing the world through the lens of property rights (referred to as the *Lochner* era in chapter 5), the U.S. Supreme Court used substantive due process as a way to protect private business owners from government regulation. Beginning with *West Coast Hotel v. Parrish*[1] in 1937, and perhaps more importantly with *United States v. Carolene Products*[2] in 1938, the Court began emphasizing civil rights over property rights.[3]

In recent years, property-rights arguments have been revived in many areas of the law, in particular with regard to the First Amendment.[4] Questions of free speech and free press are increasingly decided by questions of property, and the law and the press are central to that development.[5] The fundamental force behind this movement has come to be known as the public forum doctrine, a test courts use to decide who can use public property under what conditions. The test was first accepted by the U.S. Supreme Court in 1972 and has grown increasingly popular in the last thirty years.

This chapter will suggest that the public forum doctrine is linked in important ways to the idea of corporate rationalization. Through its reliance on property and the law's role in managing that property, the public forum doctrine provides an important avenue for corporate values to invade the public sphere. The second part of this chapter will demonstrate how those corporate values have been used by the courts to limit expression and association on public property in the United States. Courts discount the needs of the public sphere through a reliance on property, management, and an authoritarian construction of meaning that overvalues individualism.

A Brief History of the Public Forum Doctrine

The literature chronicling the history of the public forum doctrine is extensive. Rather than recounting a well-covered tale, this section provides a brief overview of several important moments in its history.

Most studies trace the doctrine's development back to the Court's 1939 decision in *Hague v. CIO*. In arguing that the government cannot constitutionally suppress speech in public parks, Justice Roberts wrote:

> Wherever the title of streets and parks may rest, they have immemorially been held in trust for the use of the public and, time out of mind, have been used for purposes of assembly, communicating thoughts between citizens, and discussing public questions. Such use of the streets and public places has, from ancient times, been a part of the privileges, immunities, rights, and liberties of citizens. The privilege of a citizen of the United States to use the streets and parks for communication of views on national questions may be regulated in the interest of all; it is not absolute, but relative, and must be exercised in subordination to the general comfort and convenience, and in consonance with peace and good order; but it must not, in the guise of regulation, be abridged or denied.[6]

While Justice Roberts's dictum is considered by many to be its foundation, a 1965 article by Harry Kalven led to the establishment of the public forum doctrine.[7] Kalven sought to carve out space for public discussion, the kind that the Supreme Court had idealized in its 1964 decision in *New York Times v. Sullivan*.[8] It is important to note, however, that Kalven's ideas differ from our current understanding of the public forum doctrine. His article, as Robert C. Post points out, was not an attempt to classify property but rather an analysis of "the underlying constitutional value of public discussion."[9]

The Supreme Court picked up on Kalven's ideas in a 1972 case, *Police Department of Chicago v. Mosley*, which concerned a statute that prohibited picketing or demonstrations, with the exception of labor picketing, within 150 feet of any primary or secondary school. In finding the statute unconstitutional, Justice Marshall wrote, "Once a forum is opened up to assembly or speaking by some groups, government may not prohibit others from assembling on the basis of what they intend to say. Selective exclusions from a public forum may not be based on content alone, and may not be justified by reference to content alone."[10]

While the Court recognized the existence of something called a public forum, it had not yet reached the idea that they could differentiate between fora by type. That was first achieved in Justice Brennan's dissenting opinion in *Lehman v. City of Shaker Heights* in 1974. The case concerned a city ordinance that allowed commercial but not political advertisements inside commuter trains operated by the city's rapid transit system. The majority of the Court upheld the policy, but Justice Brennan broke from the majority and argued that the policy was unconstitutional. A large part of his reasoning relied on the type of public forum involved in the case. For Brennan, "The determination of whether a particular type of public property or facility constitutes a 'public forum' requires the Court to strike a balance between the competing interests of the government, on the one hand, and the speaker and his audience, on the other. Thus, the Court must assess the importance of the primary use to which the public property or facility is committed and the extent to which that use will be disrupted if access for free expression is permitted."[11]

In the 1980s, the public forum doctrine began to take on its current form. In a 1983 case, *Perry Educational Association v. Perry Local Educators' Association,* the Court identified three types of public fora: the traditional public forum, the public forum created by governmental designation (what has come to be called a limited public forum), and the nonpublic forum.[12] The Court offered clear definitions for the categories two years later in *Cornelius v. NAACP Legal Defense and Educational Fund, Inc.* The traditional public forum, the Court through Justice Sandra Day O'Connor wrote, is a place that by tradition or "government fiat" is open to the public for assembly and debate. Justice O'Connor noted that this includes public streets and parks. A limited public forum can be created by government if it opens a previously nonpublic area for assembly or speech by the public, "for use by certain speakers, or for the discussion of certain subjects." As such, in a limited public forum, it would be acceptable for the government to allow certain kinds of speech while restricting others, such as in *Lehman.* The last category, a nonpublic forum, includes publicly owned areas that are not open to public debate and speech. As Justice O'Connor wrote, "We will not find that a public forum has been created in the face of clear evidence of a contrary intent, nor will we infer that the government intended to create a public forum when the nature of the property is inconsistent with expressive activity."[13]

Since the 1980s, the Court has continued to apply that interpretation to an ever-expanding list of cases. The basic structure of the public forum doctrine—

traditional public forum, limited public forum, and nonpublic forum—has become one of the central ways to interpret First Amendment issues in the public sphere.

Managing Public Life

The links between the concept of corporate rationalization and the public forum doctrine are many. Melvin Nimmer has argued that there are two lines of competing thought buried in public forum cases. One line "assumes that whether or not publicly owned premises are to be regarded as 'public forums' and hence open to the public for communication purposes turns upon factors divorced from the proposed speech itself."[14] This falls in line with the traditional understanding of the public forum doctrine, where decisions are made based on the type of property involved, not the type of speech. The other line of cases, coming primarily out of the Court's decision in *Grayned v. City of Rockford*,[15] argues that the question of whether speech should be allowed or not lies in its connection to the type of forum that is in use, and that the government needs a good reason to suppress speech. The Court has used the second line of reasoning far less frequently than the first. However, critics of the public forum doctrine often prefer the second line of reasoning mainly because the *Grayned* decision, which upheld a city's right to limit protests outside of schools if the noise might disrupt classrooms, appears to deemphasize property rights. As Justice Marshall wrote in his *Grayned* decision, "The crucial question is whether the manner of expression is basically incompatible with the normal activity of a particular place at a particular time. Our cases make clear that in assessing the reasonableness of a regulation, we must weigh heavily the fact that communication is involved; the regulation must be narrowly tailored to further the State's legitimate interest."[16] Marshall's incompatibility test allows courts to take into account the type of speech involved.

Of course, not even the *Grayned* decision breaks completely from questions of property rights. Courts do not make decisions based on an evaluation of the speech but rather on whether the speech is compatible with the property involved. In that way, property still plays a vital role in determining what types of expression will be acceptable.

Post, in one of the few attempts to rethink public forum doctrine in theoretical terms, argues that by relying on the first line of thought and not the second, the Court has carved out a "class of government property in which the First Amendment claims of the public are radically devalued and immune from independent judicial scrutiny."[17] He believes that any theoretical constitutional principle is lacking, and he attempts to articulate a theory that can explain current public forum doctrine and inform revision. Post leans heavily on organizational theory in offering his theory of public forum. In doing so, he draws a distinction between "management" and "governance": "When administering its own institutions, the government is invested with a special form of authority, which I shall call 'managerial.' Managerial authority is controlled by First Amendment rules different from those that control the exercise of the authority used by the state when it acts to govern the general public. I shall call the latter kind of authority 'governance.'"[18]

In terms that might be called Habermasian, Post seemed to suggest that instrumental (managerial) logic is acceptable when dealing with the government itself. True government property, such as private offices, can be managed under Post's theory. However, when we move to the public sphere a different type of oversight needs to be applied. Governance, where the state has less say over content, is needed over public property that is traditionally used by citizens for expression. Post claims that public forum doctrine is more about *managing* than *governing* public life, and he argues for revising the doctrine to emphasize governance. He proposes that the Court stop focusing on the character of the property, mainly because he believes that there is no theory connecting the type of property and the First Amendment, and instead focus on judicial review and institutional authority.[19] The main question facing courts in public speech cases, then, is whether the appropriate governmental role is managerial or governmental.[20]

Post's analysis identifies an important link to the idea of corporate rationalization. As he notes, the Supreme Court uses the public forum doctrine as a form of managerial control, relying on the nature of the property to determine the level of protection. And Post is correct that the great weakness of the public forum doctrine is its lack of a foundational theory. However, it's not clear whether his management-governance distinction helps resolve the problem. The determination of whether property is public hinges on social customs and how the public currently uses that space.[21] So, for Post, the Court was correct in limiting access to advertising on commuter trains in *Lehman* because there was never any expectation that the space would be made available to the public. But Post disagrees with the Court when it calls mailboxes nonpublic fora primarily because their social use suggests otherwise.[22] "Anyone who has unthinkingly dropped a note in a friend's mailbox knows . . . that in everyday life mailboxes are subject to uses other than simply the deposit of stamped mailable matter."[23]

From a discursive perspective, Post's rethinking of the public forum issue is a step forward, but it fails to break free of past ideological constraints. By substituting tradition for governmental management, courts are still not free to make decisions that will necessarily benefit discourse. Democratic discourse takes place in many sectors. Making it reliant on property, as opposed to an independent assessment of the type of speech involved, does little to settle the problems associated with the public forum doctrine. For discourse theory, the question of whether mailboxes are public fora is not tied to tradition or questions of whose property they are but rather to the nature of the material being circulated. To provide two brief examples, advertisements for consumer goods placed in mailboxes would not be protected, whereas an announcement placed in mailboxes of a debate between candidates for city council would be. The first is not inherently vital to a functioning democracy, nor is it necessarily discursive in nature. While this goes against the Supreme Court's growing protection of commercial speech,[24] discourse theory seeks to find a way to partition off sectors of public life from corporate and governmental influence. The announcement of a political debate is democratic in nature and aimed at the formation of public life. It is about citizens being able to come together to make public opinion. Discourse theory calls on judges to make independent evaluations of the type of speech that is involved rather than the type of property.

Post is correct, however, in seeing current public forum doctrine as driven solely by managerial concerns. Efficiency and social control are at the heart of that managerial concern, but so is the need to make the law appear more scientific. Courts avoid difficult questions about what the public sphere needs to thrive and work in the effort to develop criteria that will be perceived as neutral and can be "fairly" applied. Courts make independent evaluations of the type of speech and its value to democracy, but not by directly confronting the issue of the value of the speech. Instead, that is done through the cloak of property. Of course, property is not inherently a neutral concept, an idea that has roots in the New Deal and the legal realists.[25] Property is not evenly—nor fairly, some would argue—distributed in a democratic society. Relying on property thus favors those who own or are given access to that property. People who own property are going to enjoy more freedom than those who do not.

Perhaps more importantly, however, the New Deal argument that was used to end the *Lochner* era—the idea that property is a human creation and therefore could be legislated—is now being used in public forum arguments as a way to protect property rights and hinder the public sphere. As Post notes, "In the end the public realm created by public forum doctrine is nothing other than a governmentally protected public space for the achievement of private ordering."[26] Under public forum doctrine, the government sees the public sphere as something it created. Because it has created it, government has a right to control and manage it. Reducing the public sphere to private voices—a singular entity with a single message—allows the government to more easily control content. And as we have seen in other areas, a corporately rationalized system is able to subsume critique and use it for its own purposes. The following cases illustrate how the public forum doctrine has increased the management of public life while repressing the discursive needs of citizens.

Managing Debates: *Arkansas Educational Television Commission v. Forbes*

While the management of political campaigns seems to increase with each passing election, the opportunities for citizens to see interaction between candidates is decreasing. Over the past few years, political debates have increasingly focused on the major-party candidates, and the public forum doctrine has played a role in that development.

Ralph Forbes, a frequent but unsuccessful candidate for public office in Arkansas, decided in 1992 to run for a seat in Congress as an independent candidate. After collecting the required two thousand signatures required by Arkansas law, Forbes qualified for a spot on the ballot for the state's Third Congressional District. The Arkansas Educational Television Commission (AETC), a state agency that owns and operates five noncommercial television stations in Arkansas, sponsored a debate among the candidates for federal office, one of which included candidates for Forbes's district. Arguing that time constraints did not allow it to invite all candidates, AETC decided to limit the debates to "the major party candidates or any other candidate who had strong popular support." Based on those criteria, Forbes was not invited to participate.

Forbes sued, claiming that while private commercial television might be free to make content-based decisions, governmental bodies should not decide for voters who is a viable political candidate. In 1998, the U.S. Supreme Court ruled in favor of AETC, and the public forum doctrine was central to its decision.

In the eyes of the Supreme Court, the state-owned television network was a nonpublic forum not open to public use. As Justice Kennedy noted, "[B]road rights of access for outside speakers would be antithetical, as a general rule, to the discretion that stations and their editorial staffs must exercise to fulfill their journalistic purpose and statutory obligations."[27] Kennedy argued that broadcasters don't retain property rights for their own freedom so much as to meet the needs of the public.[28] That property right even covers programming that is not necessarily their own speech. Kennedy noted that broadcasters' programming decisions "often involve the compilation of the speech of third parties" but that the broadcaster does not need to "generate" the content for it to be considered a speech act protected by property rights.[29]

While Kennedy acknowledged that most programming even by public broadcasters does not fall under the purview of public forum doctrine, the issue in *Forbes* was different for two reasons: The debate was "by design a forum for political speech by the candidates," and it was "of exceptional significance in the electoral process."[30] Because of its importance to democracy, broadcasters must remain neutral and "cannot grant or deny access to a candidate on the basis of whether it agrees with a candidate's views."[31] However, because AETC did not make its debate available to all candidates for the congressional seat and relied on a candidate-by-candidate viability test, the forum was declared nonpublic by the Court.[32]

The Court went further than simply deciding that AETC's debate is a nonpublic forum, however. It argued that by excluding Forbes, AETC was actually operating in the public interest by promoting speech. The Court argued that since time limits would restrict the ability of candidates to air their views, it would be better—that is, a more efficient use of time—for the public to hear a small number of candidates. As Justice Kennedy wrote, "On logistical grounds alone, a public television editor might, with reason, decide that the inclusion of all ballot-qualified candidates would 'actually undermine the educational value and quality of debates.'"[33] The prospect of this inefficient use of the airwaves might cause public television to simply opt out of airing any political coverage, the Court feared.[34] Given the choice between a debate without Forbes and no debate at all, the Court decided that a debate without Forbes better serves the public interest. Therefore, giving the public television editors the right to exclude minority candidates increases the amount of ideas in the public sphere.

It is not hard to find the flaws in Justice Kennedy's argument. Framing the issue as a choice between a debate without Forbes or no debate at all ignores the many options open to the producers of the program. To name but two, the producers could devote more time to the program, or limit the time each candidate is allowed to speak. The Court presents no evidence that AETC ever considered dropping the debate if it was forced to include Forbes. Kennedy's argument, however, also reveals the problematic nature of relying on the public forum doctrine and property to protect freedom of speech and press and, more importantly, why it works against the needs of the public sphere.

The flaw in Kennedy's argument can be seen by taking his thinking to its logical conclusion. Let's assume that a state-owned television network wants to hold a one-hour debate between the Democratic and Republican presidential candidates in 2004. Prior to the debate, it becomes obvious that President George W. Bush will win in a landslide; John Kerry has been unable to mount a serious challenge. Based on the Court's reasoning in *Forbes*, it would be perfectly allowable—in fact, logical and efficient—for the public television station to turn over the entire hour to Bush because he is clearly the more viable candidate. Allowing an unelectable candidate to take up valuable airtime—to waste the public's time—is inherently bad for democracy. Giving Bush more time to express his ideas would actually prove beneficial for society because we can gain a greater understanding of his ideas and beliefs.

Clearly, Justice Kennedy cannot be arguing that a state-owned television station should be allowed to exclude all nonviable candidates. And it is doubtful that anyone would argue that excluding a nonviable, major-party candidate from a debate—especially for a high-level office—is a good thing. So the *Forbes* decision rests more on who Forbes was not than who he was or even whether he was a viable candidate. The most important reason for rejecting Forbes is that a major political party did not endorse him. By classifying televised political debates by government-owned media as nonpublic fora, the Court has turned over an important segment of public life to a group of people to make content-based decisions. The government employees who are privileged to have control over content decide what goes on the air and what doesn't. As we know, television plays a powerful role in American politics. Without access to television, it is difficult to run and win a major election in the United States today. Candidates, especially third-party candidates, increasingly find themselves in a Catch-22: Without media exposure they find it difficult to become viable candidates, and until they are viable candidates the media will not generally pay attention to them. Ross Perot became viable in 1992 only by ignoring media power structures and using his wealth to purchase airtime. Most third-party candidates, however, do not have access to that amount of money.

Just as disconcerting is the Court's view of public life. Under the Court's logic, the voices and ideas that make up public life are the property of broad-casters primarily because they elect to transmit them to the general public. Ignoring any idea of the publicness of public discourse, the Court frames the public sphere in individualistic terms that emphasize property and efficiency. The goal for broadcasters is to find an efficient way to inform citizens about viable democratic choices. The Court has cleared the way for broad-casters to manage public opinion by allowing them to make private decisions about public issues. By viewing the press and speech issues through a property lens, it allows those who are privileged enough to own property to set the terms of the debate—to define what freedom of the press and freedom of speech mean in modern society. The public forum doctrine is not only antidemocratic, it reflects corporately rationalized values.

Managing Public Parks: *Clark v. Community for Creative Non-Violence*

The public forum doctrine has been used by the courts not only to prevent third-party political candidates from expressing their views, but also private citizens who do not have the financial means to purchase media exposure. In 1982, the National Park Service allowed the group Community for Creative Non-violence (CCNV) to erect twenty tents in Lafayette Park and forty tents in the Mall, near the White House and the Capitol, respectively. The tents were intended to demonstrate the plight of the homeless in the United States. The National Park Service refused to allow demonstrators to sleep in the tents, citing a rule that forbid camping except in specified areas. The same group had staged a similar demonstration during the winter of 1981, with demon-strators sleeping in nine tents in Lafayette Park. The National Park Service's rule was formulated in response to that demonstration. The majority of the Supreme Court ruled that despite the fact that Lafayette Park and the Mall are public fora, the National Park Service did not violate CCNV's constitu-tional rights. Justice White's decision for the majority tells us much about how the public forum doctrine is used to promote an inactive public sphere.

Justice White recounted the purpose of the park and the Mall. He called it a park with "formal landscaping of flowers and trees." His description focuses on the park as a center of tourism and recreation, downplaying its role in public assembly and debate. He gave little power to the idea of the parks as a public forum. "Demonstrations for the airing of views or grievances are per-mitted in the Memorial-core parks, but for the most part only by Park Service permits."[35] Justice White's purpose, although he never clearly states it, is to marginalize the public-discourse nature of the parks and put an emphasis on the parks as a site not freely available for public demonstrations. As Justice Marshall noted in his dissent, missing from the majority's opinion "is any inkling that Lafayette Park and the Mall have served as the sites for some of the most rousing political demonstrations in the Nation's history."[36] At oral arguments, Marshall reminded the majority, the government admitted that on any given day there are "three or so demonstrations going on."[37]

After reviewing its history of the purpose and use of the parks, Justice White turned to the central question facing the Court: whether sleeping is a form of expression or conduct. White admitted that sleep, in this circumstance, is expressive conduct that enjoys some First Amendment protection, but not absolute protection. The government is allowed to restrict this form of speech as long as it is done through reasonable time, place, and manner restrictions, meaning that the government can restrict speech in relation to how, where, and when it is presented, but it cannot make decisions based solely on content.[38] For example, it is likely constitutional for a city to pass an ordinance restricting anyone from driving through neighborhoods at 2:00 A.M. blaring messages through a loudspeaker, while it is likely unconstitutional for a city to pass an ordinance prohibiting Democrats from driving through neighborhoods at 2:00 A.M. blaring messages through a loudspeaker. The first example is simply a limitation on when and how speech might be conducted, while the second hinders the speech of a specific group. For White, not allowing citizens to sleep in the parks is simply a time, place, and manner restriction. The National Park Service did not force CCNV to remove the structures nor to alter their message; they simply could not sleep in the park. As Justice White wrote, "It is also apparent to us that the regulation narrowly focuses on the Government's substantial interest in maintaining the parks in the heart of our Capital in an attractive and intact condition, readily available to the millions of people who wish to see and enjoy them by their presence."[39]

Perhaps more importantly, White saw "sleep speech" as less protected in this circumstance because it is more "facilitative" than expressive. That is, CCNV was using the tents and the promise of meals to lure homeless people to the demonstration. "Without a permit to sleep, it would be difficult to get the poor and homeless to participate or to be present at all," Justice White wrote.[40] Because of its facilitative nature, the sleeping ban will "effectively limit the nature, extent, and duration of the demonstration and so to that extent ease the pressure on the parks."[41]

The management of the parks is clearly the focus of the majority's concern. Allowing CCNV demonstrators to sleep in the parks creates a slippery slope; the Park Service would be unable to keep others from camping in the parks as well. Since some might have credible claims similar to CCNV, the "denial of permits to still others would present difficult problems for the Park Service."[42] The majority fully understood, and admitted, that refusing to recognize sleep speech was also a way of restricting protest.

Chief Justice Burger, in his concurring opinion, dismissed the possibility that there is any expressive component in sleeping in the parks, claiming that it is simply conduct. In an interesting turn of logic, Burger argued that this conduct interferes with the real purpose of the parks, which are open "for all the people, and their rights are not to be trespassed even by those who have some 'statement' to make."[43] He went on to label the case a "frivolous proceeding" that delayed "the causes of litigants who have legitimate nonfrivolous claims."[44]

Justice Marshall's dissenting opinion, other than recognizing sleep in this context as speech, builds on ideas central to the public forum doctrine without acknowledging that connection. For Marshall, sleep-speech should be protected because there was an intent to convey a clear message about the fate of the homeless in society, and "the likelihood was great that the political significance of sleeping in the parks would be understood by those who viewed it."[45] Marshall did not fear that the National Park Service would have administrative problems deciding whether sleep is linked with an expressive component, arguing that there is no record to suggest such a problem might exist. Marshall feared that when the government balanced the needs of the public against the First Amendment needs of smaller groups, the public would always win.

Perhaps more interestingly, in a footnote Marshall identified one of the fundamental problems associated with the public forum doctrine. He argued that even content-neutral regulations were problematic because they restrict "an inexpensive mode of communication" that affects "relatively poor speakers and the points of view that such speakers typically espouse." He noted that CCNV lacked the funds to gain access to other modes of communication and wrote, "A disquieting feature about the disposition of this case is that it lends credence to the charge that judicial administration of the First Amendment, in conjunction with a social order marked by large disparities in wealth and other sources of power, tends systematically to discriminate against efforts by the relatively disadvantaged to convey their political ideas."[46]

There are several ways to analyze the Court's decision in *Clark*. First of all, the majority's decision deemphasized the public forum test—which would have clearly placed Lafayette Park and the Mall in the category of traditional public fora—in an attempt to justify the power of the National Park Service. The *Clark* decision helps us understand the political nature of public forum decisions. The majority prefers to see the Lafayette Park and the Mall not in their historical use but rather similar to more traditional national parks, where the intent is clearly to protect the natural beauty. Since the capital's parks are more akin to the latter, protecting their beauty becomes far more important and is in the best interests of the public. Current use of the Mall adds to this argument. For example, in the fall of 2002 the National Park Service allowed fourteen houses to be built on the Mall by college students involved in the Solar Decathlon, a contest to build efficient solar homes. The houses stood for more than a week.[47]

In that same vein, the majority decision hides the Court's ethical choices behind methodologies such as the public forum doctrine and the time, place, and manner test. As corporate rationalization shows us, scientific reasoning is at the heart of the rules that govern public space. Methods that appear value-free are used to mask their lack of objectivity. The majority of the Court neatly sidesteps the main question that it faced in this circumstance: Is sleep in the context of CCNV's demonstration discursive and valuable to a democratic society? Instead of answering that question directly, the majority relied on questions of efficiency and management to avoid making the difficult ethical choices associated with public life. The unique aspect of *Clark* is that for once a justice called attention to this overtly political move. As Marshall noted, content-free rules are not nonpolitical in nature; they hurt those who have no access to resources far more than those who have access to resources. Not allowing Microsoft to use the national parks in Washington, D.C., for political messages is nothing but a minor inconvenience. It can purchase advertising, attract media attention, and distribute its message in many other ways. Groups without that economic power, however, suffer whenever they are not allowed to use public space. Content-free rules in the long run don't work to narrow the expression gap between corporations and private groups but serve to enlarge those gaps, further damaging the public sphere.

The debate over whether sleep can be seen in this context as expression is equally troubling. While not willing to go as far as the chief justice and dismiss such a thing as sleep-speech, Justice White has trouble seeing much expressive content in it. Justices White and Marshall, however, do agree on one point: the ability of the speaker to control meaning. Both agree that conduct can become speech only if the intent of the speaker is communicative in nature and if the audience understands that communicative intent. White and Marshall disagree about whether that expressive conduct is still subject to governmental restrictions. In that way, both justices downplay the power of the public sphere. The role of the audience is limited to receiving the message; in fact, the justices seem to view the audience solely as a way of justifying the freedoms of the speaker. The speaker will enjoy First Amendment protection as long as his or her speech or conduct is understood by the audience. If the audience does not understand it, there is no communication, and it is labeled as unprotected conduct. By denying a more powerful role to the public sphere—a role that allows members of the audience to create their own meaning—the justices facilitate the idea of an informed public that exists primarily to gather information rather than to act on that information.

In the end, discourse democracy and the needs of the public sphere take us to a ruling vastly different from that reached by the majority in *Clark*. Sleep, at least in this context, should be protected expression not because the message of the sleep-speech is clear, nor because we can be reasonably certain that the audience will take from it the intended message. Rather, it is protected because it is a commentary on a public problem. There is nothing in the record of the Court to suggest that CCNV was engaging in any action other than an invitation for discourse about a public problem. Discourse theory would suggest that the sleep-speech should enjoy more protection because the meaning of the message was ambiguous. Like a piece of abstract art, sleep-speech in this situation was a public invitation to create meaning, to think about what the demonstrators were trying to say. In short, the planned demonstration was an invitation to an active public.

Managing Streets: Public Parades and *Hurley*

The Court's decisions involving the use of city streets have similarly hindered the formation of an active public sphere. The Court's 1995 ruling in *Hurley v. Irish-American Gay, Lesbian, and Bisexual Group of Boston, Inc.,*[48] raises many of the same questions as *Clark*.

Two holidays have traditionally been celebrated in Boston on March 17: St. Patrick's Day and Evacuation Day (the day the British left Boston in 1776). The city has sponsored celebrations, including parades, since at least 1776, with some being noted as early as 1737. Formal sponsorship by the city of the celebration ended in 1947 when Mayor James Michael Curley granted authority to sponsor a parade to the South Boston Allied War Veterans Council, a collection of various veterans groups. Since that time, the group has annually applied for and received a permit to sponsor a parade through Boston on St. Patrick's Day.[49] Up to and including 1992, the city allowed the group to use the city's official seal and provided printing services and other direct funding of the parade, though the War Veterans Council remained the official sponsor.

In 1992, a group of gay, lesbian, and bisexuals of Irish descent formed with the expressed purpose of marching in the parade. Known as GLIB, the group hoped to, according to the Court, "express pride in their Irish heritage as openly gay, lesbian, and bisexual individuals" and to demonstrate their solidarity with other marchers in the parade.[50] Organizers denied GLIB permission to march in the 1992 parade, but a state court ordered the council to grant the marchers access. The Court noted that GLIB marched "uneventfully" in the parade, which included ten thousand participants and 750,000 spectators.[51]

The following year, GLIB once again sought permission to march and once again was denied. GLIB filed suit, and a state trial court ruled that the War Veterans Council must provide the marchers with access. The trial court based its decision on the Massachusetts public accommodation law, which prohibits "any distinction, discrimination or restriction on account of . . . sexual orientation . . . relative to the admission of any person to, or treatment in any place of public accommodation, resort or amusement."[52] The trial court noted that the council did not have any written criteria for allowing access, nor did it routinely probe the messages or views of other applicants. In the end, the trial court ruled that the parade was not a "constitutionally protected right of expressive association" but an "open recreational event" subject to the public accommodation law.[53]

The Supreme Judicial Court of Massachusetts affirmed the trial court's decision, and the case was appealed to the U.S. Supreme Court. A unanimous Court, led by Justice David Souter's opinion, overturned the decision, preferring to recognize the expressive content of the parade and, in particular, the ability of the organizers to control content. The state, the Court ruled, violated the First Amendment when it allowed speech to become a public accommodation.

A large portion of Justice Souter's decision for the majority rested on the uneasy relationship between private speech and its public nature. For Souter and the Court, "a speaker has the autonomy to choose the content of his message."[54] And since, in the words of the Court, "every participating unit affects the message conveyed by the private organizers," the ruling by the state courts interfered with the Council's First Amendment rights.

Justice Souter and the Court were willing to admit that expression is not simply a case of individual autonomy. Souter called parades "public dramas."[55] Parades, as defined by the Court, are composed of "marchers who are making some sort of collective point, not just to each other but to bystanders along the way."[56] In some way, then, the Court recognized a parade's "dependence on watchers"[57] based on the fact that the public plays some role in the creation of meaning. But what role does that public play in the creation of the meaning of speech? Is the public a passive, informed audience or an active interpreter of information?

Despite Justice Souter's acknowledgment of the public's role in the meaning of a parade, his decision falls back on liberal rights and authorial intent. The meaning of a parade exists in the minds of its organizers, thus legitimating the need to grant the organizers First Amendment protection. As Souter wrote, "Although each parade unit generally identifies itself, each is understood to contribute something to a common theme, and accordingly there is no customary practice whereby private sponsors disavow 'any identity of viewpoint' between themselves and the selected participants."[58]

The organizers and those whom they elect to put into the parade determine meaning for the audience. As the Court noted, "[T]he parade's overall message is distilled from the individual presentation along the way, and each unit's expression is perceived by spectators as part of the whole."[59] The only role for those in attendance is to watch. Members of the public receive the intended message without any expectation that they will interpret that message beyond the intent of the speaker.

Justice Souter's opinion that forcing a speaker to carry a view "contrary to one's own" compromises the "speaker's right to autonomy over the message" runs counter to discourse principles. Souter elected to focus on the instrumental nature of speech, clearing the way for a speaker to obtain expressive victory. By giving the organizers control over the streets, the Court assured victory or, at the very least, limited the possibility of alternative interpretations of that message. In addition, Souter's decision perpetuated a model of an informed public that has something done to it as opposed to a public that participates in its own formation. Discourse theory would view GLIB's desire to participate in the parade less as an infringement on the council's freedom of expression than as a discursive act that would allow audience members to take from it what they want.

The concepts of state action and public forum play an important part in the Court's opinion. Justice Souter's opinion followed the traditional view that speakers "should be free from interference by the State based on the content" of what they say.[60] The decision by the state courts declaring the parade a public accommodation thus constituted state involvement in what is and is not acceptable content for inclusion in the parade. As Souter wrote, "While the law is free to promote all sorts of conduct in place of harmful behavior, it is not free to interfere with speech for no better reason than promoting an approved message or discouraging a disfavored one, however enlightened either purpose may strike the government."[61]

Justice Souter failed to find any justification for making expression a category covered by the public accommodation law. He suggested that it could be argued that "forbidding acts of discrimination" might be used to rid a society of existing biases. However, Souter wrote that this idea "grates on the First Amendment, for it amounts to nothing less than a proposal to limit speech in the service of orthodox expression."[62] In the end, the value that comes from labeling expression a public accommodation does not offset the value of promoting individual expression.

Similarly, Justice Souter failed to find any protection for GLIB's requests to assure its involvement in the parade because of the public forum issue. While noting the lengthy history of the parade and the diverse topics that are covered by marchers,[63] Souter put individual autonomy above any right of access to a public forum. There seems little doubt that he views the streets of Boston as a public forum; however, the Court instructed GLIB to obtain its own permit and hold its own parade.[64] Even Justice Souter admitted that is not a viable option and recognized that "GLIB understandably seeks to communicate its ideas as part of the existing parade rather than staging one of its own."[65] The fact that city streets are viewed as a public forum, which the Court recognized as a part of the "privileges, immunities, rights, and liberties of citizens," did not override the expressive rights of individuals or the state's ability to interfere with that expression.[66]

GLIB attempted to use *Turner Broadcasting System, Inc., v. FCC*[67] to justify its entry into the parade, but the Court rejected the argument. In *Turner,* the Court found that congressional requirements forcing cable systems to carry locally originated television broadcasts, or what is known as must-carry rules, were constitutional. As far as must-carry regulations are concerned, cable is less a speaker than a common carrier. GLIB argued that gaining entry to the parade would not threaten "the core principle of speaker's autonomy" because the War Veterans Council, like a cable system operator, is nothing more than a conduit as opposed to a speaker.[68] In that sense, the council is providing the avenue through which groups express themselves, much as cable systems elect which programming to carry. The Court rejected the argument. As Justice

Souter wrote, "[T]his metaphor is not apt here, because GLIB's participation would likely be perceived as having resulted from the Council's customary determination about a unit admitted to the parade, that its message was worthy of presentation and quite possibly of support as well."[69]

There is little doubt that GLIB's argument was weak. Even discourse theory would recognize that. The council is clearly trying to convey a message and is in no way a common carrier similar in nature to cable system owners. Still, GLIB's argument shows the power of the marketplace metaphor and how it felt compelled to frame its arguments in those terms. The argument does not challenge the right of the council to control the street, nor the city's authorization, but instead builds its challenge on the issue that as "owner" the council is obligated to provide access.

Discourse theory takes a broader, more affirmative view of the relationship between state action and a public forum than the Court does in *Hurley*. The Court presupposed that a workable distinction exists between private speakers and state action. That distinction, however, cannot be sustained. The state is deeply involved in constituting the parade and its sponsor and therefore is using state power to protect the group's control of the streets. Discourse theory would argue that the Court's decision in *Hurley* falls short of separating state action from speech. It demonstrates how clearly the state is embedded in our understanding of freedom of expression—how central the state is to the existence of that freedom as we understand it. In choosing to value individual autonomy over a right of public discourse, the Court allows state action to sneak in through the back door. In other words, a system of expression that promotes individual autonomy is not a natural occurrence but a creation of the state. And the state has elected to promote individual rights. In the end, government is doing exactly what Justice Souter claims it should not be doing—"promoting an approved message or discouraging a disfavored one."

The purpose of freedom of expression in discourse democracy is not solely to allow individuals to express themselves (be it in a search for truth,[70] a more tolerant society,[71] or to protect the antiauthoritarian in all of us, as some theories suggest[72]) but to allow individuals to share ideas about how to live their lives. Discourse is vital because it begins the process of turning particular interests into generalizable interests.

In *Hurley*, then, discourse theory directs us to allow GLIB to gain entry to the parade because of its discursive potential and because the venue is a traditional public forum. While for Justice Souter, GLIB's application can be denied because the council "owns" the parade and the message that surrounds it, discourse theory recognizes the publicness of the parade. The infringement on the freedom of the speaker, the War Veterans Council, is relatively small in this case. GLIB could have easily been placed at the end of the parade, and organizers could have placed a banner signaling the end of their message. GLIB's stated goals for obtaining access to the parade, along with its past record of noninterference, also support its claim for entry.

What the Court did in *Hurley* is grant a group preferential treatment under the guise that the government leased the public property for a short period of time to a private group, allowing that private group to exclude certain groups.

Managing Rest Areas: Interstates and the Public Sphere

A more current example of how the discursive needs of citizens are undervalued by government is reflected in the management of rest areas along the interstate highway system. In early 2002, the National Association for the Advancement of Colored People (NAACP) began protesting South Carolina's decision to continue displaying the Confederate flag. The group began informational picketing at eight rest areas along interstates entering South Carolina, urging visitors not to stop or shop in South Carolina. A Louisiana-based group headed by the white activist David Duke, the European-American Unity and Rights Organization (EURO), was also picketing at the rest areas.[73]

South Carolina's attorney general, Charlie Condon, who was running for governor against the incumbent Democrat, threatened a lawsuit against the NAACP. "'We are asking the court to declare that the activities these two groups are now engaged in violates state and federal law regulating permissible activities at interstate rest stops and welcome centers,'" Condon said.[74] He referred to federal rules that limit activities at federally funded rest areas and noted that signs at the centers say that they are for "the convenience of motorists" and "not to be used for camping, overnight parking, sports, meetings or other group activities."[75] Condon said, "'We believe the law is clear: Highway rest stops and welcome centers are not forums like public squares or the sidewalks of ordinary streets.'"[76] Using classic slippery slope and managerial logic, Condon warned that allowing one group to protest will clear the way for others, eventually proving costly to law enforcement and hurting the state.[77] A spokeswoman for the state's Department of Public Safety said, "'There is nothing that we see that would restrict them from being there.'" And Governor Jim Hodges, through a spokesperson, said, "'The governor does not support the border patrols. He finds the patrols damaging to African-American businesses in particular.'"[78]

The judicial history of expressive activity at rest areas has been mixed. Generally, lower courts have held that rest areas are not public fora. While the cases revolved around whether newspaper publishers have a First Amendment right to sell their product in the rest areas, they are interesting for their reliance on public forum doctrine. Vending machines are allowed in rest areas under federal rules, but states are to give priority to vending machines operated by groups that provide employment or compensation to blind people.

The most influential case in this area appears to be the U.S. Court of Appeals for the Eleventh Circuit's 1991 decision in *Sentinel Communications Co. v. Watts*. The court ruled that while the *Orlando (Fla.) Sentinel* enjoys some First Amendment protection to distribute its newspaper, it does not override the public forum doctrine. The court noted, "As components of the Interstate System, safety rest areas are hardly the kind of public property that has 'by long tradition or by governmental fiat . . . been devoted to assembly and debate,'. . . . [T]hey are optional appendages that are intended, as part of the System, to facilitate safe and efficient travel by motorists along the System's highways."[79] The court went on to add that while there may be some similarity between rest areas and parks, the intent of the government was not to "open the forum to the same panoply of activity permitted in the latter fora."[80] For those reasons, the court called rest areas nonpublic fora. Despite agreeing with the nonpublic forum status of rest areas, other courts have ruled that states have failed to justify their rules excluding newspaper vending machines.[81]

While the question of whether protests at rest areas are protected by the First Amendment remains unclear, case law does seem to suggest that courts would not be sympathetic to the NAACP's claims in South Carolina. Rest areas are not simply places for drivers to rest, but also, by government fiat, a place where only commercial expression will be allowed. Travelers can face advertisements for soft drinks, hotels, tourist attractions, but public protest is not within the meaning of rest areas. As the officials for the state of South Carolina demonstrate through their comments, public expression in rest areas will cause disruptions and is not an efficient use of the space. As the governor clearly points out, his concern about the protest rests more with its impact on commerce than on whether it's a discursive activity that ought to be protected. By allowing the property to define what types of speech are allowed, and by casting rest areas as nonpublic forums that are efficient aids to interstate commerce, the public sphere has lost another site of public expression.

Conclusion

The values associated with corporate rationalization have led to a more restricted and managed public sphere. The cases and issues examined in this
chapter demonstrate that as the courts rely on those values to make decisions on the structure of public space, public life suffers. Underlying the
public forum doctrine are many ideas associated with corporate rationalization. Public forum doctrine turns questions of expression into questions
of property and, as such, favors individualism (property "owners"), management, and efficiency. By favoring property owners, which under corporate liberalism recognizes corporations as individuals, the doctrine also protects an authoritarian creation of meaning. The cases see the establishment
of meaning not as a process that citizens take part in but rather something
that is done to them. The role of citizens in the creation of meaning is to be
the audience—to passively receive the message and take in the speaker's
meaning. But the impact of public forum doctrine goes deeper than that.
Within its structure we also see a reliance on law as science, where the goal
is to develop an objective methodology that escapes the influence and criticism of values. That objective method is used to demonstrate that the law
is being applied in a fair way to all members of society. As such, the public
forum doctrine allows the courts to make political decisions that hinder an
active public sphere while still claiming to be making content-free decisions.
Property becomes one of the methodologies employed, but the expression-
conduct framework is equally powerful. The Court's declaration in *Clark*
that "sleep-speech" is facilitative and only done to lure homeless people to
the protest is a political act that pushes action to the margins of First Amendment protection. It has long ties to the idea that government can more freely
restrict the speech of organized groups that present a threat to society than
the speech of isolated individuals, an idea that is linked in important ways
to progressive legal thought.[82] The public forum doctrine serves more as a
form of social control than it does to protect freedom of expression.

7

Resisting Corporate Rationalization: Toward a Discourse Theory of the First Amendment

As this book is being written, there are almost daily news reports of corporate malfeasance in the United States. Enron, Worldcom, Arthur Anderson, and others have become synonymous with corporate greed and corruption. Corporations such as these have come to dominate our public discussions and have complicated American domestic policy. A sense of hopelessness surrounds many of the reports; as lawmakers debate legislation that will make corporations responsible citizens, one gets the sense that few people really believe much will be accomplished. While legislation might change the structure of corporations, it will not resolve the corporate domination of public life. Corporations have their place in a democratic society—their place, however, is not determining what values ought to guide public life.

Identifying that place and restricting the ability of corporations to dominate public life is a difficult task. This book argues that corporate ideology is so central to our thinking that it is difficult to even envision a different form of democracy. But all change must start somewhere; it must have some foundational element to build upon, and a discourse theory of the First Amendment provides that foundation. This chapter briefly highlights some elements that are central to a discourse theory of the First Amendment and describes how such a rethinking might influence the press and the law.

Democracy without an Active Public Sphere

At various times, U.S. Supreme Court justices have suggested ways to limit corporate influence. Justices Hugo Black and William Douglas found the

Court's application of the Fourteenth Amendment to corporations to be not only a legal fiction but also undemocratic. Justice William Brennan argued for providing nonprofit corporations more free speech rights than for-profit corporations, while Justice Sandra Day O'Connor argued for limited associational rights for groups engaged in purely commercial activities. Those ideas have failed to attract wide support from other members of the Court. While reasons can be found for why those ideas were never developed, the Court's refusal to deal with basic questions in any substantive way is even more interesting: Why should corporations be considered people under the Constitution? What role should modern-day corporations play in the realization of democracy?

Of course, the two questions have a history and are directly connected under the traditional American interpretation of free speech and press. While the First Amendment does not articulate a role for corporations (unless a theorist considers the press clause as articulating a freedom for the corporately owned press), it is most commonly interpreted through a classical liberal lens. That is, the First Amendment ensures protection from governmental interference with individual speech. Once corporations are granted status as people, it is a small step to conclude that they enjoy First Amendment privileges. It could be argued that it was legitimate for the Supreme Court to originally grant corporations status as people under the Constitution, that doing so made corporations more responsible and gave shareholders some power. It was an attempt to clean up the politics of an earlier day when corporate charters were granted based on political favors. As so often happens with judicial decisions, however, the ideology was soon separated from the practice, and today the idea of corporate personhood is used in ways that earlier courts never envisioned.

This book is concerned with identifying the obstacles to the formation of an active public—a group of individuals who come together with the goal of collecting and acting on information. Corporate rationalization is not the only impediment to that formation, but it is one that has long been ignored. It changes the way we think and talk about democracy, and it changes the way that dominant institutions within democratic society interact with the public sphere. This is not a new development, but it is a much-ignored development. The rise of corporations has long been of fundamental concern. The coming together of various movements, such as Progressivism, Taylorism, Fordism, and the rise of corporate liberalism, has opened the door for corporations to influence values within society. This book has sought to identify a number of the ways that corporate values have influenced public life, but of course there are others. Think, for example, of the way that corporations have influenced everyday language. "Corpspeak"—phrases such as "twenty-four seven," "networking," and "downsizing" (and its more sinister cousin, "rightsizing")—has infiltrated the lexicon.[1]

It could be argued that the fears identified here have been exaggerated and that there is nothing sinister or wrong with corporations wielding this much influence in a democratic society. We could conclude that corporations are like any other social force that citizens must deal with: Their influence will come and go, and we simply need to figure out how to deal with them. This ignores the fact that corporations have had tremendous staying power. This is not the first time in American history that we have had a corporate problem. The Progressive reformers also sought to limit corporate powers, only to see corporations rise again after amassing even more power. We should remember the historian Ron Chernow's observation that John D. Rockefeller Sr. went into the fight to break up Standard Oil in 1911 a millionaire and emerged a billionaire.[2]

This time around, however, something seems to have changed. Perhaps today's corporate problem is hard to put a face on—it seems anonymous and mysterious. If we have entered a new Gilded Age, as Paul Krugman suggests, it is one peopled with nondescript corporate CEOs.[3] Corporations have become covert political forces in the United States. When the Supreme Court cleared the way for corporations to exercise free speech rights, no one could have predicted how great that influence would become. In today's political world, barred from directly giving financial support to candidates, corporations have instead focused on the political process itself. The journalist David S. Broder has identified the corporate capture of the initiative movement (state referendums), or what he terms "the initiative industry." In Broder's view, money has corrupted the initiative process, but he fails to recognize how corporate ideology has contributed to that corruption. Corporations, with no allegiance to any ideology except profitability, have rationalized the referendum, the most public of elections. With the approval of the Supreme Court, companies are now hired to gather signatures to earn a spot on the initiative ballot.[4] Politics does not drive the industry. As one industry representative told Broder, "'The only time we have a problem is when we have directly competing issues out there, and then we give them [the workers] a choice: "You can work ours or you can work theirs."'"[5] Broder reports that a good signature collector can make twenty-five to fifty dollars an hour.[6]

Two things become obvious after reading Broder's account: Money has not simply changed the initiative process but the way the entire process has been rationalized. The initiative movement has been made into an efficient machine that spits out a form of democracy and is more concerned about winning than promoting any sense of what it means to be a citizen in a democracy. The industry's goal is to get the people to vote for their client, whether citizens understand the issue or not.

And second, the initial error is to assume that something like participatory democracy, which is arguably at the heart of the initiative process, can operate without a functioning public sphere. To the rationalized initiative industry, citizens are individuals to be manipulated, managed, and intellectually massaged until they vote for the industry's client. Without an active public sphere, where citizens are allowed to engage in discourse about what the issues mean to them—where they can encounter reasoned discourse about the issues and collectively work to counter the corporate influence—citizens stand very little chance against the initiative industry. Critics of this stand will argue that it idealizes citizenry—we have learned that citizens do not want to engage in discussions about issues and prefer to be entertained. Perhaps this is correct. Perhaps the elitist governmental and media system, which emphasizes top-down democracy, is the best we can do. One thing, however, is clear: Corporate ideology is at the heart of democracy, and for the people who benefit from it, there is no incentive for change.

The vital project facing democracy is how to resist corporate rationalization. Small steps can be taken that will aid that achievement. The sociologist George Ritzer has proposed a number of things citizens might do to oppose rationalization. His list includes supporting local merchants rather than retail chain stores and restaurants, using cash rather than credit cards, and always insisting on talking to a person when calling a business.[7] And while individual action might be a start, overturning corporate rationalization will take more than that. A new form of democracy requires an active public sphere that receives cultural support from powerful institutions devoted to serving that public sphere.

The United States has long endowed its citizens with constitutional protections. At best, however, those protections have been interpreted as negative rights—rights that protect the citizen from other citizens or the state.[8] Constitutional guarantees are said to prohibit institutions or people from interfering with the lives of private citizens. In that regard, the First Amendment is seen as providing a negative right: "Congress shall make no law . . . abridging the freedom of speech, or of the press. . . ." Positive rights have a more checkered history in constitutional law. The state or society's institutions are not generally mandated to aid citizens in their quests to achieve the good life.[9] Citizens have a right to speak, but it is not the state's responsibility to aid in making that speech effective.

While questions of negative liberty have dominated the discourse about the First Amendment and its role in democracy, it remains unclear whether that interpretation is the best for achieving an active public. Protection from state interference may no longer be enough to assure a politically active citizenry. What is needed is more than freedom from interference, but a type of freedom that encourages people to participate and join the conversation about democracy. The responsibility for promoting that freedom goes beyond the state. It is the responsibility of all producers of culture as well as the citizenry itself.

It does seem clear that the very idea of negative liberty limits the chances of an active public sphere. While negative liberty might provide protection from governmental interference in the public sphere, it also limits the government's ability to aid public life and ignores the role of corporate influence. Professionalization, journalist's privilege, rights of the corporate press, and access to public places all are built on the foundation of negative liberty. Even when the courts do grant affirmative rights, such as to the press in journalist's privilege, the primary benefit is for the professional press and only secondarily for the public. Such actions ultimately protect the professional press and establish it as the protector of an inactive public. The debate never deviates from a "top-down" version of democratic theory.[10]

This book has been concerned with identifying how corporations have influenced public life. Identifying the problem is only a start. The larger issue is: Where do we go from here?

Capturing the Discursive Nature of the Press

I have argued that corporate rationalization changes the way the public sphere interacts with its dominant institutions and, in turn, changes how democracy functions. Professionalization, a central component of corporate rationalization, does not come without a cost. It has a significant impact not only on the press and the law but on the public that relies on those institutions for support. Professionals cannot lose sight of their role in shaping democracy. In an attempt to legitimize their work, professionals in turn shape the public, just as they are shaped by the political economy and the culture that surrounds them.

As studies in the sociology of the professions have shown, professionals exist to deal with the abnormalities in society and to provide a cure when something goes wrong. Each profession seeks to establish for itself a jurisdiction of work over which it has complete control. For the press, that jurisdiction can be found in providing a check on the improper actions of government and the abuse of power. The paradox facing the press, however, is that it must rely on the very institution that it is to check for the granting of its professional power. As Andrew Abbott notes, jurisdictional claims have a culture and a social structure.[11] The watchdog function, as it is played out by professionals, not only helps shape how the press does its work, it also exposes the press to a power structure that it cannot control.

The story of press professionalization provides little if any role for an active public. The public is seen as a passive receiver of information, either with little interest in participation or too remote to get involved in the discussion of public affairs in an attempt to influence public opinion. As a consequence, the public turns that role over to the professional press. The result is that decisions are made absent public input about the important issues of the day, while the press collects the information the public needs and provides the analysis to put that information into context.[12] There is little left for citizens to do except consume the information put before them.

The trouble is, in the modern world, government and the press seem to have only tenuous ties to the public sphere. The professionalization movement has separated the press, the public's preeminent institution, from the public. Its function is no longer to promote and activate the public sphere—to give life to the ideas that percolate up from gatherings of private people who come together to form themselves into a public. The press's mission is best seen as an attempt to set aside an area of expert work, complete with routines and accepted styles. And that expert work is not the role of activating the public but being a provider of information, a watchdog that is reduced to seeking institutional status from the very power it is designed to watch.

The professionalization movement turns questions of public policy into technical questions that only specially trained elites are able to address. Checking government's actions and providing information about those actions to the public becomes a job for the trained journalist. Issues impacting the press are not seen as public issues but rather professional, technical issues. The press presents stories not as something to be acted on but as events that have already been completed.[13] Adopting a system rationality, the important questions for the professional press are means-end questions, questions that are at the root of privilege requests: How can the press effectively obtain more information so that it can inform the public? An active public sphere is not driven by means-end questions; it is grounded by a communicative rationality based on the desire for understanding, not efficiency. An idea needs to develop legitimacy to survive, and legitimacy is achieved through providing good reasons why one alternative is superior to another. The goal is not more information but the creation of what G. Thomas Goodnight has called a "deliberative rhetoric"—argumentation that allows individuals to test and create social knowledge to "uncover, assess, and resolve problems."[14] The press provides information, but it does not encourage citizens to act.[15] Rather than engaging citizens as rational people with a decision to make, the press presents authoritative information that demands only their attention—for a brief period—and not action.

Many in today's news media seem uninterested in aiding that discursive goal, unless it fits within the confines of increased profit margins. The rhetoric that media managers use to justify what they do increasingly emphasizes profitability and efficiency over public service. While it is debatable whether earlier media managers lived up to claims that they "were afflicting the comfortable and comforting the afflicted" or serving as a watchdog on government, few disagree that these were admirable goals. Today, media managers have mostly abandoned those old, tired clichés, preferring a more realistic and honest set of goals. For example, when John Hogan, the president and chief executive of Clear Channel's radio division (which owns some twelve hundred radio stations), was asked by the *New York Times* to explain his division's apparent conservative political agenda, he dismissed such claims as "laughable." The *Times* went on to explain the corporate ideology that drives Clear Channel: "Clear Channel, he [Hogan] said, is purely a company that builds audiences through entertainment so that advertisers can sell goods and services to them. 'We're in the business of having the largest possible audience,' Mr. Hogan said, not 'the most politically unified audience.'"[16]

That attitude is not found only at large, national media companies. The corporate ideology reaches into the smaller, more local media as well. In 1998, the local daily newspaper in Bloomington-Normal, Illinois, proudly announced its new slogan in a front-page letter from the publisher, Donald R. Skaggs. According to Skaggs, the slogan "Connecting Central Illinois" reflects the mission of the newspaper: "*The Pantagraph* connects people in a variety of ways—shoppers with merchants, parents with school news, investors with financial information."[17] Skaggs notes that the "list goes on," but apparently the other functions of the newspaper are not important enough to list. The comments of Hogan and Skaggs should be troubling to citizens. They should be praised for their honesty, but citizens who rely on the news media should be concerned that profitability and serving markets are the news media's primary concerns. Their unwillingness to even rhetorically acknowledge their democratic role should trouble us.

Corporate rationalization is reflected in the fact that media managers no longer feel the need to rely on claims of public service or aiding democracy to justify what they do. Today's media seem increasingly driven by a corporately rationalized value system.

Recasting the Press's Mission

The journalist William Greider has criticized the press for refusing to take responsibility for its role in the decline of public life. Greider describes a modern press that sermonizes about the decline of political life but does little to stop it: "A newspaper that took responsibility for its own readers would assume some of the burden for what they know and understand (and what they don't know and understand)." Greider continues: "It would undertake to reconnect them with political power and to invent forms of accountability between citizens and those in power that people could use and believe in."[18]

The desire to criticize but remain separate from reform would not surprise the many critics of the professional press.[19] But as Greider suggested, changing the press's mission requires not only reformulating its practices but also the role it plays in democracy. In essence, the press needs to rethink its view of the public. And while this book has focused on critique, it is my hope that the identification of the problem should also point toward some project for reform. Earlier in the book, four elements central to discourse democracy were identified: the creation of an active public, valuing the public creation of meaning, promoting the use of public space, and protecting expressive association. The press can play an important role in the realization of each of those.

Of the four, the idea of creating an active public has been most closely examined by the American press. James Carey has written that the press justifies its actions through the public but never really questions that relationship "'other than to say the public is not interested, or the public is dumb.'"[20] While elements of the press may view the public as being fragmented, the press still turns to the public for legitimation of its power.[21] The press claims that there is no such thing as a unified public while also claiming that it represents "the public" and is therefore entitled to greater freedom. For the press, the public has come to serve an instrumental role in democratic society. It adopts the public when it serves its needs, but ignores it when it is not needed.

The press must come to terms with what it means by the public and the role the public plays in society. It needs to move beyond the view that the public is comprised of individuals who share few similarities, all waging battles to push through their individual agendas. As Stuart Ewen has written, "For this situation to change, we need to rethink these habits of class, ethnicity, gender, and persuasion, encouraging us to fight it out over increasingly insufficient crumbs. Until a sense of difference is balanced by a sense of community, a democratic public will be unattainable."[22]

Individual differences should not be viewed as being destructive of a public but as helping to broaden the public's perspective. Avenues and techniques that will allow the formation of an active public need to be developed, and the public's potential must be recognized. The point is central to my claim that there is a qualitative difference between an informed and an active public. Information does not merely go to citizens, but in a sense it creates a public sphere. An active public collects information, but it also uses that information to participate in public life. The goal is the formation of public opinion that will guide future action. The press plays a different role in the promotion of an active public than it plays under the model of an informed public. No longer is the profession's highest calling the production of information or serving as a check on government; the goal becomes the establishment of ways and means to activate and involve the public.

Such ideas are not entirely idealistic, nor has the press always rejected them. Public journalism, one attempt to address some of these challenges, has sought to energize public life by discovering what citizens are interested in and helping them find solutions to common problems. As explained by Jay Rosen, one of the founders of the movement, the important point is that press leaders recognize that the "proper location for this discussion was assumed to be *the community itself*, rather than the halls of government."[23] Public journalism attracted a lot of attention in the 1990s, but by 2002 it seemed to have hit a plateau. Criticism came from all quarters. Journalists feared that it was just another marketing scheme, while publishers questioned whether the effort was really helping to increase profitability.[24]

Public journalism was never entirely altruistic. As newspapers faced declining profit margins and circulation, they looked for ways to recapture that share of the audience. Public journalism was envisioned as a way to do that. It was driven by the idea that a public excited about political life is more likely to turn to the press to feed that excitement.[25]

In some quarters, this call for empowering the public has been interpreted as a call for the press to become more consumer-driven.[26] But just as television news responds to its ratings, newspapers increasingly shape their coverage in response to readership surveys. The press's turn away from public-affairs reporting is often supported by the claim, "We're only giving readers what they want." Here the distinction between an informed public and an active public becomes apparent. Viewing its audience as consumers,[27] the press-as-informer asks people what stories it should cover. Readers and viewers have a certain range of issues from which to pick, but they are provided with little or no opportunity for a public discussion about those issues. Public opinion is in essence reduced to "institutional criteria."[28] Susan Herbst has argued that such efforts structure and thus limit public opinion: "Although many are no doubt dissatisfied with the media products available to them, these voices are rarely heard."[29] In the end, television ratings and readership surveys are not public opinion. They reflect the press's view of citizenship itself—the opinions of a fragmented group of individuals with few common interests, seeking to satisfy their individual desires.[30]

One example illustrates how public journalism came to confuse the two types of publics and its ties to corporate instrumental thought. In 1992, the *Star Tribune* in Minneapolis initiated what can arguably be called the classic example of public journalism. The newspaper aided the community in the creation of salons, small groups in which citizens could discuss issues. The newspaper provided a monthly topic (which groups were under no obligation to follow), aided in the formation of the groups through literature and other support, and provided some media coverage highlighting what the groups were talking about. About a hundred groups were formed, involving about two thousand citizens. However, the *Star Tribune* for a time ended its sponsorship of the discussion groups. As an editor explained in 1995, they were "a tool that is not being used right now, although it's in our toolbox."[31] She went on to explain that editors would consider restarting the discussion groups if they would help the newspaper understand the public mood.[32] In fact, the newspaper used the technique in January 2003 to discuss America's response to terrorism.[33]

The *Star Tribune* example is informative. By viewing public deliberation as a tool, something to be manipulated and used when it fits the needs of the newspaper, the newspaper is damaging the public sphere more than helping it. Public deliberation is not something to be turned on and off whenever it meets the need of a supporting institution. It needs to be nurtured.

A press that truly seeks to activate the public approaches the audience not as consumers but as citizens. The goal is to make public discussion meaningful for people, to show them that they can have some impact on the system. A press that is interested in public input creates opportunities for the formation of public opinion through public discussion. It doesn't lead the discussion but allows it to proceed and develop on its own. The mission of the press changes from concerns about being a good professional to being a good citizen.[34]

While promoting an active public is central to the realization of discourse democracy, it is not enough. The press also needs to understand the important role it plays in the creation of public meaning. It needs to understand the sociology of the news and how news not only aids in the establishment of meaning but also limits the creation of meaning. Just as the law hates ambiguity, so does journalism.[35] Rather than providing the raw material that enables citizens to figure out what events mean for them, journalism too often attempts to provide a single authoritative account of an event. This helps to ensure the power and influence of its voice within the community, but it also can distance the press from a community, such as when the press's interpretation differs significantly from public interpretations. Journalism often re-tells a story through its own lens, which is heavily influenced by corporate values. So, for example, when the press reports on stories about shopping malls, we get a lot of information on the business of malls, such as how popular they are, what new stores are opening, and how disturbances might hurt business. We don't get an understanding of how or why people use shopping malls or what the development of shopping malls means to the formation of democracy. In other words, the business of malls dominates the culture of malls in public discourse.

John J. Pauly has suggested that today's journalism would benefit by following the lead of the New Journalism movement of the 1960s, which focused less on an idealized version of democracy than on "politics and culture as it found them."[36] Pauly argues that the public needs the ability to tell and have access to the stories that are central to their lives.[37] What is needed is a more diverse type of journalism that goes beyond simply providing information. The press needs to open its pages to different ways of telling stories and different types of storytellers. The story of public life cannot always be told in a one-minute television segment, nor can it be captured in a highly formalized style of writing that emphasizes who, what, when, where, why, and how. People need to be able to tell their own stories and to be able to create their own meaning from the events that shape their world. In short, the press needs to break free of its routinized, rationalized world.

In that same vein, the press can play an important role in the protection of public space. Public space is more than parks and streets but also includes venues that have been traditionally opened for public use. Media outlets that justify their existence through their democratic mission fall into that category. While courts disagree, preferring to emphasize property rights, a newspaper or broadcast outlet is as much a public forum as any city park and ought to viewed in that manner. Admittedly this raises many questions, all of which cannot be addressed adequately here. Suffice it to say that this would not require media owners to give up all control but rather to make decisions that recognize the importance of discourse and find ways to increase discourse. Of course, this might run counter to profitability goals and might force a reevaluation of how the press is financed and organized.

Protecting public space requires the press to do more than simply open itself up to citizens, however. It also requires the press to be strong advocates in monitoring how public space is used and governed. The press ought to not only encourage the use of public space, including private places that have been generally open to the public, but also serve as sentinels to make sure that public space is used for discursive purposes. Public space should not be turned over to commercial interests, and the press can serve a vital function in monitoring that use.

And finally, the press needs to play an active role in protecting expressive association. The first three categories—promoting active citizens, valuing public meaning, and protecting public space—help achieve expressive association in important ways, but more is needed. The press needs to understand that the importance of association is not simply to make an individual's voice louder; it allows others to share ideas. The press needs to understand that within any association there are valid disagreements. Reporting about associations should display those differences not to hurt the solidarity of associations or to demonstrate some discord within them but rather to increase the range of views that come into the public sphere. Journalism too often uses associations or groups as tools for explaining social issues, such as a Democratic senator opposing a judge's nomination to the federal court because he or she is a conservative. Such labels, even if they have some validity, provide little help in understanding public life. Relying on simple political labels, the hallmarks of most political commentary today, is an efficient and easy way to explain our political world. Unfortunately, it also fails to capture the complexity of that world. It is in that complexity where we often find beliefs and values that cross the lines of association and bring the public together.

In the end, the press's mission in creating an active public is difficult and eclectic. It is at once partisan and yet open to differing views; it is a watchdog, but not elitist. In many ways, discourse democracy poses an ethical problem for society far more than it poses a legal problem. It calls on the press and the public sphere to identify ways that might enable the press to achieve those goals. C. Edwin Baker has called for substantive and procedural changes to the press to allow it to function in what he calls "complex democracy." Baker advocates a "structurally mixed system" where different economic systems and different types of media serve different needs, with government playing an important role in helping to structure that system.[38]

Government's role is important, but more is needed from the news media if democracy is to change for the better. There is a great deal of debate about the amount of corporate ownership of the media in the United States today. The Federal Communications Commission has relaxed rules restricting the number of media outlets that can be owned by any one corporation, prompting critics to call for tougher standards. The idea of corporate rationalization allows us to see that there are no quick-fix solutions to the problem presented by corporate media ownership. Restricting corporate ownership is a step in the right direction, but by itself it will do little to spark a discursive public. We must address a more fundamental question: How do we diversify the content produced by news operations that continue to be dominated by professional routines and norms? The answer will not be found by simply eliminating corporate ownership. Strategies are needed to undo the routinized, rationalized news media environment.

The public sphere needs to be "made," as Habermas writes, because "it is not 'there' anymore."[39] Journalism needs to play a different role in aiding public life. To change its mission, the press needs to move past its view of the public as something to be informed toward a view of the public as composed of citizens who can be called to public action.

The First Amendment and Discourse Democracy

While there are ways for the press to aid an active public sphere, law needs to play a supportive role in acquiring the freedoms to preserve that public sphere. Law's move away from the public sphere toward a profession that is centered on the needs of corporations and structured within corporate logic needs to be reconsidered. While commentators have noted the need to address the internal focus of the law, this section will focus on how we might retheorize First Amendment law to promote an active public sphere.

The law's interpretation of the First Amendment provides the structure for public life and the framework for thinking about public life. This framework has been evident at least since Oliver Wendell Holmes's famous articulation of the marketplace of ideas. In hindsight, it seems a strange metaphor upon which to build a democracy. Holmes's metaphor pays homage to the idea that our version of democracy is embedded in capitalism, and many would agree with this assessment. No doubt people who see corporate rationalization as a good thing would also see a democracy dedicated to supporting capitalism as a good thing. Others would argue that while it is perhaps true that democracy has become the same as capitalism, democracy should not be about making money.

As Holmes no doubt understood, markets are not inherently equal. Because of that inequality, they are also a form of social control. As Stanley Ingber has noted in his critique of the marketplace metaphor, "[I]n the United States today free speech is a device by which established interests may both refine their minor differences and promote their commonly held assumptions of truth; it is not a device to change society."[40]

Ingber's point is that the marketplace myth helps promote social stability because it is a subtle rather than an overt influence. It achieves this by turning ideological disputes into disputes about process and methodology.[41] According to Ingber, "This shift in focus screens the inherent biases of the system while it gives challengers to the status quo the impression that an avenue is open to obtain both resolution of their conflict and official support of their positions."[42]

As we saw earlier, reducing democracy to procedural issues often is used as a form of social control and a way to manage the public sphere. The law's role in shaping the idea of journalist's privilege reflects its vision of a public sphere that is incapable of representing itself. Those ideas are also reflected in public forum doctrine, where process is an overt form of social control that reduces questions of speech to questions of property.

Resisting the marketplace metaphor thus becomes an important step toward breaking the lock of corporate rationalization. Public life needs to be recognized not as a market but as a forum where reasoned discourse is the goal, where citizens seek to achieve understanding rather than expressive victory.

Envisioning an active public is the work of philosophy more than law. Institutional actors need to question the assumptions that have long governed First Amendment jurisprudence. They must understand that democratic structures should value not only the ability of citizens to receive information but what citizens do with that information. First Amendment jurisprudence needs to value not only the collection of information but also the ability of people to turn that information into action. The United States has long worried about the first part of that equation, putting into place laws that protect access to governmental meetings and information. We have worried far less about trying to figure out how people might go about turning that information into democratic action.

One of the ways that First Amendment jurisprudence has limited the action component of democracy is by limiting the ability of citizens to create meaning or, perhaps more accurately, failing to create sufficient public space for people to create their own meaning. Courts tend to view the creation of meaning through a liberal framework in which it is the audience's job to decipher a speaker's intended meaning. The work of citizens in democracy, based on that model, is comparable to that of spectators. As the U.S. Supreme Court has acknowledged, speakers need the public as an audience, but the audience's job is to receive information, not actively interpret public events. At times the Court has even seemed to suggest that messages that have a clear and unambiguous meaning—that don't too seriously tax the interpretive skills of citizens—are entitled to increased First Amendment protection. Such a legal framework does little to encourage citizens to think for themselves or engage in public discussions about the meaning of public events.

That lack of respect for public meaning making in a corporately rationalized democracy also serves as a way to manage the public sphere. The status quo is maintained by limiting the ideas that are put into the public sphere, the ability of citizens to come together to discuss those ideas, and the very possibility that alternative frameworks might be created from that discussion. As Richard Delgado and others have noted, alternative interpretations of public events are one way that disempowered groups can promote change in a democratic society.[43] Those alternative interpretations represent important discourses from voices that are often kept out of the mainstream. By treating public expression as property, something that can be owned and controlled, alternative, public interpretations are discouraged and dissent is managed. While this book has focused its critique on the public forum doctrine, much of the same analysis could be applied to copyright and intellectual property developments in the United States and the attempt by property owners—especially corporations—to control their works for longer periods of time. In important ways, this is an attempt not only to control access and profits but also to fix the meaning of a work in the public sphere.

One way to oppose this problem would be to democratize public spaces in the United States. In discourse theory, public spaces are not limited to governmental property but include public or private property that has been opened to public use. Government interference is not the sole challenge to democracy in the corporate liberal world, but powerful private groups present similarly serious challenges. As more and more of the places where fewer and fewer citizens gather are controlled by private entities, the public loses the ability to come together in places not controlled by economic concerns. While discourse theory would recognize privately owned shopping malls as public places open to public expression, the greater problem is realizing that malls are not about creating citizens but consumers. Malls are designed and configured to promote consumerism, not the exchange of ideas aimed at gaining a greater understanding among citizens. Fighting for public access to malls is a step in the right direction, but it ignores the fact that malls are not an ideal public space. They might be the new town squares, but they are town squares dominated by corporate America.

It has become increasingly difficult for disempowered groups to gain access to public space in the United States. Courts, through their use of the public forum doctrine, allow privileged, organized groups to achieve temporary ownership of public space to limit alternative public interpretations. It might be true that forcing groups to include alternative voices in their demonstrations and parades in public areas might encourage people to stop talking, to give up public expression rather than allow opinions with which they disagree. That is truly a problem for democracy. But rethinking democracy is not solely a problem for institutions but also for citizens. Citizens need to realize that closing off alternative viewpoints might temporarily allow them to achieve expressive victory, but it increasingly hinders the understanding between citizens that is central to the formation of an active public sphere.

David Kairys has noted that First Amendment rights in the United States were achieved politically long before they were achieved legally. That is, before the U.S. Supreme Court began protecting freedom of expression in 1919, citizens achieved these rights through political action. Kairys describes how workers, socialists, and other dissidents would ascend the soapbox one at a time. As each speaker was arrested and carted off to jail, another would take his or her place until the jails were full and public discourse was allowed to continue.[44] Today a different type of political action is needed. Citizens need to fight the authoritarian creation of meaning and realize that the desire to achieve expressive victory furthers the idea of corporate rationalization. Inclusion of voices with which we disagree is a radical, overtly political act in the name of discursive politics. This does not mean that citizens must be tolerant of all forms of expression. Rather, it calls on them to tolerate the types of expression that seek understanding and hope to engage in reasoned discourse. Just as the speaker seeks understanding, the person who opposes the speaker is required to be open to that form of discourse. Coercion by speaker or opponent is destructive of discourse.

Recent work on communicative ethics is central to discourse theory. Communicative ethics envisions a public ethic where citizens agree to enter discursive opportunities with the goal of trying to reach understanding. This does not mean that agreement must be achieved, nor that consensus is the logical outcome.[45] Citizens gain something by exposing themselves to alternative viewpoints, considering differing ideas, and deciding why they agree or disagree.

And finally, discourse theory recognizes a right of association. Discursive association, however, is far different from how the Court has dealt with the issue. The right to associate with others is not valuable because it gives increased power to individual voices, nor because it allows an organization to express its beliefs and identity. Such a right serves to further fragment society, to continue the corporate rationalization of public life. Discursive association recognizes the right of people to come together for the creation of public meaning. The goal is not to protect the beliefs of groups or empower individuals but to find avenues for people to exchange ideas. Discursive association is not intended to allow groups to isolate themselves from others but rather to bring people together to be exposed to differing ideas.

Fighting corporate rationalization requires the support of democratic institutions coupled with citizen activism. We need to rethink the values that guide democracy. Arguments that reduce democracy to questions of efficiency, popularity, and marketability cannot produce an active public sphere where citizens participate in their own governance. An active public sphere will not be attainable until people and institutions realize that the values that guide corporate America should not be the values that guide public life.

Notes

Introduction

1. *Abrams v. United States*, 250 U.S. 616 (1919). In his dissent, Justice Holmes wrote: "But when men have realized that time has upset many fighting faiths, they may come to believe even more than they believe the very foundations of their own conduct that the ultimate good desired is better reached by free trade in ideas—that the best test of truth is the power of the thought to get itself accepted in the competition of the market, and that truth is the only ground upon which their wishes safely can be carried out" (630).

2. Discussions of discourse democracy include John S. Dryzek, *Deliberative Democracy and Beyond: Liberals, Critics, Contestations* (New York: Oxford University Press, 2000); John S. Dryzek, *Discursive Democracy: Politics, Policy, and Political Science* (New York: Cambridge University Press, 1995); and Carlos Santiago Nino, *The Constitution of Deliberative Democracy* (New Haven, Conn.: Yale University Press, 1996).

3. See Jürgen Habermas, *The Structural Transformation of the Public Sphere: An Inquiry into a Category of Bourgeois Society,* trans. Thomas Burger (Cambridge: Massachusetts Institute of Technology Press, 1989).

4. See Ben H. Bagdikian, *The Media Monopoly,* 5th ed. (Boston: Beacon Press, 1997); Edward S. Herman and Noam Chomsky, *Manufacturing Consent: The Political Economy of the Mass Media* (New York: Pantheon, 1988); Robert W. McChesney, *Rich Media, Poor Democracy: Communication Politics in Dubious Times* (Urbana: University of Illinois Press, 1999); John McManus, *Market-Driven Journalism: Let the Citizen Beware?* (Thousand Oaks, Calif.: Sage, 1994); Herbert I. Schiller, *Culture, Inc.: The Corporate Takeover of Public Expression* (New York: Oxford University Press, 1989); Thomas Streeter, *Selling the Air: A Critique of the Policy of Commercial Broadcasting in the United States* (Chicago: University of Chicago Press, 1996); Doug Underwood, *When MBAs Rule the Newsroom: How the Marketers and Managers Are Reshaping Today's Media* (New York: Columbia University Press, 1993).

5. Internal Revenue Service, "Number of Business Income Tax Returns, by Size of Busi-

ness for Specified Income Years, 1980–2000" (May 2003), <www.irs.gov/taxstats/article/ 0,,id=96380,00/html>.

6. R. Jeffrey Lustig, *Corporate Liberalism: The Origins of Modern American Political Theory, 1890–1920* (Berkeley: University of California Press, 1982), 10.

7. Ibid.

8. Martin J. Sklar, *The Corporate Reconstruction of American Capitalism, 1890–1916: The Market, the Law, and Politics* (New York: Cambridge University Press, 1988), 13.

9. Streeter, *Selling the Air,* 40.

10. Ibid., 41.

11. Lustig, *Corporate Liberalism,* xii.

12. James Boyd White, *When Words Lose Their Meaning: Constitutions and Reconstitutions of Language, Character, and Community* (Chicago: University of Chicago Press, 1984), 266.

13. White, *Justice as Translation: An Essay in Cultural and Legal Criticism* (Chicago: University of Chicago Press, 1990), 202.

14. White, *When Words Lose Their Meaning,* 15.

15. Ibid., 264.

16. White, *Justice as Translation,* 180.

17. Quoted in Seyla Benhabib, *Critique, Norm, and Utopia: A Study of the Foundations of Critical Theory* (New York: Columbia University Press, 1986), 3.

18. See, for example, Michael Walzer, "A Critique of Philosophical Conversation," *Philosophical Forum* 21 (Fall–Winter 1989–90): 182–203.

19. White, *Justice as Translation,* 102.

20. *First National Bank of Boston v. Bellotti,* 435 U.S. 765 (1978).

21. Lustig, *Corporate Liberalism,* 193.

Chapter 1: The Rise of Corporate Rationalization

1. Alexis de Tocqueville, *Democracy in America,* trans. and ed. Harvey C. Mansfield and Delba Winthrop (Chicago: University of Chicago Press, 2000), 530–32.

2. Robert W. McChesney, *Rich Media, Poor Democracy: Communication Politics in Dubious Times* (Urbana: University of Illinois Press, 1999), 2.

3. See David Pearce Demers, *The Menace of the Corporate Newspaper: Fact or Fiction?* (Ames: Iowa State University Press, 1996).

4. Quoted in John B. Judis, *The Paradox of American Democracy* (New York: Pantheon, 2002), 243.

5. Tocqueville, *Democracy in America,* 542.

6. Lawrence M. Friedman, *A History of American Law,* 2d ed. (New York: Simon and Schuster, 1985), 188.

7. Ibid., 189.

8. Ibid., 190.

9. Ibid., 194.

10. Ibid., 195.

11. *Dartmouth College v. Woodward,* 17 U.S. 518 (1819).

12. Alfred H. Kelly, Winfred A. Harbison, and Herman Belz, *The American Constitution: Its Origins and Development*, 6th ed. (New York: W. W. Norton, 1983), 199.

13. *Santa Clara County v. Southern Pacific Railroad*, 118 U.S. 394 (1886).

14. Ibid., 396.

15. Morton J. Horwitz, "*Santa Clara* Revisited: The Development of Corporate Theory," *West Virginia Law Review* 88 (1985): 174.

16. Ron Chernow, *Titan: The Life of John D. Rockefeller Sr.* (New York: Vintage Books, 1998), 148.

17. Quoted in ibid.

18. Ibid., 297.

19. Robert H. Wiebe, *Self-Rule: A Cultural History of American Democracy* (Chicago: University of Chicago Press, 1995), 296.

20. Ibid., 296-97.

21. Ibid., 297.

22. Frederick Winslow Taylor, *The Principles of Scientific Management* (New York: Harper, 1911), 36.

23. Ibid., 38.

24. Ibid., 64.

25. Ibid., 21.

26. Ibid., 140.

27. Daniel Nelson, *Frederick W. Taylor and the Rise of Scientific Management* (Madison: University of Wisconsin Press, 1980), 168.

28. David Harvey, *The Condition of Postmodernity* (Cambridge, Mass.: Blackwell, 1990), 125-26.

29. Ibid., 126.

30. Nelson, *Frederick W. Taylor*, 186.

31. Ibid., 174-75.

32. Antonio Gramsci, *Selections from the Prison Notebooks*, trans. and ed. Quinton Hoare and Geoffrey Nowell Smith (New York: International Publishers, 1971), 303.

33. Robert H. Wiebe, *The Search for Order, 1877-1920* (New York: Hill and Wang, 1967).

34. Wiebe, *Self-Rule*, 166.

35. Ibid., 164.

36. Ibid., 177-78.

37. Ibid., 166.

38. Martin J. Sklar, *The Corporate Reconstruction of American Capitalism, 1890-1916: The Market, the Law, and Politics* (New York: Cambridge University Press, 1988), 29.

39. Wiebe, *Self-Rule*, 147.

40. Ibid., 149.

41. Thomas L. Haskell, *The Emergence of Professional Social Science: The American Social Science Association and the Nineteenth-Century Crisis of Authority* (Urbana: University of Illinois Press, 1977), 238.

42. Louis Menand, *The Metaphysical Club: A Story of Ideas in America* (New York: Farrar, Straus, and Giroux, 2001), 193-94.

43. R. Jeffrey Lustig, *Corporate Liberalism: The Origins of Modern American Political Theory, 1890–1920* (Berkeley: University of California Press, 1982), 173.

44. Walter Lippmann, *Drift and Mastery: An Attempt to Diagnose the Current Unrest* (New York: M. Kennerley, 1914).

45. Stuart Ewen, *PR! A Social History of Spin* (New York: Basic Books, 1996), 64.

46. Ewen, *Captains of Consciousness: Advertising and the Social Roots of the Consumer Culture* (New York: McGraw-Hill, 1976), 15.

47. Ibid., 197.

48. Wiebe, *Self-Rule*, 197.

49. Roland Marchand, *Creating the Corporate Soul: The Rise of Public Relations and Corporate Imagery in American Big Business* (Berkeley: University of California Press, 1998), 362.

50. Ewen, *Captains of Consciousness*, 89.

51. Thorstein Veblen, *The Theory of the Leisure Class: An Economic Study of Institutions* (New York: The Modern Library, 1934).

52. T. J. Jackson Lears, "From Salvation to Self-Realization: Advertising and the Therapeutic Roots of the Consumer Movement, 1880–1930," in *The Culture of Consumption: Critical Essays in American History, 1880–1980*, ed. Richard Wightman Fox and T. J. Jackson Lears (New York: Pantheon, 1983), 5.

53. Kevin Mattson, *Creating a Democratic Public: The Struggle for Urban Participatory Democracy during the Progressive Era* (University Park: Pennsylvania State University Press, 1998), 10.

54. Ibid., 11.

Chapter 2: Corporate Rationalization and Discourse Democracy

1. For a description of Weber's different forms of rationalization, see Stephen Kalberg, "Max Weber's Types of Rationality: Cornerstones for the Analysis of Rationalization Processes in History," *American Journal of Sociology* 85 (March 1980): 1145–79.

2. Ibid., 1158.

3. George Ritzer, *The McDonaldization of Society: New Century Edition* (Thousand Oaks, Calif.: Pine Forge Press, 2000).

4. Kalberg, "Max Weber's Types," 1158.

5. Ritzer, *McDonaldization of Society*, 11–16.

6. Seyla Benhabib, *Critique, Norm, and Utopia: A Study of the Normative Foundations of Critical Theory* (New York: Columbia University Press, 1986), 229–30.

7. Ibid., 230.

8. Ritzer, *McDonaldization of Society*, 39.

9. Apparently Gruen realized his mistake late in life. Before his death, he said of the shopping malls he helped create, "'I refuse to pay alimony to those bastard developments.'" Quoted in Eric Nelson, *Mall of America: Reflections of a Virtual Community* (Lakeville, Minn.: Galde Press, 1998), 50.

10. Ibid., 91.

11. Herbert Schiller, *Culture, Inc.* (New York: Oxford University Press, 1989), 89.

12. Richard Bernstein, *Habermas and Modernity* (Cambridge: Massachusetts Institute of Technology Press, 1985), 25.

13. The distinction was first introduced in Jürgen Habermas, *Legitimation Crisis*, trans. Thomas McCarthy (Boston: Beacon Press, 1975).

14. Jürgen Habermas, *The Theory of Communicative Action: Reason and Rationalization of Society*, trans. Thomas McCarthy (Boston: Beacon Press, 1981), 12–13.

15. James Bohman, "'System' and 'Lifeworld': Habermas and the Problem of Holism," *Philosophy and Social Criticism* 15 (1989): 387.

16. See Jürgen Habermas, "The Public Sphere," in *Jürgen Habermas on Society and Politics: A Reader*, ed. Steven Seidman, (Boston: Beacon Press, 1989), 231. It is important to note that Habermas sees a qualitative difference between today's common usage of the term "public opinion" and his idea of public opinion: "Public opinion is not representative in the statistical sense. It is not an aggregate of individually gathered, privately expressed opinion held by isolated persons. . . . Political opinion polls provide a certain reflection of 'public opinion' only if they have been preceded by a focused public debate and a corresponding opinion-formation in a mobilized public sphere" (Habermas, *Theory of Communicative Action: Reason*, 362). For Habermas, the public sphere is the "social space generated in communicative action," a "network for communicating information and points of view . . . ; the streams of communication are, in the process, filtered and synthesized in such a way that they coalesce into bundles of topically specified *public* opinions" (360).

17. Habermas, *The Theory of Communicative Action: Lifeworld and System*, trans. Thomas McCarthy (Boston: Beacon Press, 1987), 153–55.

18. Ibid., 63.

19. Habermas, "Public Sphere," 286.

20. "[I]t is not the emergence of the differentiated political and economic subsystems and their internal coordination through system integration that produces the 'loss of freedom,' but rather the penetration of an already modernized lifeworld by their logic, prompted by the selective pattern of institutionalization." Jean L. Cohen and Andrew Arato, *Civil Society and Political Theory* (Cambridge: Massachusetts Institute of Technology Press, 1995), 448.

21. Habermas, *Theory of Communicative Action: Reason*, 286.

22. Ibid., 305.

23. Ibid., 325.

24. Ibid., 305.

25. Thomas Streeter has made a similar argument in terms of media policy issues in the United States. See Thomas Streeter, *Selling the Air: A Critique of the Policy of Commercial Broadcasting in the United States* (Chicago: University of Chicago Press, 1996), 113–62.

26. Habermas, *Theory of Communicative Action: Reason*, 302.

27. Ibid., 325.

28. Bohman, "'System' and 'Lifeworld,'" 381–82.

29. Habermas, *Between Facts and Norms: Contributions to a Discourse Theory of Law and Democracy*, trans. William Rehg (Cambridge: Massachusetts Institute of Technology Press, 1996), 360.

30. Ibid., 362.

31. Ibid.

32. See Oskar Negt and Alexander Kluge, *Public Sphere and Experience: Toward an Analysis of the Bourgeois and Proletarian Public Sphere*, trans. Peter Labanyi, Jamie Owen Daniel, and Assenka Oksiloff (Minneapolis: University of Minnesota Press, 1993).

33. See Nancy Fraser, *Unruly Practices* (Minneapolis: University of Minnesota Press, 1989).

34. See Negt and Kluge, *Public Sphere and Experience*.

35. See Kenneth Baynes, "Democracy and the Rechtsstaat: Habermas's Faktizitat und Geltung," in *The Cambridge Companion to Habermas*, ed. Stephen K. White (New York: Cambridge University Press, 1995), 210.

36. Habermas, *Between Facts and Norms*, 282.

37. Ibid.

38. Baynes, "Democracy and the Rechtsstaat," 212.

39. Habermas, *Between Facts and Norms*, 122–23.

40. Ibid., 442.

41. Ibid.

42. Ibid., 445.

43. Ibid., 449.

44. Ibid., 442.

45. It should be noted that Habermas is not advocating a form of direct democracy: "[T]he communication structures of the public sphere *relieve* the public *of the burden of decision making;* the postponed decisions are reserved for the institutionalized political process" (ibid., 362).

46. For the distinction between negative and positive rights, see Isaiah Berlin, *Two Concepts of Liberty* (New York: Oxford University Press, 1958).

47. Cohen and Arato, *Civil Society and Political Theory*, 253.

48. See, for example, Thomas G. Goodnight, "The Personal, Technical, and Public Sphere of Argument: A Speculative Inquiry into the Art of Public Deliberation," *Journal of the American Forensic Association* 18 (Spring 1982): 214–27. This is also central to the arguments that ground the public journalism movement in the United States. For a good review of these ideas, see Theodore L. Glasser, ed., *The Idea of Public Journalism* (New York: Guilford, 1999).

49. Paul F. Lazarsfeld and Robert K. Merton, "Mass Communication, Popular Taste, and Organized Social Action," in *The Process and Effects of Mass Communication*, rev. ed., ed. William Schramm and Donald F. Roberts (Urbana: University of Illinois Press, 1977), 554–78. Evidence of corporate rationalization can be found in other forms of mass communication research. For example, Jesse Delia notes that mass communication in the Lazarsfeld tradition sought to single out individuals for study: "[T]he notion of the audience as atomistic, as consisting of disparate and independent individuals, is in general harmony with the research practices of many early mass communication researchers and became progressively more accepted with the shift to survey and marketing research methods." Jesse Delia, "Communication Research: A History," in *Handbook of Communication Science*, ed. Charles R. Berger and Steven H. Chaffee (Beverly Hills, Calif.: Sage, 1987), 67.

50. James Lemert has argued that this is particularly evident in the way the mass media discourage political participation, except in the area of voting. Part of this is due to journalists ignoring information that would spark participation, or what Lemert calls "mobilizing information." Journalists downplay mobilizing information, according to Lemert, because they perceive it as partisan. They believe it is dull information and that reporters are more concerned about analyzing public issues than what citizens can do about those issues. James Lemert, *Does Mass Communication Change Public Opinion after All?* (Chicago: Nelson-Hall, 1981), 93–139.

51. Walter Benjamin, *Illuminations,* ed. Hannah Arendt, trans. Harry Zohn (New York: Schocken Books, 1968), 88–89.

52. Compare the Court's decisions in *Zemel v. Rusk,* 381 U.S. 1 (1965), to *Lamont v. Postmaster General,* 381 U.S. 381 (1965). I discuss these cases in "The Supreme Court and the Creation of an (In)active Public Sphere," in *Freeing the First Amendment: Critical Perspectives on Freedom of Expression,* ed. David S. Allen and Robert Jensen (New York: New York University Press, 1995), 93–113.

53. Hannah Arendt, *The Human Condition* (Chicago: University of Chicago Press, 1958), 176.

54. *Gompers v. Bucks Stove and Range Co.,* 221 U.S. 418 (1911).

55. Thomas I. Emerson, *The System of Freedom of Expression* (New York: Random House, 1970), 8.

56. Ibid., 85–89.

57. This point is made by Michael Margolis, "Democracy: American Style," in *Democratic Theory and Practice,* ed. Graeme Duncan (Cambridge: Cambridge University Press, 1983), 117.

58. Arendt, *Human Condition,* 52–53.

59. For an analysis of the relationship between these concepts, see Robert Jensen, "First Amendment Potluck," *Communication Law and Policy* 3 (Autumn 1998): 563–88.

60. Jürgen Habermas, *The Structural Transformation of the Public Sphere: An Inquiry into a Category of Bourgeois Society,* trans. Thomas Burger (Cambridge: Massachusetts Institute of Technology Press, 1989), 159.

61. Jon Elster, "The Market and the Forum: Three Varieties of Political Theory," in *Deliberative Democracy,* ed. James Bohman and William Rehg (Cambridge: Massachusetts Institute of Technology Press, 1997), 26.

62. John Milton, *Areopagitica* (Cambridge: Cambridge University Press, 1918), 58.

63. *Abrams v. United States,* 250 U.S. 616 (1919), 22.

64. I am accepting the idea that discourse takes place in the marketplace of ideas for the sake of this argument alone. Discourse legal theory would challenge the claim that anything resembling discourse takes place when we envision, even rhetorically, speech as taking the form of a marketplace. This is most obvious in Habermas's ideas of the public sphere.

65. It should be noted that this framework does not coincide with Habermas's thought in some ways. For Habermas, the end is the achievement of some universal understanding of how people ought to live their lives. Critics such as Seyla Benhabib, however, call for making the discourse an end in itself: "It is not the *result* of the process of moral judg-

ment alone that counts but the process for the attainment of such judgment." Seyla Benhabib, "Afterword: Communicative Ethics and Current Controversies in Practical Philosophy," in *The Communicative Ethics Controversy*, ed. Seyla Benhabib and Fred Dallmayr (Cambridge: Massachusetts Institute of Technology Press, 1990), 345.

66. Lustig, *Corporate Liberalism*, 118.

67. As Holmes wrote in his dissent in *Abrams*, "Now nobody can suppose that the sur-
reptitious publishing of a silly leaflet by an unknown man, without more, would present
any immediate danger that its opinions would hinder the success of the government arms
or have any appreciable tendency to do so." *Abrams v. United States*, 250 U.S. 616 (1919), 628.
He labeled the writings of Abrams and his colleagues "poor and puny anonymities" (629).

68. Lustig, *Corporate Liberalism*, 120.

69. See Stuart Ewen, *PR! A Social History of Spin* (New York: Basic Books, 1996); and
Murray Edelman, *Constructing the Political Spectacle* (Chicago: University of Chicago
Press, 1988).

70. See, for example, *Virginia State Board of Pharmacy v. Virginia Citizens Consumer Coun-
cil*, 425 U.S. 748 (1976); *Bates v. State Bar of Arizona*, 433 U.S. 360 (1977); *Boldger v. Youngs
Drug Prod. Corp.*, 463 U.S. 60 (1983); *Central Hudson Gas and Elec. Corp. v. Public Service
Comm'n*, 447 U.S. 557 (1980); and *Cincinnati v. Discovery Network*, 113 Sup. Ct. 1505 (1993).

71. Cass Sunstein, "Free Speech Now," *University of Chicago Law Review* 59 (Winter
1992): 264.

72. Ibid., 266.

73. For a critique of the idea of markets and property, especially the role it plays in
helping to determine broadcast policy, see Streeter, *Selling the Air*, 163–216.

74. Sunstein, "Free Speech Now," 266. See also *Lloyd Corp. v. Tanner*, 407 U.S. 551 (1972);
and *Hudgens v. NLRB*, 424 U.S. 507 (1976).

75. See Sunstein, "Free Speech Now," 272. See also *CBS v. Democratic National Committee*, 412 U.S. 94 (1973); and *Arkansas Educational Television Commission v. Forbes*, 523
U.S. 666 (1998).

76. John Fiske, *Reading the Popular* (Boston: Unwin Hyman, 1989).

77. Douglas Kellner, *Media and Culture* (New York: Routledge, 1995), 37.

78. Ibid.

79. Habermas, *Theory of Communicative Action: Reason*, 275.

80. Ibid., 276–77.

81. Antonin Scalia, "Originalism: The Lesser Evil," *University of Cincinnati Law Review*
57 (1989): 864.

82. *Arkansas Educational Television Commission v. Forbes*, 523 U.S. 666 (1998).

83. *Spence v. Washington*, 418 U.S. 405 (1974), 410.

84. Ibid., 410–11.

85. *West Virginia State Board of Education v. Barnette*, 319 U.S. 624 (1943), 632–33. Perhaps the Court's acceptance of an open meaning of the American flag is tied directly to
the lack of a clear, accepted idea of what the flag actually means. There is no individual
or single group that has the power to establish its meaning.

86. *CBS v. Democratic National Committee*, 412 U.S. 94 (1973).

87. See, for example, *Buckley v. Valeo*, 424 U.S. 1 (1976) (per curiam).

88. The Court has long distinguished between types of public-owned property in determining how much expressive activity is permitted on that property and the government's role in controlling that expressive activity. See Harry Kalven Jr., "The Concept of the Public Forum: *Cox v. Louisiana*," *Supreme Court Review* 1 (1965): 1–32; and Robert C. Post, *Constitutional Domains: Democracy, Community, Management* (Cambridge, Mass.: Harvard University Press, 1995).

89. Joshua Cohen, "Freedom of Expression," *Philosophy and Public Affairs* 22 (Summer 1993): 247. Owen Fiss makes a similar argument in *Liberalism Divided* (Boulder, Colo.: Westview, 1996), 49.

90. *Pruneyard Shopping Center v. Robbins*, 447 U.S. 74 (1980).

91. Ibid., 81.

92. Sunstein, "Free Speech Now," 309. Sunstein writes, "[I]f no one sees the political content, it is hard to understand why the speech should be allowed" (304).

93. Habermas, *Between Facts and Norms*, 368.

94. Ibid., 369.

95. Ibid., 370.

96. *Roberts v. United States Jaycees*, 468 U.S. 609 (1984), 619.

97. Ibid., 618–20. See also Madhavi Sunder, "Cultural Dissent," *Stanford Law Review* 54 (December 2001): 538.

98. *Boy Scouts of America v. Dale*, 530 U.S. 640 (2000), 647.

99. Daniel Farber, "Speaking in the First Person Plural: Expressive Associations and the First Amendment," *Minnesota Law Review* 85 (June 2001): 1495.

100. *Roberts v. United States Jaycees*, 468 U.S. 609 (1984), 633–34.

101. See Cohen and Arato, *Civil Society and Political Theory;* and Stanley Ingber, "The First Amendment, Intermediate Institutions, and a Democratic Personality," *Valparaiso University Law Review* 26 (Fall 1991): 71–88.

102. Habermas, *Between Facts and Norms*, 442.

103. Ibid., 378.

104. Ibid., 280. On the role of the courts, Habermas writes: "The court may not assume the role of a regent who takes the gaze of a robust legal public sphere—a citizenry that has grown to become a 'community of constitutional interpreters'—the constitutional court can at best play the role of a tutor" (280).

105. Ibid., 378.

106. Ibid., 379.

107. Ibid.

108. Habermas, *Structural Transformation*, 209.

109. Quoted in Stephen K. White, *The Recent Work of Jürgen Habermas: Reason, Justice, and Modernity* (Cambridge: Cambridge University Press, 1988), 117.

Chapter 3: Professionalization of the Press and Law

1. Walter Lippmann, *Public Opinion* (New York: Free Press, 1965), 233.

2. James W. Carey, "Reconceiving 'Mass' and 'Media,'" in *Communication as Culture: Essays on Media and Society* (Boston: Unwin Hyman, 1988), 78.

3. Lippmann, *Public Opinion*, 212.

4. Carey, "Reconceiving 'Mass' and 'Media,'" 78.

5. Eliot Freidson, *Professional Powers: A Study of the Institutionalization of Formal Knowledge* (Chicago: University of Chicago Press, 1986), 21.

6. Ibid.

7. Ibid., 22.

8. Ibid., 24.

9. Ibid., 23.

10. Magali Sarfatti Larson, *The Rise of Professionalism: A Sociological Analysis* (Berkeley: University of California Press, 1977), 4–5.

11. For example, all of the thirteen contemporary professions listed by Harold L. Wilensky formed professional associations between 1840 and 1897. See Harold L. Wilensky, "The Professionalization of Everyone?" *American Journal of Sociology* 70 (Sept. 1964): 143. Further evidence is provided by Burton J. Bledstein, who notes that during those same years, specialization within the medical profession led to the creation of ten new professional associations. See Burton J. Bledstein, *The Culture of Professionalism: The Middle Class and the Development of Higher Education in America* (New York: Norton, 1976), 85.

12. Andrew Abbott, *The System of Professions: An Essay on the Division of Expert Labor* (Chicago: University of Chicago Press, 1988), 4. Most nonhistorical studies on the profession of journalism tend to follow this approach. For example, see Randal A. Beam, "Journalism Professionalism as an Organizational-Level Concept," *Journalism Monographs* 121 (June 1990): 1–43; Bruce Garrison and Michael Salwen, "Professional Orientations of Sports Journalists," *Newspaper Research Journal* 10 (1989): 77–84; Karl A. Idsvoog and James L. Hoyt, "Professionalism and Performance of Television Journalists," *Journal of Broadcasting* 21 (1977): 97–109; Jack McLeod and Searle H. Hawley Jr., "Professionalization among Newsmen," *Journalism Quarterly* 41 (Fall 1964): 529–39; David Weaver and G. Cleveland Wilhoit, *The American Journalist: A Portrait of U.S. News People and Their Work* (Bloomington: Indiana University Press, 1986); Donald S. Weinthal and Garrett J. O'Keefe, "Professionalization among Broadcast Newsmen in an Urban Area," *Journal of Broadcasting* 18 (1974): 193–209; Swen Windahl and Karl Erik Rosengren, "Newsmen's Professionalization: Some Methodological Problems," *Journalism Quarterly* 55 (1978): 466–73.

13. Abbott, *System of Professions*, 5.

14. Larson, *Rise of Professionalism*, xii–xiii.

15. Ibid., 116.

16. Ibid., 117.

17. Ibid., 134.

18. Ibid., 133–34.

19. Ibid., 140.

20. Ibid., 142.

21. Ibid., 145. Some have referred to this as "new class theory," where members of the bureaucracy have become a new social class. For a review of literature in this area, see Freidson, *Professional Powers*, 42–60.

22. Larson, *Rise of Professionalism*, 227.

23. Bledstein, *Culture of Professionalism*, xi.

24. Ibid., 105.

25. Ibid., 101.

26. Ibid., 102.

27. Abbott, *System of Professions*, 59.

28. Ibid., 62–63.

29. Ibid., 64.

30. Ibid., 60.

31. Ibid.

32. Ibid., 88.

33. Ibid.

34. Ibid., 70–71.

35. Ibid., 135.

36. Thomas E. Patterson, "Irony of the Free Press: Professional Journalism and News Diversity" (paper delivered at the annual meeting of the American Political Science Association, September 3–6, 1992, Chicago). See also Thomas E. Patterson, *Out of Order* (New York: Knopf, 1993).

37. Stephen A. Banning, "'Truth Is Our Ultimate Goal': A Mid-Nineteenth-Century Concern for Journalism Ethics," *American Journalism* 16 (Winter 1999): 17–39.

38. Hazel Dicken-Garcia, *Journalistic Standards in Nineteenth-Century America* (Madison: University of Wisconsin Press, 1989), 257.

39. ASNE's code of ethics has a colorful history. Shortly after approving the code of ethics, ASNE began an investigation of the publisher of the *Denver Post*, Frederick G. Bonfils, and his connection with the Teapot Dome scandal. After a three-year investigation and Bonfils's threats to sue the organization for slander, Bonfils resigned from ASNE, and it agreed to drop the investigation. According to one ASNE member, the case established for all time that "'ASNE did not have the muscle and lacked the authority to punish anyone.'" Quoted in Alice Fox Pitts, *Read All about It! Fifty Years of ASNE* (Easton, Penn.: American Society of Newspaper Editors, 1974), 30.

40. For views on the subject that differ widely, see, for example, Edwin Emery and Michael B. Emery, *The Press and America: An Interpretive History of the Mass Media* (Englewood Cliffs, N.J: Prentice Hall, 1984); David T. Z. Mindich, *Just the Facts: How 'Objectivity' Came to Define American Journalism* (New York: New York University Press, 1998); Frank Luther Mott, *American Journalism: A History of Newspapers in the United States* (New York: MacMillan, 1950); Dan Schiller, *Objectivity and the News: The Public and Rise of Commercial Journalism* (Philadelphia: University of Pennsylvania Press, 1981); and Michael Schudson, *Discovering the News: A Social History of American Newspapers* (New York: Harper, 1978).

41. Dan Schiller, "An Historical Approach to Objectivity and Professionalism in American News Reporting," *Journal of Communication* 29 (Autumn 1979): 47.

42. John C. Nerone, "The Mythology of the Penny Press," *Critical Studies in Mass Communication* 4 (1987): 377.

43. Ibid., 401.

44. Ibid.

45. Douglas Birkhead, "The Power in the Image: Professionalism and the 'Communications Revolution,'" *American Journalism* 1 (Winter 1984): 1–2.

46. Quoted in Douglas Birkhead, "Presenting the Press: Journalism and the Professional Project," Ph.D. dissertation, University of Iowa, 1982, 259.

47. Birkhead, "Power in the Image," 11–12.

48. Jürgen Habermas, *The Structural Transformation of the Public Sphere: An Inquiry into a Category of Bourgeois Society,* trans. Thomas Burger (Cambridge: Massachusetts Institute of Technology Press, 1989), 185.

49. Jim Lehrer, "Returning to Our Roots," The Red Smith Lecture in Journalism (University of Notre Dame, September 2002), 17.

50. "Coverage on Home Turf," *On The Media,* National Public Radio, October 11, 2002.

51. W. Lance Bennett, *News: The Politics of Illusion,* 4th ed. (New York: Longman, 2001), 151.

52. Mark Fishman, *Manufacturing the News* (Austin: University of Texas Press, 1988), 44.

53. Ibid.

54. James W. Carey, "The Communications Revolution and the Professional Communicator," in "The Sociology of Mass Media Communicators" (special issue), ed. Paul Halmos, *The Sociological Review Monograph* (1969), 27.

55. Ibid., 28.

56. For example, see Warren Breed, "Social Control in the Newsroom," in *Mass Communications,* ed. Wilbur Schramm (Urbana: University of Illinois Press, 1960), 178–94; Fishman, *Manufacturing the News;* Robert S. Fortner, "The Journalist's Albatross: Objectivity, Critical Reporting, and Social Responsibility," *Journal of Communication Inquiry* 6 (Winter 1981): 69–85; Herbert J. Gans, *Deciding What's News: A Study of CBS Evening News, NBC Nightly News, Newsweek, and Time* (New York: Vintage Books, 1979); Mary S. Mander, "Narrative Dimensions of the News: Omniscience, Prophecy, and Morality," *Communication* 10 (1987): 51–70; John Soloski, "News Reporting and Professionalism: Some Constraints on the Reporting of the News," *Media, Culture, and Society* 11 (April 1989): 207–28; Gaye Tuchman, *Making News: A Study in the Construction of Reality* (New York: Free Press, 1978).

57. Jeffery A. Smith, *Printers and Press Freedoms: The Ideology of Early American Journalism* (New York: Oxford University Press, 1988), 162.

58. Ibid., 122–23.

59. Thomas C. Leonard, *The Power of the Press: The Birth of American Political Reporting* (New York: Oxford University Press, 1986), 56.

60. Ibid., 53.

61. Schudson, *Discovering the News,* 58.

62. Ibid., 60.

63. Schiller, *Objectivity and the News,* 10.

64. Ibid., 48.

65. Schudson, *Discovering the News,* 68–69.

66. Schiller, *Objectivity and the News,* 49.

67. Ibid., 54.

68. Ibid., 10.

69. Dicken-Garcia, *Journalistic Standards,* 107. Timothy Gleason has traced the rise of

the press's claim to watchdog status back into nineteenth-century press law. Even though judges were reluctant to grant the press that status, and to some degree remain hesitant to do so, many of those arguments have been carried over into the twentieth-century debate. Timothy Gleason, *The Watchdog Concept: The Press and the Courts in Nineteenth-Century America* (Ames: Iowa State University Press, 1990), 99.

70. For example, the sociologist Herbert J. Gans has argued that the American press's enduring values can be traced to turn-of-the-century Progressivism. See Herbert J. Gans, *Deciding What's News*, 204–6.

71. Walter Lippmann, *Liberty and the News* (New York: Harcourt, Brace, and Howe, 1920), 71. It should be noted that Lippmann apparently did see a danger in journalism becoming too professional. He noted that while "it might correct certain evils, the general tendency would be to turn the control of the news over to unenterprising stereotyped minds soaked in the traditions of a journalism always ten years out of date" (81).

72. Ibid., 75.

73. For elaboration on this point, see Schudson, *Discovering the News*, 153.

74. Ibid., 128.

75. Ibid., 129.

76. Ibid., 134.

77. Ibid., 6.

78. Christopher P. Wilson, *The Labor of Words: Literary Professionalism in the Progressive Era* (Athens: University of Georgia Press, 1985), 11–12.

79. Schudson, *Discovering the News*, 119.

80. Wilson, *Labor of Words*, 3.

81. Ibid.

82. Ibid.

83. Leonard, *Power of the Press*, 193–94.

84. Ibid., 198.

85. Ibid., 196.

86. Ibid., 202.

87. Ibid., 223.

88. Wilson, *Labor of Words*, 17.

89. James Carey, "Journalists Just Leave: The Ethics of an Anomalous Profession," in *Ethics and the Media*, ed. Maile-Gene Sagen (Iowa City: Iowa Humanities Board, 1987), 13.

90. Ibid., 16.

91. Floyd Abrams, "The Press Is Different: Reflections of Justice Stewart and the Autonomous Press," *Hofstra Law Review* 7 (Spring 1979): 591.

92. I refer to this as a "so-called right" because the existence of a public's right to know is far from clear. David M. O'Brien, in his constitutional history of the claim, writes, "There exists no historical basis for the proposition that the First Amendment was designed to guarantee to individuals and to the press an affirmative constitutional right to demand access to government facilities or materials." David M. O'Brien, *The Public's Right to Know: The Supreme Court and the First Amendment* (New York: Praeger, 1982), 53.

93. *Branzburg v. Hayes*, 408 U.S. 665 (1972), 721.

94. For a review of a right to know and its place in early constitutional debates in the

United States, see Jeffery A. Smith, *War and Press Freedom: The Problem of Prerogative Power* (New York: Oxford University Press, 1999), 30–35.

95. See "The Right to Know," *New York Times,* January 23, 1945, 18. While Cooper is given credit for the popularization of the term, the concept has a long legal and political history. For histories of the concept, see O'Brien, *Public's Right to Know;* and Peter Dennis Bathory and Wilson Carey McWilliams, "Political Theory and the People's Right to Know," in *Government Secrecy in Democracies,* ed. Itzhak Galnoor (New York: Harper Colophon Books, 1977), 1–21.

96. Kent Cooper, *The Right to Know* (New York: Farrar, Straus, and Cudahy, 1956), xii–xiii.

97. Harold L. Cross, *The People's Right to Know* (New York: Columbia University Press, 1953), 123.

98. Gleason sees it as a move towards community-based rights and argues that it "places the press in a subservient relation to the public." For Gleason, the watchdog concept provides little power to individual reporters but in effect gives the public editorial control over the press. Gleason, *Watchdog Concept,* vii.

99. While the commission, also known as the Hutchins Commission, touched on many of the themes contained in the theory, it was Theodore Peterson who brought the ideas together under the term "social responsibility theory." See Theodore Peterson, "The Social Responsibility Theory of the Press," in Fred S. Siebert, Theodore Peterson, and Wilbur Schramm, *Four Theories of the Press* (Urbana: University of Illinois Press, 1956). See especially Peterson's claim that under the social responsibility theory, the press "should safeguard the rights of the individual by serving as a watchdog against government" (74).

100. For elaboration of this point, see Jerilyn S. McIntyre, "Repositioning a Landmark: The Hutchins Commission and Freedom of the Press," *Critical Studies in Mass Communication* 4 (1987): 137. However, it should be noted that while the theory itself provides a philosophy for the press, the philosophy that grounds social responsibility theory remains a curious mix of Christian and classical humanism. See Paul Mark Fackler, "The Hutchins Commissioners and the Crisis in Democratic Theory, 1930–1947," Ph.D. dissertation, University of Illinois at Urbana-Champaign, 1981.

101. See, for example, J. Edward Gerald, *The Social Responsibility of the Press* (Minneapolis: University of Minnesota Press, 1963), 183–84. Gerald sees journalists as either leaders in their own right or as "agents for" leaders to improve society.

102. Quoted in McIntyre, "Repositioning a Landmark," 147.

103. Quoted in ibid., 148.

104. William E. Hocking, *Freedom of the Press: A Framework of Principle* (Chicago: University of Chicago Press, 1947), 199.

105. Peterson, "Social Responsibility Theory of the Press," 100.

106. William J. Miller, "What's Wrong with the Newspaper Reader," *Nieman Reports* 1 (February 1947): 2.

107. Recent work in press theory builds on Blasi's work. For example, C. Edwin Baker has noted that the watchdog theory is at the core of elitist theories of democracy, but he calls for a complex democracy that incorporates the many functions of the press, includ-

ing the watchdog function. See C. Edwin Baker, *Media, Markets, and Democracy* (Cambridge: Cambridge University Press, 2002), 129–35.

108. Vincent Blasi, "The Checking Value in First Amendment Theory," *American Bar Foundation Research Journal* (1977): 528.

109. Ibid., 541. Floyd Abrams follows much the same argument, claiming that the press is a distinct institution and thus entitled to special constitutional protection. Abrams argues that even if the press rarely fulfills its watchdog role, it is the only institution "that can serve on a continuing basis as an open eye of the public." Abrams, "Press Is Different," 592.

110. Blasi, "Checking Value," 542.

111. Ibid., 605.

112. There is a strain of this thought that gives more weight to self-government and the power of the citizenry. For example, Alexander Meiklejohn, who was influential in the thought of the former Supreme Court Justice William Brennan, attempted to design protections for speech that bear on issues important to self-governance: "What is essential is not that everyone shall speak, but that everything worth saying shall be said." See Alexander Meiklejohn, *Political Freedom* (New York: Harper and Brothers, 1960), 26. Meiklejohn has been seen as not providing enough protection for unpopular free speech and being unrealistic in his assessment of people's interest in public policy. Meiklejohn and Brennan were hindered by their inability to provide a distinction between the public and private sphere. For a discussion of this point, see Martin Edelman, *Democratic Theories and the Constitution* (Albany: State University of New York Press, 1984), 211–44.

113. Vincent Norris, for example, has described the American press as a "watchdog that nips at the heels while carefully avoiding the jugular." See Vincent Norris, "Like It or Not, the Sword Is Mightier Than the Pen," *Public Communication Review* 1 (Winter 1982): 15.

114. In C. Edwin Baker's earlier work, he acknowledges the participatory nature of speech for society, as do many First Amendment theorists, but he draws a clear distinction between press rights and speech rights. For example, Baker sees his Liberty Model as primarily concerned with protecting speech for self-fulfillment or speech that is "essential to a democratic, participatory process of change." C. Edwin Baker, "Scope of the First Amendment Freedom of Speech," *UCLA Law Review* 25 (1978): 991. Exactly what role Baker sees individuals playing in societal change, however, is unclear.

115. See, for example, Herbert Marcuse, *One-Dimensional Man* (Boston: Beacon Press, 1964). Marcuse writes: "[T]echnology also provides the great rationalization of the unfreedom of man and demonstrates the 'technical' impossibility of being autonomous, of determining one's own life. For this unfreedom appears neither as irrational nor as political, but rather as submission to the technical apparatus which enlarges the comforts of life and increases the productivity of labor. Technological rationality thus protects rather than cancels the legitimacy of domination and the instrumentalist horizon of reason opens on a rationally totalitarian society" (85).

116. For a description of how Habermas defines the distinction between purposive-rational action and social interaction, see Thomas McCarthy, *The Critical Theory of Jürgen Habermas* (Cambridge: Massachusetts Institute of Technology Press, 1988), 26.

117. Kim Lane Scheppele, "Forward: Telling Stories," *Michigan Law Review* 87 (August 1989): 2085.

118. Ronald H. Coase, "The Problem of Social Cost," *Journal of Law and Economics* 3 (1960): 1–44. Some studies have found this to be the most cited legal article. See Fred R. Shapiro, "The Most Cited Law Review Articles Revisited," *Chicago-Kent Law Review* 71 (January 1996): 767.

119. Guido Calabresi, "Some Thoughts on Risk Distribution and the Law of Torts," *Yale Law Journal* 70 (1961): 499–553.

120. Richard A. Posner, *The Economics of Justice* (Cambridge, Mass.: Harvard University Press, 1983), 66.

121. Richard A. Posner, *Economic Analysis of Law,* 2d ed. (Boston: Little, Brown, 1977), 312–13.

122. Peter J. Hammer, "Free Speech and the 'Acid Bath': An Evaluation and Critique of Judge Richard Posner's Economic Interpretation of the First Amendment," *Michigan Law Review* 87 (November 1988): 511.

123. Hand is in many ways an enigma. In 1917, he put forward a standard that is widely considered to be one of the most protective free speech standards ever set by a court. Hand wrote in *Masses Publishing Co. v. Patten,* 244 F.535 (SDNY, 1917), that speech can only be restricted by government when there is a "direct incitement to violent resistance" (540). The direct-incitement test, however, had a short life, as an appellate court overturned his *Masses* decision. Hand was also the author, some twenty-seven years later, of a far more restrictive standard. In a case deciding whether the government can punish the speech of members of the Communist Party under the Smith Act, Hand drew a careful distinction between the freedom of speech for people who work within the system and those who don't. He ruled that because the members of the Communist Party were operating outside of the system, by teaching and advocating the violent overthrow of the government, they were not entitled to protection. The result is a more restrictive version of the clear-and-present-danger test. As Hand noted, courts should determine "whether the gravity of the evil, discounted by its improbability, justifies such invasion of free speech as is necessary to avoid the danger." *United States v. Dennis,* 183 F.2d 201 (1950), 212. According to critics of such tests, Hand puts too much power in the hands of judges to try and predict future events. How do judges determine the probability of an event? The U.S. Supreme Court, however, adopted Hand's refinement. As Chief Justice Fred Vinson wrote, "More we cannot expect from words." *Dennis v. United States,* 341 U.S. 494 (1951), 502.

124. Richard A. Posner, "Free Speech in an Economic Perspective," *Suffolk University Law Review* 20 (Spring 1986): 8.

125. Posner, *Economic Analysis of Law,* 10.

126. Richard A. Posner, *The Problematics of Moral and Legal Theory* (Cambridge, Mass.: Belknap Press, 1999), 203.

127. Ibid., 206.

128. Ibid., 243–44.

129. Lawrence M. Friedman, *A History of American Law,* 2d ed., (New York: Simon and Schuster, 1985), 20.

130. Ibid., 21.

131. Ibid., 23.

132. Ibid., 97–98.

133. Ibid., 97.

134. Colin Croft, "Reconceptualizing American Legal Professionalism: A Proposal for Deliberative Moral Community," *New York University Law Review* 67 (December 1992): 1281.

135. Ibid., 1282.

136. England's Jeremy Bentham was an intellectual influence in this movement. Bentham was concerned about the clutter that had become known as the common law and supported procedural changes in the law. See Friedman, *History of American Law,* 392. Bentham also offered to help codify American law, but James Madison rejected his offer in 1816. See "Note, *Swift v. Tyson* Exhumed," *Yale Law Journal* 284 (1969): 61–73.

137. David Dudley Field, "What Shall Be Done with the Practice of the Courts," in *Law and American History: Cases and Materials,* ed. Stephen B. Presser and Jamil S. Zainaldin (St. Paul, Minn.: West, 1980), 407.

138. Friedman, *History of American Law,* 403.

139. Ibid., 397.

140. Ibid.

141. Ibid., 406.

142. Ibid., 407.

143. Field, "What Shall Be Done," 425.

144. Ibid., 426.

145. Morton J. Horwitz, "The Rise of Legal Formalism," *The American Journal of Legal History* 19 (1975): 255.

146. See David Dudley Field, "Magnitude and Importance of Legal Science," in *Law and American History: Cases and Materials,* ed. Stephen B. Presser and Jamil S. Zainaldin (St. Paul, Minn.: West, 1980), 651–56.

147. Friedman, *History of American Law,* 613.

148. Ibid., 617.

149. Horwitz, "Rise of Legal Formalism," 256.

150. Friedman, *History of American Law,* 617.

151. Larson, *Rise of Professionalism,* 169.

152. Ibid., 170.

153. Ibid., 127.

154. Ibid., 168.

155. Thomas L. Haskell, "Persons as Uncaused Causes: John Stuart Mill, the Spirit of Capitalism, and the 'Invention' of Formalism," in *The Culture of the Market: Historical Essays,* ed. Thomas L. Haskell and Richard F. Teichgraeber III (Cambridge: Cambridge University Press, 1993), 502.

156. Herbert Hovenkamp, "The Mind and Heart of Progressive Legal Thought," *Iowa Law Review* 81 (October 1995): 152.

157. See Herbert Hovenkamp, "Knowledge about Welfare: Legal Realism and the Separation of Law and Economics," *Minnesota Law Review* 84 (April 2000): 816.

158. Hovencamp, "Mind and Heart of Progressive Legal Thought," 155.

159. Ibid., 157.

160. See Wilfrid E. Rumble Jr., *American Legal Realism: Skepticism, Reform, and the Judicial Process* (Ithaca, N.Y.: Cornell University Press, 1968), 4–8. See also Philip P. Wiener, *Evolution and the Founders of Pragmatism* (Cambridge, Mass.: Harvard University Press, 1949); and Morton White, *Social Thought in America: The Revolt against Formalism* (Boston: Beacon, 1957).

161. Holmes, "Book Review (of the Second Edition of Langdell's Casebook)," *American Law Review* 14 (1880): 233–35.

162. Ibid.

163. For a description of what became known as the "Brandeis Brief," argued before the Supreme Court in *Muller v. Oregon,* 208 U.S. 412 (1908), see Alfred H. Kelly, Winfred A. Harbison, and Herman Belz, eds., *The American Constitution: Its Origins and Development,* 6th ed. (New York: W. W. Norton and Co., 1983), 456.

164. Roscoe Pound, "Law in Books and Law in Action," *American Law Review* 44 (1910): 36.

165. Rumble, *American Legal Realism,* 10.

166. Pound, "The Scope and Purpose of Sociological Jurisprudence," *Harvard Law Review* 25 (1912): 515.

167. Ibid., 467.

168. See Karl Llewellyn, "Some Realism about Realism—Responding to Dean Pound," *Harvard Law Review* 44 (1931): 1222.

169. Ibid.

170. Rumble, *American Legal Realism,* 28.

171. Jerome Frank, *Law and the Modern Mind,* 6th ed. (Gloucester, Mass.: Peter Smith, 1970), x.

172. Ibid., x–xi.

173. Ibid.

174. Ibid., xii.

175. James Boyle, "The Politics of Reason: Critical Legal Theory and Local Social Thought," *University of Pennsylvania Law Review* 133 (April 1985): 707.

176. Hovencamp, "Knowledge about Welfare," 851.

177. Ibid., 858.

178. J. M. Balkin, "Some Realism about Pluralism: Legal Realist Approaches to the First Amendment," *Duke Law Journal* 1990 (June): 381.

179. Ibid., 386.

180. Cass R. Sunstein, *Democracy and the Problem of Free Speech* (New York: Free Press, 1993), 33.

181. Haskell, "Persons as Uncaused Causes," 502.

182. Ibid., 501.

183. "Use of Profiling to Discover Would-Be Terrorist," *Morning Edition,* National Public Radio, February 12, 2002.

184. Larson, *Rise of Professionalism,* 177.

185. J. M. Balkin, "What Is Postmodern Constitutionalism?" *Michigan Law Review* 90 (June 1992): 1974.

186. Ibid.

Chapter 4: Defining a Professional Mission

1. Skip Hollandsworth, "The Inmate: Why Has Vanessa Leggett Been in Jail Longer Than Any Journalist in U.S. History? Herein Lies the True Crime," *Texas Monthly* (December 2001), <www.texasmonthly.com./mag/issues/2001–12–01/reporter.php>.

2. Ibid.

3. Amicus brief in Re: Grand Jury Subpoena to Vanessa Leggett, Reporters Committee for Freedom of the Press (October 6, 2004), <www:rcfp.org/news/documents/Leggett.html>.

4. Ibid.

5. For example, Magali Sarfatti Larson argues that average professionals are seen as possessing "cognitive superiority" that "distinguishes all of them from the laity." Magali Sarfatti Larson, *The Rise of Professionalism: A Sociological Analysis* (Berkeley: University of California Press, 1977), 47.

6. Quoted by the Associated Press in a press release by the Reporters Committee for Freedom of the Press (October 6, 2004), <http://www.rcfp.org/news/2001/0818inregr.html>.

7. For this study, ninety state and federal appellate-level cases, between 1897 and 2003, involving the issue of journalist's privilege were identified through two methods: a LexisNexis computerized search and the index of *Media Law Reporter.*

8. The Supreme Court refused to review the decision of the U.S. Court of Appeals, Second Circuit. That decision, written by Circuit Judge Potter Stewart, has been read as recognizing a qualified privilege, at least in noncivil cases, where the government must prove relevance and materiality to gain disclosure. See *Garland v. Torre,* 259 F 2d 545 (2d Cir. 1958), cert. den. 358 U.S. 910 (1958), 549–50.

9. James Brigham, *The Cult of the Court* (Philadelphia: Temple University Press, 1987), 205–6.

10. One of the few studies that has connected the idea of journalist's privilege with professionalization is Mark Osiel, "The Professionalization of Journalism: Impetus or Impediment to a 'Watchdog Press,'" *Sociological Inquiry* 56 (Spring 1986): 163–89.

11. Andrew Abbott, *The System of Professions: An Essay on the Division of Expert Labor* (Chicago: University of Chicago Press, 1988), 62–63. Abbott notes that the legal system is one of three areas where professionalization claims are made, the others being public opinion and the workplace.

12. *Branzburg v. Hayes,* 408 U.S. 665 (1972).

13. I use the phrase "little guidance" advisedly, because while the Supreme Court had not explicitly dealt with the issue of journalist's privilege prior to *Branzburg,* a great number of cases were interpreted by lower courts as influencing the question.

14. *Ex parte Nugent,* 18 Fed. Cas. 471 (D.C. Cir., 1848).

15. See, for example, *People ex rel. Phelps v. Fancher,* 2 Hun. (N.Y.) 226, 4 Thomp. and

C. 467 (Sup. Ct. N.Y., 1st Dept., 1874); and *Pledger v. State,* 77 Ga. 242, 3 S.E. 320 (Sup. Ct. Ga., 1887). In one of the earliest cases, W. F. G. Shanks, the editor of the *New York Tribune,* refused to identify the author of an article to a grand jury, claiming that it was an office regulation not to "'give the name of writers of articles published.'" Quoted by the court in *People ex rel. Phelps v. Fancher,* 468.

16. The evolving view of federal and state courts towards the press also played a role. The historian Margaret Blanchard argues that the U.S. Supreme Court has been formulating its policy on the institutional press since the late 1800s, carefully drawing a connection between speech and press by anchoring the institutional press's rights on the rights of individuals. The press began a campaign in the 1930s and 1940s to gain the Court's blessing for its role as the agent that represents the public. Margaret A. Blanchard, "The Institutional Press and Its First Amendment Privileges," in *The Supreme Court Reporter* (Chicago: University of Chicago Press, 1978), 227. Blanchard makes much the same finding in relation to state courts. See Margaret Blanchard, "Filling in the Void: Speech and Press in State Court prior to *Gitlow,*" in *First Amendment Reconsidered: New Perspectives on the Meaning of Freedom of Speech and Press,* ed. Bill F. Chamberlin and Charlene J. Brown (New York: Longman, 1982), 14–59.

17. *People v. Durrant,* 116 Calif. 179 (Sup. Ct. Calif., 1897); and *Ex Parte Lawrence,* 116 Calif. 298 (Sup. Ct. Calif., 1897).

18. Of the seventeen appellate-level, post-1900 cases identified for this study, nine came before 1960 and eight in the twelve-year period prior to the *Branzburg* ruling. An appellate-level court did not uphold a claim of journalist's privilege until 1963. *In re Taylor,* 193 A.2d 181 (Sup. Ct. Pa., 1963). This is not to say, however, that the press lost all privilege cases. Even though there was no recognition of a common law privilege, some judges refused to compel disclosure or instituted very weak penalties for failure to disclose information. See Paul Marcus, "The Reporter's Privilege: An Analysis of the Common Law, *Branzburg v. Hayes,* and Recent Statutory Developments," *Arizona Law Review* 25 (1983): 820.

19. *Plunkett v. Hamilton,* 70 S.E. 781 (Sup. Ct. Ga., 1911), 785.

20. *Ex parte Holliway,* 199 S.W. 412 (Sup. Ct. Mo., 1917), 414.

21. Ibid.

22. Quoted by the Court, *Elwell v. United States,* 275 F.772 (7th Cir., 1921), 776. Elwell continued: "'I regret that I must decline to answer the question. . . . I decline to answer, because my answer might tend to incriminate me. I regret I cannot explain how or why my answer might tend to incriminate me, because such explanations might tend to incriminate me'" (777). Of main concern to Elwell was Illinois's criminal libel statute.

23. *Clein v. State,* 52 So. 2d 117 (Sup. Ct. Fla., 1950), 118–19.

24. Ibid.

25. *In re Taylor,* 193 A.2d 181 (Sup. Ct. Pa., 1963), 183.

26. *State v. Buchanan,* 436 P.2d 729 (Sup. Ct. Ore., 1968), 730.

27. *Ex parte Lawrence,* 116 Calif. 298 (Sup. Ct. Calif., 1897), 125.

28. See *Plunkett v. Hamilton,* 70 S.E. 781 (Sup. Ct. Ga., 1911); and *Joslyn v. People,* 184 Pac. 375 (Sup. Ct. Colo., 1919), 377.

29. *In re Grunow,* 85 A. 1011 (Sup. Ct. N.J., 1913), 1012.

30. *Ex parte Holliway,* 199 S.W. 412 (Sup. Ct. Mo., 1917), 415.

31. *People ex. Rel. Mooney v. Sheriff of New York County,* 269 N.Y. 291 (Ct. App. N.Y., 1936), 416.

32. *State v. Donovan,* 129 N.J. Law 478 (Sup. Ct. N.J., 1943), 426.

33. *In re Taylor,* 193 A.2d 181 (Sup. Ct. Pa., 1963), 185.

34. Ibid.

35. *Bursey v. U.S.,* 466 F. 2d 1059 (9th Cir., 1972), 1083–84.

36. *State v. Knops,* 183 N.W. 2d 93 (Sup. Ct., Wis., 1971), 98–99.

37. Maurice Van Gerpen argues that the social unrest of the 1960s and 1970s caused more subpoenas to be issued seeking information that the press possessed, thus bringing the privilege issue to the forefront. In addition, the privilege debate was spurred in the early 1970s by greater television coverage of events that created government's desire for access to the film and the press's increasing resistance to cooperating with government, especially presubpoena requests for evidence. Maurice Van Gerpen, *Privilege Communication and the Press,* (Westport, Conn.: Greenwood, 1979), 29–30.

38. *Branzburg v. Pound,* 461 S.W.2d 345 (Ct. App. Ky., 1970).

39. *In re Pappas,* 266 N.E.2d 297 (Sup. Ct. Mass., 1971).

40. *United States v. Caldwell,* 434 F.2d 1059 (9th Cir., 1972).

41. Justice Douglas's dissenting opinion is not included in this study. While interesting, it has generally been unable to attract support from lower courts.

42. Paul Marcus has called Justice White's opinion "a disappointment" and Justice Powell's concurring opinion "confusing." Justice Powell seems to agree with Justice Stewart's dissent, yet he voted with Justice White. Marcus, "Reporter's Privilege," 829–31.

43. *Branzburg v. Hayes,* 408 U.S. 665 (1972), 681.

44. Ibid., 695.

45. Ibid., 692.

46. Ibid., 695.

47. Ibid.

48. Ibid., 697–98.

49. Ibid., 707.

50. Ibid., 709.

51. Ibid., 710.

52. Ibid.

53. Ibid.

54. Ibid., 725.

55. Ibid.

56. Ibid., 746.

57. Ibid.

58. Ibid., 726–27.

59. Ibid., 729.

60. Ibid., 738.

61. Ibid., 733.

62. Ibid., 739.

63. See *CBS v. Superior Court*, 4 Med. L. Rptr. 1569 (Ct. App. Calif., 1st Dist., 1978), 1573. Even though the court ruled that neither right is "entitled per se to precedence," it ordered CBS to turn over tapes of an undercover drug arrest for *in camera* review.

64. See, for example, *In re Farber*, 4 Med. L. Rptr. 1360 (Sup. Ct. N.J., 1978); *Grand Forks Herald v. District Court*, 8 Med. L. Rptr. 2269 (Sup. Ct. N.D., 1982); *Tofani v. Maryland*, 9 Med. L. Rptr. 2193 (Ct. App. Md., 1983); *Beach v. Shanley*, 9 Med. L. Rptr. 1991 (Sup. Ct. N.Y., 3d Dept., 1983); *In re Grand Jury Proceedings*, 810 F.2d 580 (6th Cir., 1987); *Delaney v. Los Angeles Superior Court*, 15 Med. L. Rptr. 1815 (Ct. App. Calif., 2d Dist., 1988); and *In re Letellier*, 578 A.2d 722 (Sup. Jud. Ct. Me., 1990).

65. *Beach v. Shanley*, 9 Med. L. Rptr. 1991 (Sup. Ct. N.Y., 3rd Dept., 1983), 1993.

66. *New York v. LeGrand*, 4 Med. L.Rptc. 2524 (Sup. Ct. N.Y., App. Div., 1979), 2526.

67. Ibid., 2528.

68. Ibid., 2527. In 1993, the U.S. Court of Appeals for the Ninth Circuit followed much the same logic in denying protection to a Washington State University doctoral student. The student, who had written articles and a book on the environmental movement, had refused to testify before a grand jury investigating damage to the university's animal research laboratories. The suspect believed to be responsible for the damage had been staying at the student's house. The court not only refused to recognize him as a journalist but also refused to recognize a First Amendment protection in these circumstances. *In re Grand Jury Proceedings*, 5 F.3d 397 (1993).

69. *Reporters Committee for Freedom of the Press v. AT&T*, 593 F.2d 1030 (D.C. Cir., 1978), 1049.

70. *U.S. v. Cuthbertson*, 630 F.2d 139 (3d Cir., 1980).

71. *Tofani v. Maryland*, 9 Med. L. Rptr. 2193 (Ct. App. Md., 1983), 2203.

72. *In re Letellier*, 578 A.2d 722 (Sup. Jud. Ct. Me., 1990), 727.

73. *In re Haden-Guest*, 5 Med. L. Rptr. 2361 (Sup. Ct. N.Y., Bronx County, 1980), 2361.

74. *Reporters Committee for Freedom of the Press v. AT&T*, 593 F.2d 1030 (D.C. Cir., 1978), 1062.

75. *U.S. v. Cuthbertson*, 630 F.2d 139 (3d Cir., 1980), 1981; *Wisconsin ex rel. Green Bay Newspaper v. Circuit Court, Branch 1*, 9 Med. L. Rptr. 1889 (Sup. Ct. Wis., 1983), and *In re Special Grand Jury Investigation*, 11 Med. L. Rptr. 1142 (Sup. Ct. Ill., 1984).

76. *U.S. v. Criden*, 633 F.2d (3d Cir., 1980), 346.

77. *Hammarley v. Superior Court*, 4 Med. L. Rptr. 2055 (Ct. App. Calif., 3d Dist., 1979).

78. *U.S. v. Criden*, 633 F.2d (3d Cir., 1980), 356.

79. Pashman dissent, *In re Farber*, 4 Med. L. Rptr. 1360 (Sup. Ct. N.J., 1978), 1371.

80. *Delaney v. Superior Court*, 50 Calif. 3d 785 (Sup. Ct. Calif., 1990), 808. The court quotes approvingly from the ballot argument for the California shield law. In this case, even though the court recognized the privilege of the reporter to protect eyewitness information, it used a variation of Stewart's test to determine that the information would aid in the defendant's defense and ruled that the information must be produced.

81. *In re Rutti*, 5 Med. L. Rptr. 1513 (Ct. App. Ohio, 5th Dist., 1979), 1515.

82. *In re Vrazo*, 6 Med. L. Rptr. 2410 (Sup. Ct. N.J., Camden County, 1980).

83. *Ohio v. Geis*, 7 Med. L. Rptr. 1676 (Ct. App. Ohio, Franklin County, 1981).

84. *Tennessee v. Shaffer,* 17 Med. L. Rptr. 1489 (Ct. App. Tenn., 1990), 1494. *In camera* allows a judge to examine evidence privately within his or her chambers.

85. *Zelenka v. Wisconsin,* 4 Med. L. Rptr. 1055 (Sup. Ct. Wis., 1978); *In re Wright,* 11 Med. L. Rptr. 1937 (Sup. Ct. Idaho, 1985).

86. While Justice Stewart's dissent has attracted the most interest, Justice Douglas's opinion is not without influence. His influence can be seen in a Washington appeals court decision granting an absolute privilege to journalists under the state constitution. It viewed the state constitution as not a guide to public policy but a "command, the breach of which cannot be tolerated." *Washington v. Rinaldo,* 9 Med. L. Rptr. 2529 (Ct. App., Div. 1, 1983), 2531. The Washington Supreme Court refused to recognize an absolute privilege, preferring a qualified privilege based on Stewart's dissent. See *Washington v. Rinaldo,* 10 Med. L. Rptr. 2448 (Sup. Ct. Wash., 1984).

87. *Reporters Committee for Freedom of the Press v. AT&T,* 593 F.2d 1030 (D.C. Cir., 1978), 1084.

88. *In re Rutti,* 5 Med. L. Rptr. 1513 (Ct. App. Ohio, 5th Dist., 1979), 1515.

89. *In re Wright,* 11 Med. L. Rptr. 1937 (Sup. Ct. Idaho, 1985), 1943–44.

90. Ibid., 1945.

91. Morton J. Horwitz, "The Constitution of Change: Legal Fundamentality without Fundamentalism," *Harvard Law Review* 107 (November 1993): 98–99.

92. Ibid., 99.

93. Robert M. Cover, "Foreward: *Nomos* and Narrative," *Harvard Law Review* 97 (November 1983): 57.

94. Horwitz, "Constitution of Change," 100.

95. See Frank I. Michelman, "Foreward: Traces of Self-Government," *Harvard Law Review* 100 (1986): 15.

Chapter 5: Corporate Ownership and the Press

1. Tim McGuire, the former editor of the *Star-Tribune* in Minneapolis, estimates that as many as fifty millionaires attended the 2000 ASNE convention. See Leonard Downie Jr. and Robert G. Kaiser, *The News about the News* (New York: Knopf, 2002), 93.

2. Ibid., 68.

3. In 1938, Justice Black argued that the purpose of the Fourteenth Amendment was to "protect weak and helpless human beings." *Connecticut General Life Insurance Co. v. Johnson,* 303 U.S. 77 (1938), 87. Despite that intent, Black noted that during the first fifty years of the amendment, "less than one-half of one percent invoked it in protection of the Negro race, and more than fifty per cent asked that its benefits be extended to corporations." Black believed that the Court added corporations to the meaning of the Fourteenth Amendment without warning, thus depriving states of the privilege of regulating corporations (89). In 1949, Justice Douglas also rejected the idea that corporations are people under the Fourteenth Amendment: "We are dealing with a question of vital concern to the people of the nation. It may be most desirable to give corporations this protection from the operation of the legislative process. But that question is not for us. It is for the people. If they want corporations to be treated as humans are treated, if they want to grant corporations this large

degree of emancipation from state regulations, they should say so. The Constitution provides a method by which they may do so. We should not do it for them through the guise of interpretation." *Wheeling Steel Corp. v. Glander,* 337 U.S. 562 (1949), 581.

4. *First National Bank of Boston v. Bellotti,* 435 U.S. 765 (1978), 780

5. Gregory A. Mark, "The Personification of the Business Corporation in American Law," *University of Chicago Law Review* 54 (1987): 1441–84; Carl J. Mayer, "Personalizing the Impersonal: Corporations and the Bill of Rights," *Hastings Law Journal* 41 (1990): 577–667.

6. Mayer, "Personalizing the Impersonal," 627. This is a controversial interpretation and one that has been directly challenged by several members of the current Court. David Rocklin writes that if the Court's decision in *Grosjean v. American Press Co.,* 297 U.S. 233 (1936), is read in conjunction with *Hague v. CIO,* 307 U.S. 496 (1939), they "seem to indicate that only corporations possessing free press rights would be accorded free speech rights." David Rocklin, "Note and Comment: Non-profit Corporate Political Speech," *Chicago-Kent Law Review* 63 (1987): 163.

7. David Lange, "The Speech and Press Clauses," *UCLA Law Review* 23 (1975): 77–119.

8. Sanford A. Schane, "The Corporation Is a Person: The Language of a Legal Fiction," *Tulane Law Review* 61 (February 1987): 565.

9. Ibid., 566.

10. Ibid., 567.

11. Ibid.

12. Ibid., 568.

13. *Bank of United States v. Deveaux,* 9 U.S. 61 (1809).

14. *Santa Clara County v. Southern Pacific Railroad,* 118 U.S. 394 (1886).

15. Mayer, "Personalizing the Impersonal," 582. The Court first granted corporations Bill of Rights protections in *Noble v. Union River Logging R.R.,* 147 U.S. 165 (1893). In the case, the Court granted a corporation Fifth Amendment due process rights. The Court had granted Fourth Amendment protections to corporations in *Hale v. Henkel,* 201 U.S. 43 (1906), but it limited those rights in *United States v. Morton Salt Co.,* 338 U.S. 632 (1950).

16. *Lochner v. New York,* 198 U.S. 45 (1905).

17. Alfred H. Kelly, Winfred A. Harbison, and Herman Belz, *The American Constitution: Its Origins and Development,* 6th ed. (New York: W. W. Norton, 1983), 416. The authors argue that while substantive due process is not inherently conservative "in a socioeconomic sense," it may be "antidemocratic" and is an instrument "of power that can be used for different political purposes."

18. See Mayer, "Personalizing the Impersonal." Others have argued that the Court's power in this area was far more subtle and complex. For example, Kelly, Harbison, and Belz note that between 1887 and 1910, 558 cases challenging state legislation under the due process clause came before the Court, and the Court sustained eighty-three percent of the cases. The authors believe that this can be explained by the fact that justices "did not have complete discretion to decide things according to their own political and social values. Most cases could be disposed of under established precedent and rules of law." The power of the Court to determine the reasonableness of the legislation "greatly increased

the policy-making capability of the judiciary without making it supreme." Kelly, Harbison, and Belz, *American Constitution*, 416–17.

19. *West Coast Hotel Co. v. Parrish*, 300 U.S. 379 (1937).

20. Mayer, "Personalizing the Impersonal," 602–3.

21. Daniel Bell, *The Coming of the Post-Industrial Society* (New York: Basic Books, 1973); James Boyle, *Shamans, Software, and Spleens: Law and the Construction of the Information Society* (Cambridge, Mass.: Harvard University Press, 1996); Martin T. Sklar, *The Corporate Reconstruction of American Capitalism, 1890–1916: The Market, the Law, and Politics* (Cambridge: Cambridge University Press, 1988); Thomas Streeter, *Selling the Air: A Critique of the Policy of Commercial Broadcasting in the United States* (Chicago: University of Chicago Press, 1996).

22. Mayer, "Personalizing the Impersonal," 620.

23. The commercial speech doctrine holds that commercial speech enjoys less protection than political speech under the Constitution. In *Valentine v. Chrestenson*, 316 U.S. 52 (1942), the Court ruled that a man who was distributing handbills advertising tours of a submarine was engaging in "purely commercial advertising" and had no First Amendment protection.

24. *Central Hudson Gas and Electric Corp. v. Public Service Commission of New York*, 447 U.S. 557, 574 (1980).

25. Ibid., 574.

26. Ibid., 589.

27. *Virginia Board of Pharmacy v. Virginia Citizens Consumer Council, Inc.*, 425 U.S. 748 (1976).

28. *Bates v. State of Arizona*, 433 U.S. 350 (1977).

29. *First National Bank of Boston v. Bellotti*, 435 U.S. 765 (1978).

30. Ibid., 776.

31. Ibid., 776–77.

32. Ibid., 783.

33. Ibid.

34. Ibid., 805.

35. Ibid., 807.

36. Ibid., 808.

37. Ibid., 809.

38. Ibid., 810.

39. Justice Anthony Kennedy has made this point. See *FEC v. Beaumont*, 2003 U.S. Lexis 4595 (2003) (concurring opinion by Kennedy).

40. Ibid., 18.

41. *Buckley v. Valeo*, 424 U.S. 1 (1976).

42. *FEC v. Beaumont*, 2003 U.S. Lexis 4595 (2003), 29.

43. Ibid., n.8.

44. *First National Bank of Boston v. Bellotti*, 435 U.S. 765 (1978), 781.

45. Ibid., 808.

46. Ibid., 796.

47. Ibid., 796–97.

48. Randall A. Bezanson, "The New Free Press Guarantee," *Virginia Law Review* 63 (1977): 731–88; Lange, "Speech and Press Clauses"; Melvin B. Nimmer, "Is Freedom of the Press a Redundancy: What Does It Add to Freedom of Speech?" *Hastings Law Journal* 26 (1975): 639–58; Potter Stewart, "Or of the Press," *Hastings Law Journal* 26 (1975): 631–43; William W. Van Alstyne, "The Hazards to the Press of Claiming a 'Preferred Position,'" *Hastings Law Journal* 28 (1977): 76170.

49. *First National Bank of Boston v. Bellotti,* 435 U.S. 765 (1978), 802.

50. Ibid., 798.

51. *Grosjean v. American Press Co.,* 297 U.S. 233 (1936).

52. Ibid., 244.

53. Ibid., 249.

54. Ibid., 250.

55. Stewart, "Or of the Press," 633–34.

56. Jeffery A. Smith writes: "The wording of the Constitution and contemporary discussion left little doubt that the aim of both those who wanted a written guarantee and those who did not was to deny the legislative, executive, and judicial branches any power over the press." Jeffrey A. Smith, *War and Press Freedom: The Problem of Prerogative Power* (New York: Oxford, 1999), 35.

57. Lange, "Speech and Press Clauses."

58. It is often argued that cases such as *Branzburg v. Hayes,* 408 U.S. 665 (1972), as well as a series of cases known as the Prison Access cases (*Pell v. Procunier* 417 U.S. 817 [1974]; *Saxbe v. Washington Post,* 417 U.S. 843 [1974]; and *Houchins v. KQED,* 438 U.S. 1 [1978]) support the contention that the Court is not willing to grant the press a privileged status. That is not entirely the case. While the Court was hesitant to say that the press enjoys a special constitutional status, it did allow—and has routinely allowed—the state and federal governments to carve out special privileges and rights for the institutional press. These range from recognizing state shield laws to waiving search and copying costs under the Freedom of Information Act.

59. *FEC v. Massachusetts Citizens for Life, Inc.,* 479 U.S. 238 (1986), 250.

60. Ibid., 251.

61. Ibid., 259.

62. Ibid., 264.

63. Ibid., 268.

64. *Austin v. Michigan State Chamber of Commerce,* 494 U.S. 652 (1990), 662–63.

65. Michigan Campaign Finance Act, §169.206(3)(d).

66. *Austin v. Michigan State Chamber of Commerce,* 494 U.S. 652 (1990), 666.

67. Ibid., 667.

68. Ibid.

69. Ibid., 668.

70. Ibid., 691.

71. Ibid.

72. Ibid., 692.

73. Ibid., 712.

74. Ibid., 713.

75. *Los Angeles Police Department v. United Reporting Publishing*, 528 U.S. 32 (1999), 5.

76. Ibid., 5–6.

77. Ibid., 8.

78. Ibid., 15.

79. Ibid., 17.

80. Ibid., 16.

81. Ibid., 17.

82. Ibid., 23.

83. Ibid., 24–25.

84. Ibid., 25.

85. *Judicial Watch, Inc., v. U.S. Department of Justice*, 133 F. Supp. 2d 52 (2000), 53.

86. Ibid., 53–54.

87. Robert W. McChesney sees this idea as being problematic: "Of course, in prac-tice, professional journalism has never enjoyed the independence from corporate or commercial pressure suggested by its rhetoric." Robert W. McChesney, *Rich Media, Poor Democracy: Communication Politics in Dubious Times* (Urbana: University of Illinois Press, 1999), 49.

88. Ben H. Bagdikian notes that profit margins of daily newspapers are "two or three times higher than average profits of the Fortune 500 top corporations." The average profit for publicly traded news companies in 1994 was 20 percent. Ben H. Bagdikian, *The Media Monopoly*, 5th ed. (Boston: Beacon Press, Boston, 1997), xxii.

89. John McManus, *Market-Driven Journalism: Let the Citizen Beware?* (Thousand Oaks, Calif.: Sage, 1994); Douglas Underwood, *When MBAs Rule the Newsroom: How the Market-ers and Managers Are Reshaping Today's Media* (New York: Columbia University Press, 1993).

90. Similar questions have troubled courts in other areas of the law. For example, courts have several times been asked to decide who qualifies for the media exemption from search and copying costs under the federal Freedom of Information Act. In 1989, the U.S. Court of Appeals for the District of Columbia defined the news media as "a person or entity that gathers information of potential interest to a segment of the public, uses its editori-al skills to turn the raw materials into a distinct work, and distributes that work to an audience." The court also ruled that the fact that most news media are for-profit organi-zations does not eliminate its protections. *National Security Archive v. U.S. Department of Defense*, 880 F. 2d 1381 (1989), 1387.

91. Scalia held this view long before he was appointed to the Court. As an assistant at-torney general in the U.S. Department of Justice in 1975, he testified against a proposed federal shield law for journalists. Scalia told a House of Representatives committee that the First Amendment "does not mean freedom for newspapers and publishing houses, but rather freedom to publish." *Newsmen's Privilege: Hearings before the Subcommittee on Courts, Civil Liberties, and the Administration of Justice of the Committee on the Judiciary, House of Representatives*, 1975, 94th Cong. 1st Sess., 1, 8.

92. Stuart Ewen, *PR! A Social History of Spin* (New York: Basic Books, 1996), 414.

93. Jürgen Habermas, "There Are Alternatives," *New Left Review* 231 (1998): 8.

94. Ibid., 9.

95. Thomas Linzey, "Killing Goliath: Defending Our Sovereignty and Environmental Sustainability through Corporate Charter Revocation in Pennsylvania and Delaware," *Journal of Environmental Law and Politics* 6 (1997): 33.

96. Ibid., 47.

97. Ibid.

98. Ibid., 37.

99. Linzey, "Awakening a Sleeping Giant: Creating a Quasi-Private Frame of Action for Revoking Corporate Charters in Response to Environmental Violations," *Pace Environmental Law Review* 13 (Fall 1995): 255.

100. An attempt to revoke the charter of the California petroleum company Unocal failed when the state attorney general refused to initiate proceedings. For details on this action and others, see the web page for Ending Corporate Governance, <http://www.ratical.org/corporations/index.html>.

101. Richard Grossman, "Revoking the Corporation," *Journal of Environmental Law and Litigation* 11 (1996): 141.

102. Ibid.

103. Owen Fiss, *Liberalism Divided: Freedom of Speech and the Many Uses of State Power* (Boulder, Colo.: Westview, 1996), 150.

104. For example, in *Arkansas Educational Television Commission v. Forbes*, 523 U.S. 666 (1998), the Court relied on property arguments in ruling that a state-owned television network could hold political debates and exclude third-party candidates.

105. In *Pruneyard Shopping Center v. Robins*, 447 U.S. 74 (1980), the Court ruled that California could interpret its constitution to give citizens access rights to privately owned shopping malls. The Court recognized that states may interpret their constitutions freely as long as their decisions promote, rather than negate, federal rights.

106. R. Randall Rainey and William Rehg, "The Marketplace of Ideas, the Public Interest, and Federal Regulation of the Electronic Media: Implications of Habermas's Theory of Democracy," *Southern California Law Review* 69 (1996): 1973.

107. Ibid., 1974.

108. Ibid., 1980.

109. Ibid., 1975–76.

Chapter 6: Public Television, Parks, Parades, and Rest Areas

1. *West Coast Hotel v. Parish*, 300 U.S. 379 (1937).

2. *United States v. Carolene Products Co.*, 304 U.S. 144 (1938).

3. In his now-famous footnote, Justice Stone wrote: "There may be narrower scope for the operation of the presumption of constitutionality where legislation appears on its face to be within a specific prohibition of the Constitution, such as those of the first ten amendments, which are deemed equally specific when held to be embraced within the Fourteenth. . . . [P]rejudice against discrete and insular minorities may be a special condition, which tends seriously to curtail the operation of those political processes ordinarily to be relied upon to protect minorities, and which may call for a correspondingly more searching judicial inquiry" (ibid., 152).

4. David Schultz argues that the Rehnquist Court, and in particular Justice Antonin Scalia, are engaged in revitalizing property arguments: "It is a move, much more with Scalia than with Rehnquist, toward a post–*Carolene Products* jurisprudence, where some type of rethinking of the property and civil rights dichotomy is being explored. Such a rethinking seems premised upon breaking with the use of different levels of analysis presently used to review the legislative process, depending upon whether or not economic or civil rights claims are at issue." David Schultz, "Scalia, Property, and *Dolan v. Tigard:* The Emergence of a Post-*Carolene Products* Jurisprudence," *Akron Law Review* 29 (Summer 1995): 32.

5. Thomas Streeter makes this argument in "Some Thoughts on Free Speech, Language, and the Rule of Law," in *Freeing the First Amendment,* ed. David S. Allen and Robert Jensen (New York: New York University Press, 1995), 43.

6. *Hague v. Committee for Industrial Organization,* 307 U.S. 496 (1939), 515–16.

7. Harry Kalven Jr., "The Concept of the Public Forum: *Cox v. Louisiana,*" *Supreme Court Review* 1 (1965): 1–32.

8. *New York Times v. Sullivan,* 376 U.S. 254 (1964).

9. Robert C. Post, "Between Governance and Management: The History and Theory of the Public Forum," *UCLA Law Review* 34 (June–August 1987): 1718.

10. *Police Department of Chicago v. Mosley,* 408 U.S. 92 (1972), 96.

11. *Lehman v. City of Shaker Heights,* 419 U.S. 298 (1974), 312.

12. *Perry Education Association v. Perry Local Educators' Association,* 460 U.S. 37 (1983), 45.

13. *Cornelius v. NAACP Legal Defense and Educational Fund, Inc.,* 473 U.S. 788 (1985), 803.

14. Melville B. Nimmer, *Nimmer on Freedom of Speech: A Treatise on the Theory of the First Amendment* (New York: M. Bender, 1984).

15. *Grayned v. City of Rockford,* 408 U.S. 104 (1972).

16. Ibid., 116–17.

17. Post, "Between Governance and Management," 1766.

18. Ibid., 1776.

19. Ibid., 1777.

20. Ibid., 1784.

21. Ibid., 1795–96.

22. Ibid., 1794.

23. Ibid., 1795. The case is *U.S. Postal Service v. Council of Greenburgh Civic Associations,* 453 U.S. 114 (1981).

24. See, for example, *Virginia State Board of Pharmacy v. Virginia Citizens Consumer Council,* 425 U.S. 748 (1976); *Bates v. State Bar of Arizona,* 433 U.S. 360 (1977); *Boldger v. Youngs Drug Prod. Corp.,* 463 U.S. 60 (1983); *Central Hudson Gas and Elec. Corp. v. Public Service Comm'n,* 447 U.S. 557 (1980); and *Cincinnati v. Discovery Network,* 113 Sup. Ct. 1505 (1993).

25. For a good review of this concept, see Cass R. Sunstein, *Democracy and the Problem of Free Speech* (New York: Free Press, 1993), 37–38.

26. Post, "Between Governance and Management," 1800.

27. *Arkansas Educational Television Commission v. Forbes,* 523 U.S. 666 (1998), 673.

28. Ibid., 674. Justice Kennedy wrote: "Public and private broadcasters alike are not only

permitted, but indeed required, to exercise substantial editorial discretion in the selection and presentation of their programming."

29. Ibid.

30. Ibid., 675.

31. Ibid., 676.

32. Ibid., 680.

33. Ibid., 681.

34. Ibid.

35. *Clark v. Community for Creative Non-Violence,* 468 U.S. 288 (1984), 291.

36. Ibid., 303.

37. Ibid., n.2.

38. Ibid., 293.

39. Ibid., 296.

40. Ibid.

41. Ibid.

42. Ibid., 297.

43. Ibid., 300.

44. Ibid., 301.

45. Ibid., 305.

46. Ibid., 314, n.14.

47. "Solar Decathlon," *Weekend Edition Saturday,* National Public Radio, September 28, 2002. The host of the show, Scott Simon, noted that although the students inhabited the houses at all hours during the construction, National Park Service rules prohibited them from living or sleeping in them once finished.

48. *Hurley v. Irish-American Gay, Lesbian, and Bisexual Group of Boston, Inc.,* 515 U.S. 557 (1995).

49. Ibid., 560–61. The Court notes that no other applicant had ever applied for a permit.

50. Ibid., 561

51. Ibid.

52. *Mass. Gen. Laws* § 272:98 (1992).

53. *Hurley v. Irish-American Gay, Lesbian, and Bisexual Group of Boston, Inc.,* 515 U.S. 557 (1995), 563.

54. Ibid., 573.

55. Ibid., 568.

56. Ibid.

57. Ibid.

58. Ibid., 576.

59. Ibid., 577.

60. Ibid., 579.

61. Ibid.

62. Ibid.

63. For example, Justice Souter noted that banners have been carried with such slogans as "England get out of Ireland" and "Say no to drugs." In addition, he noted that in previous years the Veterans Council had rejected applications from the Ku Klux Klan and ROAR, an antibusing group (ibid., 579, 562).

64. Ibid., 578.

65. Ibid., 570.

66. Ibid., 579.

67. *Turner Broadcasting System, Inc. v. FCC,* 512 U.S. 622 (1994).

68. *Hurley v. Irish-American Gay, Lesbian, and Bisexual Group of Boston, Inc.,* 515 U.S. 557 (1995), 575.

69. Ibid.

70. See Zechariah Chafee Jr., *Free Speech in the United States* (Cambridge, Mass.: Harvard University Press, 1941).

71. See Lee C. Bollinger, *The Tolerant Society: Freedom of Speech and Extremist Speech in America* (New York: Oxford University Press, 1986).

72. See Steven H. Shiffrin, *The First Amendment, Democracy, and Romance* (Cambridge, Mass.: Harvard University Press, 1990).

73. Vincent Breeding, the national director of EURO, denied that the group was involved in a protest: "'It was just a display of Southern hospitality.'" Quoted in "Attorney General: Using Rest Stops for Border Patrols Violates State Law," *Rock Hill (S.C.) Herald,* March 19, 2002, 1A.

74. Quoted in ibid.

75. Ibid.

76. Quoted in Warren Wise, "Condon Sues over Picketing; Protests at State Welcome Centers Called Illegal," *Charleston (S.C.) Post and Courier,* March 19, 2002, 1B.

77. Warren Wise, "Hodges Pressed on Boycott," *Charleston (S.C) Post and Courier,* March 5, 2002, 3B.

78. Quoted in ibid.

79. *Sentinel Communications Co. v. Watts,* 936 F.2d 1189 (1991), 1203.

80. Ibid.

81. See *Jacobsen v. Howard,* 904 F. Supp. 1065 (1995), 1071 ("The Court concludes that South Dakota's statutes are not reasonable because they completely prohibit, rather than regulate, First Amendment activity"); and *Jacobsen v. Howard,* 109 F.3d 1268 (1997), 1274 ("The state has presented no credible explanation why the distribution of newspapers at an interstate rest area is incompatible with the state's interests in providing places of safety, rest, and information to interstate travelers").

82. R. Jeffrey Lustig makes this point in *Corporate Liberalism: The Origins of Modern American Political Theory, 1890–1920* (Berkeley, Calif.: University of California Press, 1982), 119.

Chapter 7: Resisting Corporate Rationalization

1. Janet Kidd Stewart, "Corpspeak Clouding Up Picture of VIP B-Stuff," *Chicago Tribune,* April 8, 2001, sec. 2, 3.

2. Ron Chernow, *Titan: The Life of John D. Rockefeller Sr.,* (New York: Vintage Books, 1998), 556.

3. Paul Krugman, "For Richer," *New York Times Magazine,* October 20, 2002, 62.

4. *Buckley v. American Constitutional Law Foundation, Inc.,* 525 U.S. 182 (1999). See also *Meyer v. Grant,* 486 U.S. 414 (1988).

5. Quoted in David S. Broder, *Democracy Derailed: Initiative Campaigns and the Power of Money* (New York: Harcourt, 2000), 59.

6. Ibid., 63.

7. George Ritzer, *The McDonaldization of Society: New Century Edition* (Thousand Oaks, Calif.: Pine Forge Press, 2000), 226–27.

8. For a description of negative and positive liberty, see Isaiah Berlin, *Four Essays on Liberty* (New York: Oxford University Press, 1969).

9. In media law, there are exceptions—exceptions that trouble many liberal thinkers. For example, the Federal Communications Commission has over the years granted some positive rights to citizens in regard to radio and television broadcasting. For a critique of these decisions, see David Kelley and Roger Donway, "Liberalism and Free Speech," in *Democracy and the Mass Media,* ed. Judith Lichtenberg (Cambridge: Cambridge University Press, 1990), 66–101. For a critique of that view, see David Kairys, "Freedom of Speech," in *The Politics of Law: A Progressive Critique,* ed. David Kairys (New York: Pantheon Books, 1982), 140–71.

10. Susan Herbst has argued that our society continues to move away from "bottom-up" strategies towards "top-down" strategies of public opinion, with the latter controlled by "state or private industry forces." Susan Herbst, "Classical Democracy, Polls, and Public Opinion: Theoretical Frameworks for Studying the Development of Public Sentiment," *Communication Theory* 1 (August 1991): 232.

11. Andrew Abbott, *The System of Professions* (Chicago: University of Chicago Press, 1988), 59.

12. This idea is supported by research that documents what can be termed the agenda-setting function of the media. See Maxwell McCombs and Donald Shaw, "The Agenda-Setting Function of Mass Media," *Public Opinion Quarterly* 36 (Summer 1972): 176–87. Some would argue that the press doesn't set the agenda as much as it follows the lead of its influential sources, what Mark Fishman calls "manipulated journalism." Fishman's description of the creation of a crime wave raises questions about who actually sets the agenda, the press or the government. See Mark Fishman, *Manufacturing the News* (Austin: University of Texas Press, 1988).

13. Daniel Hallin, in his critique of a CBS newscast, puts it this way: "CBS speaks to its audience as a provider of authoritative information. It solicits nothing beyond their attention, solicits of them no active role regarding the political material reported; indeed the authoritative and detached style of the report and the finality of the sign-off leave the impression that the matters discussed are essentially closed, at least until the next broadcast." See Daniel Hallin, "The American News Media: A Critical Theory Perspective," in *Critical Theory and Public Life,* ed. John Forester (Cambridge: Massachusetts Institute of Technology Press, 1985), 135.

14. G. Thomas Goodnight, "The Personal, Technical, and the Public Spheres of Argument: A Speculative Inquiry into the Art of Public Deliberations," *Journal of the American Forensic Association* 18 (Spring 1982): 214.

15. Goodnight makes this argument in regard to the mass media (ibid., 226).

16. John Schwartz and Geraldine Fabrikant, "War Puts Radio Giant on the Defensive," *New York Times,* March 31, 2003, C1.

17. Donald R. Skaggs, "Pantagraph Connects with New Slogan," *(Bloomington-Normal, Ill.) Pantagraph,* February 15, 1998, 1.

18. William Greider, *Who Will Tell the People: The Betrayal of American Democracy* (New York: Simon and Schuster, 1992), 304.

19. For example, see James S. Ettema and Theodore L. Glasser, "Narrative Form and Moral Force: The Realization of Innocence and Guilt through Investigative Journalism," *Journal of Communication* 38 (Summer 1988): 8–26. The authors argue that investigative journalists are blind to their own moral choices, cloaking them in the professional ideology of objectivity.

20. Quoted in "Dialogue," *Center Magazine* 20 (March–April 1987): 17.

21. As Carey writes, "The public is totem and talisman, and an object of ritual homage." See James Carey, "The Press and the Public Discourse," *Center Magazine* 20 (March–April 1987): 4. Habermas also notes that democratic states still count on an intact public opinion, even if they don't really believe it exists, "because it is still the only accepted basis for the legitimation of political domination." See Jürgen Habermas, *The Structural Transformation of the Public Sphere: An Inquiry into a Category of Bourgeois Society,* trans. Thomas Burger (Cambridge: Massachusetts Institute of Technology Press, 1989), 237.

22. Stuart Ewen, *PR! A Social History of Spin* (New York: Basic Books, 1996), 414.

23. Jay Rosen, "Making Journalism More Public," *Communication* 12 (1991): 272–73.

24. For example, Leonard Downie of the *Washington Post* refers to public journalism as something akin to what "'our promotion department does.'" Richard Aregood, the editorial-page editor of the *Philadelphia Daily News,* criticizes public journalism for letting readers set the press's agenda. Quoted in T. Case, "Public Journalism Denounced," *Editor and Publisher,* November 12, 1994, 14. And William Woo, the former editor of the *St. Louis Post-Dispatch,* wonders whether the mission of public journalism is compatible with the professional values of objectivity and detachment. Woo worries that public journalism calls for the press to abandon the nonvoter or the nonparticipant who will become "'not merely a second-class citizen but also a second-class reader.'" Quoted in M. L. Stein, "Beware of Public Journalism," *Editor and Publisher,* May 6, 1995, 18.

25. Rosen, "Making Journalism More Public," 270.

26. For example, the *Charlotte (N.C.) Observer* has put forward what it calls "consumer-oriented campaign news." Editors have attempted to find ways to involve readers in shaping the paper's political coverage, especially in the types of stories that are selected and the use of opinion polls. For a review of the paper's attempts, see Elizabeth Kolbert, "Paper Adjusts Reporting by Asking Its Readers," *New York Times,* June 21, 1992, 14.

27. Habermas argues that media institutions have moved farther from the public sphere into the "private sphere of commodity exchange." The public sphere has been altered by the entry of privileged, private interests that are packaged to represent truly public interests. Habermas, *Structural Transformation,* 188–89.

28. Ibid., 238.

29. Herbst, "Classical Democracy," 231.

30. Opinion of this type might best be described, as C. Wright Mills terms it, as "mass opinion." Mills argues that (1) fewer people express opinions than receive them, (2) communications are so organized that individuals cannot answer back, (3) the realiza-

tions of opinion in action is controlled by authorities, and (4) the mass has no autonomy from institutions. See C. Wright Mills, *The Power Elite* (London: Oxford University Press, 1956), 304.

31. Author's interview with Pam Fine, news leader, *Minneapolis Star Tribune* (July 10, 1995), Minneapolis.

32. Author's interview with Pam Fine.

33. More than six hundred state residents met to discuss terrorism. The project was jointly sponsored by Twin Cities Public Television.

34. John Durham Peters and Kenneth Cmiel make a similar argument in their call for an increased recognition of the public sphere in media ethics. See John Durham Peters and Kenneth Cmiel, "Media Ethics and the Public Sphere," *Communication* 12 (1991): 209.

35. As the former Supreme Court Justice William Brennan once wrote, "Unlike literary critics, judges cannot merely savor the tensions or revel in the ambiguities inherent in the text—judges must decide." William Brennan, "The Constitution of the United States: Contemporary Ratification," *South Texas Law Review* 27 (1986): 434.

36. John J. Pauly, "Journalism and the Sociology of Public Life," in *The Idea of Public Journalism,* ed. Theodore L. Glasser (New York: Guilford, 1999), 148.

37. Ibid., 149.

38. C. Edwin Baker, *Media, Markets, and Democracy* (Cambridge: Cambridge University Press, 2002), 283–84.

39. Habermas, *Structural Transformation,* 201.

40. Stanley Ingber, "The Marketplace of Ideas: A Legitimizing Myth," *Duke Law Journal* 1984 (February 1984): 76.

41. Ibid., 80–81.

42. Ibid., 81–82.

43. Delgado has argued that narrative not only builds community but can provide "counterstories" that might help construct a new world: "They can show that what we believe is ridiculous, self-serving, or cruel. They can show us the way out of the trap of unjustified exclusion. They can help us understand when it is time to reallocate power. They are the other half—the destructive half—of the creative dialectic." Richard Delgado, "Storytelling for Oppositionists and Others: A Plea for Narrative," *Michigan Law Review* 87 (August 1989): 2415. See also Kim Lane Scheppele, "Forward: Telling Stories," *Michigan Law Review* 87 (August 1989): 2073–98.

44. David Kairys, "Freedom of Speech," in *The Politics of Law: A Progressive Critique,* ed. David Kairys (New York: Pantheon, 1982), 156.

45. This differs from Habermas's idea of discourse ethics. For a description of those differences, see Seyla Benhabib, "Afterword: Communicative Ethics and Current Controversies in Practical Philosophy," in *The Communicative Ethics Controversy,* ed. Seyla Benhabib and Fred Dallmayr (Cambridge: Massachusetts Institute of Technology Press, 1990), 341.

Index

DAVID S. ALLEN, a former journalist, is an associate professor in the Department of Journalism and Mass Communication at the University of Wisconsin–Milwaukee. He is the coeditor, with Robert Jensen, of *Freeing the First Amendment: Critical Perspectives on Freedom of Expression* (1995). His research has appeared in journals such as *Communication Law and Policy,* the *Journal of Mass Media Ethics, Free Speech Yearbook, Journalism: Theory, Practice, and Criticism,* and *Angelaki: Journal of the Theoretical Humanities.*

THE HISTORY OF COMMUNICATION

The University of Illinois Press
is a founding member of the
Association of American University Presses.

———————————————————————

Composed in 10.5/13 Adobe Minion
with Meta display
by Celia Shapland
for the University of Illinois Press
Manufactured by Thomson-Shore, Inc.

University of Illinois Press
1325 South Oak Street
Champaign, IL 61820-6903
www.press.uillinois.edu